This is an updated and substantially revised edition of Peter Matthews's well-known *Morphology*, first published in 1974. It includes chapters on inflectional and lexical morphology, derivational processes and productivity, compounds, paradigms, and much new material on markedness and other aspects of iconicity. As in the first edition, the theoretical discussion is eclectic and critical: its scope ranges from the ancient grammarians to the work of Chomsky and his followers, the disintegration of the classical Chomskyan scheme, and the renewed standing of morphology and historical linguistics in recent years. The examples are drawn from English and other European languages, both ancient and modern. The work will appeal to both specialists in particular languages – it contains much original material – and students of general linguistics.

For this new edition much now obsolete discussion has been removed and replaced by discussion of current issues, and the further reading sections have been thoroughly updated.

# CAMBRIDGE TEXTBOOKS IN LINGUISTICS

*General Editors:* J. BRESNAN, B. COMRIE, W. DRESSLER,
R. HUDDLESTON, R. LASS, D. LIGHTFOOT, J. LYONS,
P. H. MATTHEWS, R. POSNER, S. ROMAINE, N. V. SMITH,
N. VINCENT

# MORPHOLOGY

Second edition

# MORPHOLOGY

## Second edition

## P. H. MATTHEWS

PROFESSOR OF LINGUISTICS
UNIVERSITY OF CAMBRIDGE

CAMBRIDGE
UNIVERSITY PRESS

Published by the Press Syndicate of the University of Cambridge
The Pitt Building, Trumpington Street, Cambridge CB2 1RP
40 West 20th Street, New York, NY 10011–4211, USA
10 Stamford Road, Oakleigh, Melbourne 3166, Australia

First published 1974
Second edition 1991
Reprinted 1993

Printed in Great Britain at the University Press, Cambridge

*British Library cataloguing in publication data*

Matthews, P. H. (Peter, Hugoe) *1934*—
Morphology, 2nd ed. – (Cambridge textbooks in linguistics)
I. Language. Morphology
1. Title
415

*Library of Congress cataloguing in publication data*

Matthews, P. H. (Peter Hugoe)
Morphology/P. H. Matthews. – 2nd edn.
    p.    cm. – (Cambridge textbooks in linguistics)
Includes index.
ISBN 0 521 41043 6 (hardback). – ISBN 0 521 42256 6 (pbk.)
1. Grammar, Comparative and general – Morphology. 1. Title.
11. Series.
P241.M3 1991
415 – dc20   90-24762 CIP

ISBN 0 521 41043 6 hardback
ISBN 0 521 42256 6 paperback

UP

# CONTENTS

Contents

# PREFACE TO THE FIRST EDITION

This was first conceived as a partial *editio minor* of my recent *Inflectional Morphology* (in the Cambridge Studies in Linguistics). But it has become, I think, a little more interesting. I hope that it will be of value to specialists in particular European languages, as well as to postgraduate and undergraduate students of general linguistics.

I am very grateful to my colleagues R. W. P. Brasington, D. Crystal, G. C. Lepschy, F. R. Palmer, K. M. Petyt and Irene P. Warburton, who read the book in typescript and have helped me to make a number of corrections and improvements. I look forward with pleasure to a fresh collaboration with the University Printers, who set my first book so beautifully.

*July* 1973                                                           P. H. M.

# PREFACE TO THE SECOND EDITION

The first edition took me one year flat; the second has taken, off and on, four. I can only hope that, if it shows, it shows in the right way.

I am grateful to Frank Palmer, who commented on the typescript for me, and to my wife, Lucienne Schleich, to whom I have read aloud most of it. I am also grateful to Claudia Ventura for lending me a typewriter while I was on holiday.

*July* 1990                                                           P. H. M.

# PRINCIPAL REFERENCES

ADAMS = V. Adams, *An Introduction to Modern English Word-Formation* (London, Longman, 1973).

ALINEI = 'Round table on word formation and meaning', ed. M. Alinei, *Quaderni di Semantica* 5 (1984), pp. 43–142, 275–365.

ANDERSON, 'Where's morphology?' = S. R. Anderson, 'Where's morphology?', *LIn* 13 (1982), pp. 571–612.

ANTTILA = R. Anttila, *An Introduction to Comparative Linguistics*, 2nd edn (Amsterdam, Benjamins, 1989).

ARONOFF = M. Aronoff, *Word Formation in Generative Grammar* (Cambridge, Mass., MIT Press, 1976).

BAUER, *Morphology* = L. Bauer, *Introducing Linguistic Morphology* (Edinburgh, Edinburgh University Press, 1988).

BAUER, *Word-formation* = L. Bauer, *English Word-formation* (Cambridge, Cambridge University Press, 1983).

BENVENISTE = E. Benveniste, *Problèmes de linguistique générale* (Paris, Gallimard, 1966).

BLOOMFIELD = L. Bloomfield, *Language*, British edn (London, Allen and Unwin, 1935).

BYBEE = J. L. Bybee, *Morphology: a Study of the Relation between Meaning and Form* (Amsterdam, Benjamins, 1985).

BYNON = T. Bynon, *Historical Linguistics* (Cambridge, Cambridge University Press, 1977).

CARSTAIRS = A. Carstairs, *Allomorphy in Inflexion* (London, Croom Helm, 1987).

CHOMSKY, 'Nominalization' = N. Chomsky, 'Remarks on nominalization', in R. Jacobs & P. Rosenbaum (eds.), *Readings in English Transformational Grammar* (Waltham, Mass., Ginn, 1970), pp. 184–221. Reprinted in N. Chomsky, *Studies on Semantics in Generative Grammar* (The Hague, Mouton, 1972), pp. 11–61.

CHOMSKY, *Structures* = N. Chomsky, *Syntactic Structures* (The Hague, Mouton, 1957).

CHOMSKY & HALLE = N. Chomsky & M. Halle, *The Sound Pattern of English* (New York, Harper and Row, 1968).

COLLINS[2] = *Collins Dictionary of the English Language*, ed. P. Hanks, 2nd edn (London, Collins, 1986).

CORBIN = D. Corbin, *Morphologie dérivationelle et structuration du lexique*, 2 vols. (Tübingen, Niemeyer, 1987).

DRESSLER, *Leitmotifs* = W. U. Dressler (ed.), *Leitmotifs in Natural Morphology* (Amsterdam, Benjamins, 1987).

DRESSLER, *Morphonology* = W. U. Dressler, *Morphonology: the Dynamics of Derivation* (Ann Arbor, Mich., Karoma, 1985).

FISIAK = J. Fisiak (ed.), *Historical Morphology* (The Hague, Mouton, 1980).

GIMSON = D. Jones, *Everyman's English Pronouncing Dictionary*, 14th edn by A. C. Gimson (London, Dent, 1977).

GOODWIN = W. W. Goodwin, *A Greek Grammar*, 2nd edn (London, Macmillan, 1894).

GUILBERT = L. Guilbert, *La Créativité lexicale* (Paris, Larousse, 1975).

HAMMOND & NOONAN = M. Hammond & M. Noonan (eds.), *Theoretical Morphology* (New York, Academic Press, 1988).

HARRIS = Z. S. Harris, *Methods in Structural Linguistics* (Chicago, University of Chicago Press, 1951). Later reissued under the title *Structural Linguistics*.

HOCKETT, *Course* = C. F. Hockett, *A Course in Modern Linguistics* (New York, Macmillan, 1958).

HOCKETT, 'Models' = C. F. Hockett, 'Two models of grammatical description', *Word* 10 (1954), pp. 210–31. Reprinted in *RiL*, pp. 386–99.

*IJAL* = *International Journal of American Linguistics*.

*Inflectional Morphology* = P. H. Matthews, *Inflectional Morphology: a Theoretical Study Based on Aspects of Latin Verb Conjugation* (Cambridge, Cambridge University Press, 1972).

*JL* = *Journal of Linguistics*.

LASS = R. Lass, *Phonology* (Cambridge, Cambridge University Press, 1984).

LEES = R. B. Lees, *The Grammar of English Nominalizations* (Bloomington, Ind., supplement to *IJAL*, 1960).

LEWIS = G. L. Lewis, *Turkish Grammar* (Oxford, Clarendon Press, 1967).

*Lg* = *Language*.

*LIn* = *Linguistic Inquiry*.

LYONS, *Introduction* = J. Lyons, *Introduction to Theoretical Linguistics* (Cambridge, Cambridge University Press, 1968).

LYONS, *Semantics* = J. Lyons, *Semantics*, 2 vols. (Cambridge, Cambridge University Press, 1977).

MARCHAND = H. Marchand, *The Categories and Types of Present-day English Word-formation*, 2nd edn (Munich, Beck, 1969).

MARTINET = A. Martinet, *Eléments de linguistique générale* (Paris, Colin, 1960). English translation, *Elements of General Linguistics*, by E. Palmer (London, Faber, 1964).

MAYERTHALER = W. Mayerthaler, *Morphologische Natürlichkeit* (Wiesbaden, Athenaion, 1980).

MIRAMBEL = A. Mirambel, *La Langue grecque moderne : description et analyse* (Paris, Klincksieck, 1959).

NORMAN = J. Norman, *Chinese* (Cambridge, Cambridge University Press, 1988).

*OED* = *The Oxford English Dictionary*, ed. Sir James Murray *et al.*, 1st edn (Oxford, Clarendon Press, 1933).

*OEDS* = *A Supplement to the Oxford English Dictionary*, ed. R. W. Burchfield, 4 vols. (Oxford, Clarendon Press, 1972–86).

PALMER = F. R. Palmer, *The English Verb*, 2nd edn (London, Longman, 1988).

PAUL = H. Paul, *Prinzipien der Sprachgeschichte*, 5th edn (Halle, Niemeyer, 1920).

PLANK = F. Plank, *Morphologische (Ir-)Regularitäten: Aspekte der Wortstrukturtheorie* (Tübingen, Gunter Narr, 1981).

QUIRK *et al.* = R. Quirk, S. Greenbaum, G. Leech & J. Svartvik, *A Comprehensive Grammar of the English Language* (London, Longman, 1985).

*RiL* = *Readings in Linguistics I*, ed. M. Joos (Chicago, University of Chicago Press, 1966). Formerly *Readings in Linguistics* (New York, American Council of Learned Societies, 1957).

*RiL II* = *Readings in Linguistics II*, ed. E. P. Hamp, F. W. Householder & R. Austerlitz (Chicago, University of Chicago Press, 1966).

ROBINS, *Linguistics* = R. H. Robins, *General Linguistics: an Introductory Survey*, 4th edn (London, Longman, 1989).

ROBINS, 'WP' = R. H. Robins, 'In defence of WP', *TPhS* 1959, pp. 116–44. Reprinted in R. H. Robins, *Diversions of Bloomsbury* (Amsterdam, North-Holland, 1970), pp. 47–77.

SAPIR = E. Sapir, *Language* (New York, Harcourt Brace, 1921).

SAUSSURE = F. de Saussure, *Cours de linguistique générale*, Edition critique par T. de Mauro (Paris, Payot, 1972). English translation, *Course in General Linguistics*, by R. Harris (London, Duckworth, 1983).

SCALISE = S. Scalise, *Generative Morphology* (Dordrecht, Foris, 1984).

SEBEOK = T. A. Sebeok (ed.), *Current Trends in Linguistics*, vol. XIII: *Historiography of Linguistics* (The Hague, Mouton, 1975).

*TPhS* = *Transactions of the Philological Society*.

TRUBETZKOY = N. S. Trubetzkoy, *Grundzüge der Phonologie* (Prague, 1939). French translation, *Principes de phonologie*, by J. Cantineau (Paris, Klincksieck, 1949). English translation, *Principles of Phonology*, by C. A. M. Baltaxe (Berkeley/Los Angeles, University of California Press, 1969).

ULLMANN = S. Ullmann, *Semantics* (Oxford, Blackwell, 1962).

WURZEL = W. U. Wurzel, *Flexionsmorphologie und Natürlichkeit* (Berlin, Akademie-Verlag, 1984). English translation, *Inflectional Morphology and Naturalness*, by M. Schentke (Dordrecht, Luwer, 1989).

# I

# What is morphology?

Branches of linguistic theory: morphology as the study of 'forms of words'. Morphology in antiquity, and in nineteenth century: flectional, isolating and agglutinating languages. Morphology in structural linguistics: fusion of morphology with syntax (Bloomfield, Chomsky); and with generative phonology. Revival of morphology since 1970s; morphology and historical linguistics.
*The scope of morphology.* Double articulation of language; grammar vs phonology. Morphemes. Categories and inflections: inflections as markers, alternation of inflections. Compounds, word-formation. Limits of analysis: where should the division of words stop?
*Morphology and general linguistic theory.* Is a general theory possible? Theories of motivation; of laws and universals. Problems of universality; different models appropriate to different languages.

In the traditional view of language, words are put together to form sentences. The words differ from each other in both sound and meaning: *clock* and *gong*, for example, denote different sorts of object and are distinguished by different consonants at the beginning and end. Hence the sentences too will differ in sound and meaning, *The clock has been sold* being distinguished from *The gong has been sold* as a function of the words *clock* and *gong*. However, not only the words but also the construction and the 'forms of words' will vary from one individual sentence to another. *The gong has been sold* has a Passive construction, with *the gong* as Subject; contrast the Active *He has sold the gong*, in which it is Object. In both sentences, *gong* is Singular, and when it is the Subject the Auxiliary is *has*. Contrast *The gongs have been sold*, where *gongs* is Plural. In such examples, the choice between different forms of words – between the endings of *gongs* and *gong* on the one hand and *have* and *has* on the other – varies independently of the variation in construction (Passive versus Active). But in other cases the construction itself requires that a word should be in one form rather than another. For example, in *He hit them*, the word *them* is Object and must therefore appear in what is traditionally called the 'Accusative' Case. Contrast *They have sold the gong*, where the same Pronoun is Subject and must therefore appear as the 'Nominative' *they* instead. In describing a language all four varying facets – sounds, constructions, meanings and forms of words – have to be given due attention.

In the same spirit, the field of linguistic theory may be said to include at least four major subfields. The first is concerned with the study of speech sounds, a subject which in modern structural linguistics is handled on two theoretical levels. Of these the level of **phonology** is concerned with the functioning of sound-units within the systems of individual languages, whereas that of **phonetics** is concerned with the nature and typology of speech sounds in themselves. The second major subfield is that of **syntax** (from a Greek word meaning a 'putting together' or 'arranging' of elements), which traditionally covers both the constructions of phrases and sentences and also the features of meaning which are associated with them. For example, the Interrogative (*Has he sold the gong?*) is different both in construction and in meaning from the Non-Interrogative or Declarative (*He has sold the gong*). The third subfield of **semantics** then reduces to the study of word meanings – to which perhaps we may add the meanings of idioms (see chapter 5) or of special phrases generally. Traditionally, the problems of semantics have often been assigned to the dictionary. However, the oppositions of word meanings also lend themselves to structural analysis, most notably in specific 'semantic fields' such as those of kinship, colour terms, occupations, types of skill and knowledge, and so on. In addition, the limits of syntax and semantics have frequently been disputed both within and between the various structural schools. According to some, constructional meanings would also belong to semantics – syntax being reduced to the formal distribution of words and groups of words. Other writers make a further distinction between semantics, as a study of the meanings of words and sentences in the abstract, and **pragmatics**, as that of sentences used in specific situations. According to others, syntax itself is partly a matter of word meanings: for example, it is implicit in the meaning of 'to sell' or 'to hit' that it can take an Object. On many such issues, the debate continues in full vigour.

The last major subfield is that of **morphology**, and it is this that forms the central theme of this book. The term itself is a Greek-based parallel to the German *Formenlehre* (the 'study of forms'), and like many linguistic terms is nineteenth-century in origin, the first references for this sense in the *OED* being from the 1860s (s.vv. 'morphology', 'morphological', 'morphologically'). As a biological term it is older by at least thirty years (the first references for English in the *OED* being to 1830), and its linguistic sense was at first conceived in the same intellectual framework. It must be remembered that the science of language was at that time influenced by the evolutionary model of Darwin's *On the Origin of Species* (published in 1859). But the parallel between linguistics and biology is now seen as spurious. Philologists have long given up the hope (expressed so seductively in Max Müller's Oxford lectures of 1889) that by studying the 'evolution' of words in Indo-European, and their 'four or five hundred' basic roots in particular, the 'world-old riddle of the origin of language' can be solved.[1] On a less fanciful level, we no longer think of languages as organisms, which are born and grow and compete with each other. 'Morphology', therefore, is simply a term for that branch of linguistics which is concerned with the 'forms of words' in different uses and constructions. What precisely this means will be distinguished more carefully in the next section of this chapter.

The analysis of words has had varying fortunes in twentieth-century linguistic theory. In antiquity it was paramount: both Latin and Greek show complex variations in the forms of words, and their classification, into Cases such as Nominative or Accusative, into Numbers such as Singular and Plural, into Tenses such as Present, Past Perfect and so on, took the lion's share of ancient grammars. As we will see in chapter 10, ancient ideas are still worth debating. In the nineteenth century it lay at the heart of comparative linguistics. In the light of the ancient Indian analysis of Sanskrit, itself a masterwork in our field, it was possible to confirm and make precise its relationship to the classical languages of the West. As the understanding of other languages grew, it became attractive to group them into types. In Latin or Greek, each word is a whole but may subsume a range of distinguishable meanings. For example, a Verb has a time

---

[1] F. M. Müller, *Three Lectures on the Science of Language and its Place in General Education* (repr. Benares, Indological Book House, 1961), p. 32.

reference (Past, Present or Future); it may identify an action from the viewpoint of one who performs it (Active) or one who experiences it (Passive); it will predicate the action of the speaker (1st Person), or of the person spoken to (2nd Person), and so on. These are the defining instances of what was called, and is still called, a **flectional** language. In Chinese, each word seemed invariable and each meaning seemed to have its own word. It was therefore identified as an **isolating** language. In Turkish, which we will look at in some detail in a later chapter, words may subsume several meanings but they are not fused into a whole. Its type was accordingly **agglutinating**. This typology is partly from the same source as the Darwinesque froth which we referred to in the last paragraph. But it is easy to skim off what was wrong and retain what was worthwhile.

In the twentieth century many structural linguists have attached far less importance to the word. One reason is that they could not devise an operational definition of it. As we will see in chapter 11, there is no single watertight criterion which will identify word boundaries in whatever language. Another reason is that part of morphology was assimilated to syntax. Take, for example, the word *trying*. It consists of a form *try-* followed by a form *-ing*: in phonetic transcription, [traɪ]+[ɪŋ].[2] Likewise *tried*, or [traɪd], consists of [traɪ] followed by [d]. Now take the sentence *They are trying hard*. It consists of the word *they* followed by three further words: *they+are+trying+hard*. At either level we might apply the terminology that Bloomfield used in his great work of the 1930s (BLOOMFIELD, ch. 10). In *They are trying hard*, the form *hard* is 'selected' and is 'ordered' after *trying*. That is the only possible order: one would not say, for example, *They are hard trying*. In *trying*, the form *-ing* is likewise selected and is ordered after *try-*. That is again the only possible order: there is no word *ingtry* or [ɪŋtraɪ]. If we limit ourselves to concepts of selection and order, it seems that both the word and the sentence can be analysed in the same way.

Bloomfield himself retained a division between morphology and syntax. But other and later structuralists were more radical. In Europe, Hjelmslev firmly rejected it. In the United States,

---

[2] Transcriptions of English (Southern British 'Received Pronunciation') will normally follow Gimson's revision of Daniel Jones's pronouncing dictionary (GIMSON).

Harris's 'morphology' covered formal patterning at both levels, and the word, with other familiar units such as the syllable and the sentence, was demoted to vanishing point (HARRIS). According to a form of grammatical theory that had emerged by the beginning of the 1960s, the word was merely one term in a hierarchy of units. In *They are trying hard*, the words *are* and *trying* (two units at 'word level' in the overall grammatical hierarchy of English) would constitute a phrase *are trying* (one unit at 'phrase level'). At the same level, *they* and *hard* are both one-word phrases. Likewise, at a higher level, the three phrases *they*, *are trying* and *hard* form a clause (one unit at 'clause level'). That clause is, in turn, the only element of a one-word sentence. Now syntax traditionally deals with the last three rungs in this hierarchy (phrase, clause and sentence). Morphology traditionally deals with the word. But just as the phrase *are trying* has as its elements *are* and *trying*, so the word *trying* has as its elements *try-* and *-ing*. The word *hard* has no internal structure; neither has the phrase *hard*. If we put things in this way, the natural conclusion is that morphology has no claim to separate treatment, any more than, if we may coin some barbarisms, 'phrase-ology' or 'clause-ology'.

The late 1950s also saw the development of transformational grammar. In Chomsky's first book (CHOMSKY, *Structures*), Harris's influence was still very strong, and in its treatment of the word, as in some other matters, it is an apotheosis of his ideas. With Harris, Chomsky began by assuming that a word like *trying* was a sequence of two separate units (*try-* + *-ing*). In *They are trying hard*, these are part of a larger sequence which is superficially four words. But let us now compare *are trying* with, for example, *have tried*. In both we can replace *try-* with, for example, *cry* or *wail*: *are crying* or *have cried*, *are wailing* or *have wailed*. But in *are trying* we cannot simply replace *are* with *have*: there is no sentence *They have trying hard*. The *are* and the *-ing* go together, and are opposed as a whole to the *have* and the *-ed* of *have tried*. In the same way, the more complex *have been trying* may be analysed into the three interlocking members *try-*, *be* and *-ing*, *have* and *-en*. The reason, again, is that in standard English one cannot say [*They*] *have being trying* (replacing *-en* in the member *have* + *-en* with *-ing*), or *have be trying* (dropping *-en* altogether), or *been trying* (dropping *have* but holding everything else constant), and so on. *Have* and *-en*, *be* and *-ing* are pairs of dependent variables.

This analysis is natural on semantic grounds also. In *are trying*, the *are* and *-ing* together mark what may be called the 'Present Progressive' Tense, as opposed, for example, to the Simple or Non-Progressive Present in *They try hard*. Likewise, the *have* and *-ed* of *have tried* mark what is normally called the 'Present Perfect', and in *have been trying* we have a combination of the Auxiliaries, with associated *-en* and *-ing*, that marks both 'Perfect' and 'Progressive' together. At an abstract level it is these concepts of Tense ('Present', 'Progressive', 'Perfect') that the analyst is above all concerned with. But at the same time the Verbal element *try-* or *tri(e)-* (*trying* and *tried* shorn of their endings) may be linked on its own with the separate word *hard*. *Hard* is an Adverb that sits easily with *try-*, whereas others (e.g. *mellifluously* or *away*) sit with difficulty at best; this fact is independent of the remainder of the Verb phrase, *They have tried away* being as awkward as *They are trying away*, but *They have gone away*, by contrast, being as natural as *They are going away*. The rest of the phrase may even be absent in certain Non-Finite constructions ([*We have made them*] *try hard*), co-ordinate structures ([*They'll try, and*] *try hard*), and so on. One cannot find a converse case in which *try-* is dropped from the phrase instead (*are -ing hard* or *are hard-ing*). Now *try-* and *hard* must, of course, be recognised as independent variables. But in a weaker sense they still go together against *are* and *-ing*.

We thus arrive at an analysis which cuts clean across the conventional boundaries between words. The construction is no longer *were + trying + hard* (two-word Verbal phrase and Adverb *hard*), but rather [*are -ing*] + [*try- hard*] or – we might be tempted to say – '*try hard*' in the Present Progressive. A few years later, Chomsky introduced a theory of grammar in which 'deep' syntax was distinguished from 'surface' syntax. It was only in the surface structure of this sentence that *trying* would be established as a unit. In deep structures this and many other words would be dismembered. Their parts were independently linked to whatever other elements they might be judged to go with, whether these were whole phrases, or words on their own, or the disjecta membra of other words.

But that was not all. For if a large part of morphology was by then assimilated into syntax, the same school arbitrarily assigned the rest of it to phonology. In Chomsky's account, a grammar or **generative grammar** was a series of rules relating meanings of sentences to the phonetic forms of sentences. These rules were of several sorts: for example, there were rules which described deep structures and other rules which related deep structures to surface structures. The term 'phonology' was then applied to a further series of rules, which in turn related surface structures to phonetic forms. One partial surface structure is, for example, *try-+-ing*. From that the rules of phonology, or specifically **generative phonology**, would derive a phonetic form which, if it is to represent my own speech, might begin with a rounded affricate, followed, after the [ɹ] glide, by a long monophthong. The details of all this are water under the bridge. What is important is that, by definition, Chomsky's scheme of grammar had no place for morphology. A part of grammar that had traditionally had its own rules and its own structures was eaten up completely by transformational syntax on the one hand and generative phonology on the other.

So far as structuralist theories were concerned, morphology was at an all-time low when I wrote the first edition of this book. But since then its standing has been restored. This is due, in part, to the disintegration of the classical Chomskyan scheme; by the end of the 1970s, it was clear that one could not cram everything about a language into a series of unidirectional rules relating successive levels of structure. But another factor is the renewed interest in historical linguistics. In its heyday, structuralist theory had been either primarily or exclusively synchronic. It was assumed, firstly, that a given state of a language is best studied in abstraction from its history. That step was, in itself, spectacularly fruitful. But a second assumption, for which authority could also be found in Saussure, was that changes from one state to another are individual, isolated events. Therefore a theorist might proceed without accounting for them. We may distinguish two structuralist attitudes towards diachrony. For some scholars, it belonged to another discipline: in HARRIS, p. 5, 'descriptive linguistics' explicitly excludes it. For others, a synchronic theory might help to explain changes: one thinks immediately of the work of Martinet on diachronic phonology.[3] But it did not have to do so. A theory of language was not rejected merely because the insights of historical philologists contradicted it.

By the beginning of the 1980s this spurious wall between linguistic theory and philology was in ruins. But it was then very difficult to pretend that morphology was not there. To a historian, a morphological change is clearly different from, in particular, a sound change. The latter is phonetically natural and it often has a purely phonetic cause. It will also tend to operate regardless of grammatical categories. But a morphological change is typically motivated by analogy, for which parallels in grammar are the mainspring. By contrast, its phonetic character is irrelevant. Let us take two simple illustrations which will underline these differences. Firstly, in my speech and that of many other speakers of British Received Pronunciation, the triphthong [aɪə], as in *fire*, is monophthongised. Phonetically this is very natural, a more complex articulation being averaged to a simpler. At the same time, it does not respect the grammatical class or structure of the words involved. Thus it applies to Nouns and Verbs (*tyre* and *tire*), to the Comparative form of an Adjective (*higher*), to Nouns derived from Verbs (*buyer*). In both respects it is a typical sound change. Secondly, in some dialects of English a Past Tense *dove* has replaced *dived*: the formal relationship between Past and Present was apparently remodelled on the analogy of *drove* and *drive* or *throve* and *thrive*. Conversely, a child can easily say *drived* instead of *drove*. In explaining such alterations, one does not ask whether the phonetic change (of [aɪvd] to [əʊv] or [əʊv] to [aɪvd]) is inherently plausible. What matters are its morphological conditions. To a historian of languages these differences are fundamental. But they are precisely those which, in a synchronic context, the generative phonologists forgot or ignored. It is not surprising that when their notions were applied to diachrony the experiment rapidly went the way of all follies.

Our understanding of syntactic changes is far less secure. But one motivating principle is that, if two elements stand in a close semantic relationship, they will also tend to be adjacent in sentences. For example, the category of Prepositions in European

---

[3] A. Martinet, *Economie des changements phonétiques* (Berne, Francke, 1955).

languages has developed from what may prehistorically have been an independent class of Adverbs. These came into closer relationship with Nouns or Noun Phrases and, as part of the same process, they became fixed in a position before Nouns or Noun Phrases. However, this principle does not apply to alleged syntactic elements within words. For example, there is no pressure in English for the *-ing* of *are trying* to move nearer to *are*. In discussing this phrase, I have tried to give a fair account of the original Chomskyan argument. But in historical linguistics it is misleading to think of the word as no more than a superficial unit. In the history of English the verb 'to be', as a whole, has developed into an Auxiliary which stands in a grammatical relationship to, among others, the *-ing* forms of verbs, also as wholes.

Diachronic morphology will not be treated systematically, since it is covered in another book in this series (BYNON). But it is one very good reason for taking the field as a whole more seriously than many structuralists, Chomskyan and pre-Chomskyan, once took it.

## THE SCOPE OF MORPHOLOGY

So far I have merely hinted at the subject-matter of morphology; and, to some readers, it may seem that I have allowed these introductory paragraphs to run ahead of the argument. Let us therefore get back to basics. If we wish to begin with a definition, we can say that **morphology** is, briefly, the branch of grammar that deals with the internal structure of words. But although the word is a unit which is familiar in our culture, the notion that it has an internal structure is not. To put the definition in context, we will have to begin by looking more generally at different levels of linguistic patterning.

One of the most important properties of human language is the one that we shall describe as that of **double articulation**. Another common way of referring to it is to say that language has a **dual** structure, or that as a form of communication it has the property of **duality**. Any simple example in speech or writing will make this characteristic clear. If we take the first sentence of W. B. Yeats's 'Sailing to Byzantium':[4]

That is no country for old men

we can say, first of all, that it consists of seven words, *that, is, no* and so on. These combine to form phrases: *old men* is one phrase, and according to most writers would itself be part of a larger phrase *no country for old men*. Such phrases and clauses are articulated according to definite rules. If we put the final Noun into the Singular:

That is no country for old man

the result can be understood and could conceivably be poetry, by some standards. But strictly the Singular phrase (*old man*) ought to have an Article. The sentence could be intuitively corrected – say to the form:

That is no country for an old man

– and that would be more in accordance with English syntax. It is the job of the linguist to discover and elucidate these rules, distinguishing them from patterns of style etc. and testing their adequacy against the actual facts of usage.

This is the first level of organisation – the **first** or **primary articulation** of language – in which words or similar elements are related to each other in syntactic patterns. It is this that is referred to as the level of syntax or of grammar – the term 'grammar' being used here in the most restricted of its senses in linguistics. But the words *that, is* and so on have another internal organisation of their own. *That* consists of four separate letters, *t, h, a* and *t*; when spoken, [ðæt], it can be analysed into a consonant, vowel and further consonant which are assigned to the phonemes symbolised by 'ð', 'æ' and 't'. Likewise *is* [ɪz] may be analysed into two letters or two phonemes, and so on for the remainder. The units which are basic to the primary articulation of language are thus distinguished and identified by combinations of smaller units, letters or phonemes. Moreover, these combinations are in turn subject to rule. A native English word cannot begin, for example, with the consonants *cv* [kv], although it could begin

---

[4] From *The Tower* (1928); in *Collected Poems*, 2nd edn (London, Macmillan, 1950), p. 217.

with *cl*, *qu* [kw] or the like. It is not merely that a word such as *cvab* ([kvæb] or [kvɒb]) does not happen to exist. To the author's knowledge *quab* does not exist either, but there is no reason why it should not do so in the future. It is not an elegant acronym, and perhaps not the word to choose for a new soft drink or washing powder. But if an embarrassed reader were to tell me that it is in fact a four-letter word, which for some reason I have not encountered even on National Service, I could just believe them. Another suggestion is that it might be a suitable name for a weed-killer! We can react in these ways because it is a possible English word, and we can sense its resemblance to other words. But if someone were to blush at *cvab* I would wonder whose army they had been in.

These smaller patterns of organisation form a **second** or **secondary articulation** of language – the level of phonology if, as normally, we are talking of sound-structure and not in terms of the spelling. Now perhaps some might wish to argue that it is phonology that is properly 'primary' and grammar that is properly 'secondary'; in so far as this is an issue of substance it need not concern us here. The important point is that the levels are distinguished, and it is this property which is referred to as that of duality or double articulation. For some scholars the distinction of units alone (words or the like on one side, phonemes etc. on the other) is a central 'design feature', serving to set human language apart from the communication of animals, or so-called 'natural languages' apart from many artificial 'languages' (the 'language' of arithmetical formulae, for instance).

If that were all, there would be no place for morphology. We would simply state which combinations of phonemes could form words, and list in a dictionary those which actually were words; there would be no other sense in which a notion of 'word-structure' would be meaningful. But of course it is not all. If we take a little more of Yeats's poem:

> The young
> In one another's arms, birds in the trees
> – Those dying generations – at their song,
> The salmon-falls, the mackerel-crowded seas,
> Fish, flesh, or fowl, commend all summer long
> Whatever is begotten, born, and dies.

we at once find several words with parts which function separately. *Arms, birds, trees, generations, -falls* and *seas* share an ending *s* ([z]) by which, as Plural Nouns, they are distinguished from the corresponding Singulars *arm, bird* and so on. This -*s* is an example of what is usually called a **morpheme**. Similarly, *dies* has a morpheme -*s* which distinguishes it from *dying* (with a different morpheme -*ing* or [ɪŋ]) and from *die* (with no corresponding morpheme) or *died*; compare *tried, trying* and *try* in our earlier illustration. In general, then, we may proceed to specify the structure of this set of words by saying that any member (*bird* or *birds, dies, die* or *dying*) consists of a minimal Noun or Verb, followed either by no morpheme at all (*bird* or *die*) or by whichever of a series of morphemes (Plural -*s* etc.) suits.

According to a common proposal one would then say that it is not words, in fact, that form the basis of the primary articulation. In *birds in the trees* there are not four basic units but six (or five with one appearing twice). The words *birds* and *trees* are themselves combinations of units – the second unit being identified by the letter '*s*' or the phoneme symbolised by '*z*' – in much the way that, as we said, the phrase *old men* is a combination of *old* and *men*. If we could tear ourselves away from word spelling a student of grammar might find it more convenient to write the example as follows:

bird s in the tree s

The term 'morpheme' is then applied to each of these units. In our example, the first unit (*bird*) is one morpheme. It is followed by a second morpheme (*s*), which in turn is followed by a third morpheme (*in*) and so on. This is the starting-point for the structuralist analyses which we referred to earlier. In such analyses the morpheme is the minimal, indivisible or primitive unit; grammar is the study of the arrangements of morphemes within utterances; and the word is at best one of a hierarchy of complex or non-minimal units which also includes the phrase and the clause.

We will return to the morpheme in chapter 6. But for the moment there is a problem which we can easily illustrate with the same material. Let us return, for example, to *men* in the first line of Yeats's poem. In meaning, this is Plural, just as *birds* or *trees* is

Plural, and just as the meanings of these are opposed to those of the Singulars *bird* and *tree*, so that of *men* is opposed to that of the Singular *man*. We might display this as a proportional series:

man:men = bird:birds = tree:trees

But this holds for the meanings only. In form the difference between *man* and *men* lies in the vowels: Singular -*a*- but Plural -*e*-. But in the other pairs it lies in the presence or absence of -*s*. Another example is *those* at the beginning of the third line. In meaning, the Plural *those* stands to the Singular *that* (contrast *that dying generation*) as *these* stands to *this*:

that:those = this:these

But the formal distinctions differ again: phonetically, [æt] versus [əʊz] and [ɪs] versus [iːz]. Now for syntactic purposes a grammarian will want to treat the oppositions between Singular and Plural as one and the same. For example, in *those dying generations* the plural *those* agrees with the Plural *generations* in just the way that, in *these dying men*, Plural *these* agrees with Plural *men*. Traditionally the words are assigned to the same **categories**: *man, bird*, etc. to the Singular category and *men, birds*, etc. to the Plural category. But they differ in their **inflections**. In *birds* or *trees*, the Plural inflection involves a morpheme -*s*. In *men* it involves a vowel -*e*- which is different from that of the Singular.

Similar points can be made for the Verbs in the same passage. In the line:

Whatever is begotten, born, and dies

there are two words, *begotten* and *born*, which grammarians traditionally assign to the category 'Past Participle'. If we then cite the final couplet of this verse:

Caught in that sensual music all neglect
Monuments of unageing intellect.

we find another, *caught*, and in the corresponding lines of the second verse:

And therefore I have sailed the seas and come
To the holy city of Byzantium.

there are two more, *sailed* and *come*. We can establish a series in which these words are opposed to the corresponding Presents:

sail : sailed = bear : born = beget : begotten
= catch : caught = come : come

But there is again no constant inflection. *Sailed* has the regular pattern; compare *die : died* or *try : tried*. But the final consonant is different in *born* and *begotten*, and the vowels which precede it are different from those of the Present: [bɔː] plus [n] versus [beə], [bɪgɒt] plus [n] versus [bɪget]. *Caught* [kɔːt] and *catch* [kætʃ] differ in everything except the first consonant. Finally, between Present *come* and Past Participle *come* there is no formal distinction at all.

In syntax we will talk simply of the category 'Past Participle'. For example, in *I have sailed the seas and come* the two Participles are the same in respect of their relationship to the Auxiliary *have*. Morphology is then concerned with two sorts of variation in the 'forms of words'. In one case, inflections distinguish different categories: thus Past Participle *sailed* from Present *sail* or Present Participle *sailing*. We will say that the inflections **mark** the categories. Thus, in *sailed*, the presence of *-ed* at the end of the word marks the Past Participle, and also (in a construction such as *I sailed the seas*) the Past Tense. In the other case, different inflections mark the same category: thus the *e* in *men* and the *-s* in *seas* both mark Plural. We will say that the inflections **alternate**. In the Plural in English there is an **alternation** involving several inflections, of which Yeats's lines have supplied no more than a selection. Thus in *mice* and *lice* Plural is marked by a diphthong [aɪ] ([maɪs], [laɪs]), in *children* it is marked by *-ren* and by the vowel [ɪ], and so on.

But morphology is not only concerned with inflections. There are other aspects of word structure which can be illustrated in the same poem, and which shade away into patterning of finer and finer subtlety. For a straightforward example take *whatever*. This is one word, with a single accent ([wɒt'evə]). But it is in turn composed of two smaller words. In meaning, *whatever* is to *what* as *whichever* is to *which* or *whenever* to *when*. But *what* is itself a word in, say, *What was she wearing?* Likewise *ever* is a word in constructions like *if you ever see her*. A word whose parts may

themselves be words in other contexts is traditionally called a
**compound**. Another example in the text is *salmon-falls*. This is
written with a hyphen, and when we read the poem it too will be
given a single accent: ['sæmənfɔːlz], not ['sæmən 'fɔːlz]. In that
respect at least it behaves like one word. But its internal structure
subsumes not only the Plural inflection *-s*, but also *salmon* and
*fall*.

However, this second example is not quite as straightforward as
the first. We can look in any dictionary and find an entry for
*whatever*: it has been a single grammatical unit since the Middle
Ages, and the range of constructions into which it enters (in
*Whatever is begotten, Whatever book you choose, I have no notion
whatever, Bring your typewriter or whatever*) is peculiar to it. But
the first three dictionaries I have looked at say nothing about
*salmon-falls*. Its status as a unit is less clear, and for many readers
it will be a new combination of words. It will accordingly be
construed in the same way that one might understand a syntactic
combination: for example, *The salmon are leaping*. *Mackerel-
crowded* is still more clearly a nonce form. There are other
hyphenated forms which establish the pattern: for example, *snow-
covered, chocolate-filled, diamond-studded*. But in ordinary speech
there are limits on the combinations that one might use. For
example, one would not ordinarily say *I went out into a people-
crowded street* instead of *I went out into a street crowded with people*.
Part of the genius of the poet is the ability to transcend such
limits.

Another aspect of word structure will be treated under the
heading of **word-formation**. Take, for example, *unageing*. On
the face of it, this might be analysed into a morpheme *un-* plus
*ageing*, in much the sense that *died* consists of *die* plus the
morpheme *-d*. The latter has *-d* as its ending, whereas the former
has *un-* as its 'beginning'. But is it quite the same sort of case? We
will normally think of *died* and *die* as forms of the 'same word'
(see chapter 2 for this sense of 'word'). We would not expect them
to have separate entries in a dictionary, and a statement about the
meanings and syntactic uses of '*die*' would be taken to cover the
Past Tense as well as the Present. We would likewise identify
forms of the word '*age*' in both *It has aged* and *It will age*. But do
we want to say that *unageing* is merely another form of the same

word – the Negative form of the Participle, as it were, in contrast to the Positive *ageing* (e.g. in *He is ageing*)? Surely the answer is No. Indeed, whatever we think of *ageing* or *dying* in a Verbal construction of the type *He's ageing* or *He's dying*, do we still want to say that they are forms of the Verbs '*age*' or '*die*' when they appear in the phrase *his ageing father* or in Yeats's *those dying generations*? Again, a dictionary provides a rough practical test of our intuitions. We would certainly expect entries for *dying* and *undying*, and at least in a full dictionary for *ageing* and *unageing* also. The reader will find, for example, that the first pair have separate headings in the *Shorter OED*, and all four are in the *OED* proper. With many other forms in *-ing* the issue is even plainer. Take, for example, the Adjective in *a trying day*. This has its own meaning and its own range of constructions, which differ from those of *trying* as a form of the Verb '*try*'. For instance, it can be followed by the Preposition *to*: *The day was very trying to all concerned*. This is not possible with the Verb '*try*' (*They tried to all concerned*).

Nevertheless, the Verb and Adjective are related. We cannot say that the Phrase *a trying day* has nothing whatever to do with the use of *tries* in *I find this weather tries me very hard*, or that *dying generations* and *unageing intellect* have nothing whatever to do with '*die*' and '*age*'. Moreover, it is a relationship of meaning as well as form: it is not simply that *dying* or the like are Adjectives which happen to have a Verbal sort of ending. If we now take the word *generations* it is formally no more than a Noun. It has the Plural ending of *trees*, *arms*, etc., and in a phrase such as *three generations ago* it may function as a straightforward time word, as such just a little more imprecise than *five decades ago* and much more so than the potentially exact *fifty years ago*. In *the modern generation* or *later generations* it is still a straight Noun, though of a slightly different class. But at the same time it is related in form to the Verb *generate*, and may be used with a definite Verbal nuance: thus *Electricity is clean, but its generation makes a mess* (effectively with Object *it = electricity*; compare *generating it*), or less explicitly in *the act of generation*. In Yeats's poem this relationship is clearly exploited. Although *those dying generations* has the syntactic construction of *later generations*, *that sensual music* and so on, the underlying Verbal sense of *generate* may still be caught and put in opposition to the sense of '*die*' in *dying*. Similarly, the Adjective *sensual* (in the last couplet of this verse) has a formal and semantic connection with *sense* (compare *the gratification of the senses*) which brings it closer to its opposite *intellect* (compare *intellectual*). Yet an Adjective it remains.

Naturally, there are limits beyond which such analyses cannot be pushed. In one of Aldous Huxley's stories, a character feels like saying 'Bow-wow-wow!' when he hears the word 'cynic'.[5] Here (as often in Huxley's work), the resources are purely etymological – *cynic* being from a Greek Adjective formed from the word for 'dog' (κύων *kýɔːn*, Genitive κυνός *kynós*). So far as English is concerned, there is neither a formal nor a semantic connection between *cynic* on the one hand and *dog* or any comparable Noun on the other. But what of the other English Nouns in -*ic*? *Music* in Yeats's poem has an etymological connection with *Muse*, just as *panic*, for example, is connected with *Pan*. The latter pair have no link in modern English, and indeed the god Pan will mean little to many speakers. But are *Muse* and *music* entirely divorced? There is certainly a morphological element, -*ic*, in Adjectives such as *horrific* or *melancholic*. Admittedly, no Nouns in -*ic* have a truly transparent analysis. But if a writer invokes an interplay between music and the Muses can we say with absolute confidence that it is etymology and not word-structure that he is playing with? One can also find instances in ordinary conversation where a speaker has reanalysed a word. It is a worn-out gibe that feminists avoid the form -*man*- at all costs: thus *Personchester* for *Manchester* or *huperson* for *human*. But in a radio interview[6] something written by a woman was referred to, apparently in all seriousness, as 'a manifesto, or rather a woman-festo'. Momentarily at least, the speaker had treated *manifesto* as a compound of *man* and (*i*)*festo*.

The limits of morphological analysis can be illustrated with more humdrum examples. In *farmer* or *actor* we recognise an element -*er* or -*or* (phonetically both [ə]); the words have an obvious relationship to *farm* and to at least one sense of *act*. Well, let us go along the High Street. The *baker* is in origin someone who 'bakes', the *banker* runs a 'bank', the *furniture remover* 'removes furniture', and so on. What then of the *butcher*, the

---

[5] The Gioconda Smile', *Collected Short Stories* (London, 1957), p. 93.
[6] BBC, Radio 4, 16 May 1986.

*grocer*, or the *ironmonger*? One answer might be that *butcher*, for instance, is indeed *butch-* plus *-er*; since this '*butch-*' is not connected in meaning with any other '*butch*', it would be established as a (so-called) 'partially independent' element, distinct from *-er* but nevertheless unable to enter into any other combination. Likewise *groc(e)-* and *mong-* would be extracted as elements which are restricted to *grocer*, *groceries*, *ironmonger* and the like. The other answer, of course, is that words such as *butcher* are morphologically simple; but why, one then asks, do even simple 'occupation' Nouns so often end in *-er*? One can fruitlessly prolong the discussion of this kind of patterning.

But there will come a point at which no analyst will wish to pursue the chopping-up process further. Let us consider the points of the compass: *East*, *West*, *North* and *South*. The first two are opposite to each other on the dimension of longitude, and the words both end in *-st*. The others are opposite on the dimension of latitude, and both end in *-th*. Shall we therefore divide each into successive parts: an ending *-st* or *-th* for the 'East/West' or 'North/South' co-ordinate, preceded by four 'partially independent' elements *Ea-*, *We-*, *Nor-* and *Sou-*? Indeed, shall we say that *Sou-* (phonetically [saʊ]) recurs independently in *Sou-wester*? In fact, we will not support such analyses. Even if there is something here worth saying, the pattern is too restricted to fall profitably within the morphological domain. Another case that is often discussed is that of phonaesthetic (loosely onomatopoeic) groupings: to take a well-known example, is the *-mp* or *-ump* of *bump*, *thump*, etc. a separable element? If we separated it consistently, any attractions the analysis might have would rapidly dissolve. But can one say with precision where the domain of morphological analysis should end? If these are limiting cases, then are there general criteria by which the line is drawn? On the face of it, each of the cases which we have mentioned raises slightly different problems.

Such marginal uncertainties concern word-formation and compounds in particular. As we will see more clearly in later chapters, these can in some respects be taken together in opposition to inflections. In another and more obvious sense, compounding (since it involves a combination of words) is opposed to inflection and word-formation. But for the moment we have shown sufficiently that the study of word-structure must include all three.

## MORPHOLOGY AND GENERAL LINGUISTIC THEORY

One reason for studying morphology is simply that it is there: it is a facet of language that has to be described and is a source of absorbing practical problems. But linguistics is not only concerned with practical description. We must also ask how far a general theory of morphology is possible.

The aim of such a theory will be to elucidate certain principles that apply to the structure of words in all languages. Take, for example, the order of inflectional morphemes. In English, they are at the ends of words (-*s* in *seas*, -*ing* in *dying*, and so on). In many other languages they are at the beginning: we will cite some forms in chapter 7 from Navaho, which is one of the Athabaskan family in North America. But in most cases there is at least a degree of consistency. In particular, it is unusual to find that the same individual category is marked sometimes here and sometimes there. Let us suppose, for the sake of argument, that English is an unknown language which we are investigating for the first time. So far we have found Plural morphemes at the ends of words: -*s* in *seas*; also, among others, -*ren* in *children*. We would not then expect to find others – still less, for example, the same morpheme -*s* – at the beginning. Of course, we might; in linguistics there are always exceptions. But that would not represent a common pattern.

As they stand, these are just observations. But it is not difficult to see that such facts might also have an explanation. If a category is always marked in the same place, it is more easily perceived, or more easily recognised by children learning the language, or contributes generally to a more orderly system. The patterns are in that way **motivated**. All else being equal, it is natural or logical that, where there are several inflections, they should tend to occupy the same position. We may then appeal to similar arguments in accounting for the ways in which a language changes. For example, a language might at one stage have a few inflections at the beginnings of words but most at the end.

Ancient Greek was one such (see examples in chapters 8 and 9). Later it might change so that all are at the end. There are many factors to which a historian might look for explanation, but this form of motivation could be one.

The foundation of such arguments is doubtful and it might well be asked whether they are truly explanatory. Note, in particular, that at no point in this argument have we been dealing with anything stronger than a tendency. But is there a tighter theory that will cover every language? To be tighter it will have to be restrictive: it will have to set a limit to the possible structures that a language may have. It will accordingly identify not tendencies but **laws**, not patterns which we observe in languages but ones which a language must in some sense conform to. If it is true of all languages we will say that it is **universal**. In linguistics generally, such theories are particularly associated with Chomsky. According to Chomsky, certain restrictions are genetically inherited as part of the normal make-up of the human mind. They guide and limit a child's acquisition of language; therefore there is a very strong pressure for all languages to follow them.

But once we start to look for laws the differences between languages are more refractory. Two laws that we might at first sight take to be universal are (1) that all languages have words; (2) that all languages have morphemes. We may refer to these as **formal principles**: they concern the basic form of a language. But what exactly do they mean? Languages, as we have said, are doubly articulated; and, according to different conceptions, either the word or the morpheme is the basic unit of the primary articulation. Suppose that it is the word. In that case there are languages of the isolating type in which a word has no inflectional structure: Classical Chinese, in the words of a recent survey, was 'an almost perfect example'.[7] Hence the morpheme, if defined as a unit of inflection, is not universal. Alternatively, let us say that morphemes are the indivisible semantic units. Now in agglutinating languages these are easily identified: as we will see in chapter 6, a word in Turkish is a sequence of distinct parts, each of which has a separate grammatical function. But in flectional languages they are not: in Ancient Greek the parts of words are

---

[7] NORMAN, p. 84. Norman's brief account of the language is notably clear and useful.

less distinct, and when they can be separated as forms it is unusual for a single function to be associated with them. The term 'morpheme' might still be applied to them, but the criteria for the unit would be different. It can also be applied to an indivisible semantic unit in an isolating language; but then the status of the word is problematic. If we examine these principles carefully, either their substance dissipates or their universality is in doubt.

This typology of languages is more than a century old, and in the interval it has been modified and elaborated. It is also a typology of extremes: many languages (such as English) are not so clearly characterised. However, one way to avoid sacrificing substance to universality is to develop formal principles that hold, in the first instance at least, for a particular type. In some languages semantic properties will be predicated directly of the word. That is the traditional way of describing Ancient Greek and Latin, and it was originally conceived by speakers of those languages. Inflections are formal elements within the word, and we must then consider how its internal structure should be specified. In fact, there are alternatives; it may be that at this point different subtypes of language are distinguished by different formal principles, and that the classic flectional type is only one of them. In other languages, similar semantic properties will be predicated of morphemes. In some the word will also be established as a central unit, whose internal structure is governed by formal principles which differ from those applying to syntactic constructions. That broadly characterises the agglutinating type. In others morphemes will enter directly into syntactic relations, and these are the type that we would call isolating. Marginal cases will remain. But the more detailed the principles, the more the typology will be sharpened.

This is the way in which in practice, different languages have been described. In an influential article of the mid 1950s, Hockett pinpointed three **models** of grammatical analysis in general – three different 'frames of reference' (to adapt his words) within which an analyst might 'approach the grammatical description of a language and state the results of his investigation' (first sentence of HOCKETT, 'Models'). In the terms which we are using, these are particular sets of formal principles. Of Hockett's three, one, which he called the 'Word and Paradigm' model, evidently

21

referred to the traditional description of the older European languages. Another, which he labelled 'Item and Arrangement', is a model in which morphemes are the basic units of meaning and in which they were arranged linearly. The third ('Item and Process') is one in which the structure of a word is specified by a series of operations; as we will see in chapter 7, this is one effective way to describe inflections. Hockett said little about the first model; but between the others he could not choose definitively. In part, at least, it was a matter of a grammarian's general outlook. But one reason why the outlook of grammarians differs is that they tend to be specialists in particular types of system. An 'Item and Arrangement' model has, in practice, been effective in Chinese. It has few attractions for a specialist in Latin, and not just through inculcated theoretical prejudice.

To speak in this way is not to renounce the prospect of identifying other, more general principles. It may be that some are more abstract and will cut across models. Another possibility is that certain principles in morphology may correlate with principles in syntax or in other branches of description. Such correlations would themselves be principles of a higher order. But before we are tempted to launch into flights of speculation, we should recall that morphology is also a practical subject. For particular languages or families of languages, various particular models or techniques of description have proved illuminating. It is at this level that an introduction can be most helpful.

RELATED READING

There are few general introductions to morphology: for readers who do not like mine, BAUER, *Morphology* is the natural alternative; for those who know German, there is an older text by H. Bergenholtz & J. Mugdan, *Einführung in die Morphologie* (Stuttgart, Kohlhammer, 1979). At a higher level WURZEL should be read, especially for an historical perspective. On historical morphology see further BYNON; ANTTILA, especially ch. 5; also FISIAK, which is a cut above most conference proceedings.

For an up-to-date survey of technical work within the generative school see A. Spencer, *Morphological Theory* (Oxford, Blackwell, 1991), which has unfortunately appeared too late for detailed reference. HAMMOND & NOONAN is a useful sampling of recent work in morphology, at least in the United States.

On nineteenth-century classifications see A. Morpurgo Davies, 'Language classification', in SEBEOK, pp. 606–716 (typological classes pp. 652ff.). Other papers in SEBEOK are sporadically useful for the history of the subject. For a later typology, which stands as a monument without that much productive influence, see SAPIR, ch. 6. My own approach to the issue springs from an inaugural lecture by C. E. Bazell, *Linguistic Typology* (London, School of Oriental and African Studies, 1958; reprinted in P. D. Strevens (ed.), *Five Inaugural Lectures*, London, Oxford University Press, 1966).

For Hjelmslev's view of morphology and syntax see L. Hjelmslev, *Prolegomena to a Theory of Language* (trans. F. J. Whitfield, 2nd edn, Madison, University of Wisconsin Press, 1961), pp. 26, 59. But this is a difficult work; much easier is his *Language: an Introduction* (Madison, University of Wisconsin Press, 1970), also trans. F. J. Whitfield. Bloomfield's mature view is in a classic book (BLOOMFIELD) which all students of linguistics should read; for commentary I hope I may anticipate the publication of a study of my own, 'Bloomfield's morphology and its successors', to appear in *TPhS*.

For the semantics of the English Verb see, for example, PALMER. Chomsky's treatment first appeared in CHOMSKY, *Structures*, pp. 38–42; current textbook version in A. D. Radford, *Transformational Grammar* (Cambridge, Cambridge University Press, 1988), pp. 401ff. We will return to generative phonology in the reading for chapter 8; for the moment LASS, ch. 9, may stand as a sufficient obituary.

The importance of double articulation was first stressed by Martinet: for a textbook account see MARTINET, § 1.8, but note that his term 'moneme', for a unit of the first articulation (§ 1.9), is not general. 'Duality' is Hockett's term: see HOCKETT, *Course*, p. 574. For its place among 'design features' see LYONS, *Semantics*, I, pp. 70ff.

Ch. 8 of BAUER, *Morphology*, is a useful discussion of the limits to the recognition of morphemes: for the slide into etymology see pp. 116ff. The term 'partially independent element' is from HARRIS, p. 177. On phonaesthetic groupings see ULLMANN, pp. 82ff.; briefly, but in a useful theoretical perspective, in LYONS, *Semantics*, I, p. 104. Words in *-ump* are among the examples introduced by BLOOMFIELD, p. 245; others, in profusion, are discussed with insight in a group of papers by D. L. Bolinger: see his *Forms of English* (ed. I. Abe & T. Kaneyiko, Tokyo, Hokuou Publishing Company, 1965), part 2, chs. 2–5.

For motivated patterns see chapter 12. For Chomsky's current conception of 'universal grammar' see his *Knowledge of Language* (New York, Praeger, 1986), noting especially the theory of parameters (pp. 146ff.). I have discussed its development in my contribution to N. E. Collinge (ed.), *An Encyclopaedia of Language* (London, Routledge, 1990), pp. 112–38.

# 2
# Word, word-form and lexeme

Different senses of the term 'word': words and lexemes; homonymy, syncretism, lexical homonymy; words and word-forms. *Practical illustrations.* Need to draw distinctions: in lexicography; in counting word frequency; in concordances; in study of collocations; in semantic theory. *Lexical and inflectional morphology.* Word-formation as lexeme formation; likewise compounding. Word-formation and compounding as branches of lexical morphology. Paradigms; inflectional morphology the study of paradigms. Categories: morphosyntactic categories; morphosyntactic categories vs morphosyntactic properties.

The reader may have noticed that the term 'word' has been used in two, or perhaps three, different senses. We said, first of all, that the opening sentence of Yeats's poem:

That is no country for old men

was made up of seven words, and that each of these was made up of varying numbers of letters or phonemes. Likewise in a line of Latin poetry about a river:

Labitur et labetur in omne volubilis aevum

'It glides past and will continue to glide past, rolling on for all time' (Horace, *Epistles*, 1, 2. 43) we will distinguish a seven-letter word *labitur* '[it] glides', a two-letter word *et* 'and', and so on. The ancient grammarians would already have analysed the line in this way, saying more precisely that *labitur* was built up of the three syllables *la, bi* and *tur*, and that it was these in turn which were built up of the letters *l, a*, etc. Similarly, the English word *country* could, in the first instance, be divided phonetically into the syllables [kʌn] and [tri], with stress on the first. In all this we are describing a 'word' in terms of phonological units: syllables and ultimately letters or phonemes, considered as the primitives or minimal elements (in the Ancient Greek philosophers' term the *stoikheîa*) of the secondary articulation of language. Let us refer to this, for the moment, as a characteristic of the 'word' in sense 1.

At the same time we said, for example, that *dies* and *died* (two different words in sense 1) are nevertheless varying forms of the SAME word '*die*'. Similarly, *man* and *men* are two different forms (Singular and Plural) of the one word '*man*', and in the line of Horace which we have cited there are two different forms *labitur* 'glides' and *labetur* '[it] will glide', of the one word which we look up in the dictionary as '*labor*' ('slip', 'glide', etc.). The distinction is perhaps more familiar in this type of language than in English, since we are used to seeing the different forms of words (the forms being the 'words' in sense 1) set out systematically for learning purposes. We will look up Latin '*amo*' ('love') in a dictionary, but we know that this subsumes a battery of forms which may be classified as 1st Person, 2nd Person and 3rd Person (*amo* 'I love', *amas* 'you [Sg.] love', *amat* '[he] loves'), and then again as Present or Perfect (*amo* 'I love', *amavi* 'I loved, have loved') and so on. So, if we came across a particular form such as *amat* or *amavi* in a particular passage of literature we might ask 'What exactly is the force or significance of "*amo*" here?', meaning not the individual form *amo* (the word in sense 1), but the dictionary word '*amo*' to which it and *amat*, and *amavi*, and many other variant forms belong.

The words which we have been writing in inverted commas ('*amo*', '*labor*', '*die*' or '*man*') are plainly words in a different sense from that in which our assemblages of syllables, letters or phonemes (*died, labitur, man* or *amo* specifically) are words. Let us, for the moment, simply refer to this as the 'word' in sense 2. It should be obvious that the word in sense 2 is not, as such, composed or built up of any kind of smaller element. It is instead an ABSTRACT unit. It belongs to the grammatical or primary articulation of language, and when we talk about its properties they are most usually characteristics of syntactic classification (for instance, the word '*die*' is a Verb) or of meaning (for example, '*die*' is in one sense opposite in meaning to '*live*'). Again, if we say that '*man*' and '*die*' are very common words in English the statement is neutral not only between the variants *man* or *men, die* or *died*, etc., but also between the written forms *man* etc. (which are analysable in terms of letters), and the spoken [mæn] etc. (which are analysable in terms of phonemes).

This point may perhaps need underlining. When we look up

'*amo*' or '*labor*' in a Latin dictionary we do, of course, expect to find them in alphabetical order. We therefore open the book at the beginning or towards the middle and scan the page headings for '*a*' or '*am*', for '*l*', '*lab*', and so on. And perhaps we are mildly narked if we look up the Adjective '*volubilis*' (as in our Horatian example) under '*v*' and find that, following the ancient style in which *v* and *u* were the same letter, it has been entered as '*uolubilis*' instead. In this practical sense it may seem that '*labor*' and '*volubilis*' or '*uolubilis*' are indeed composed of letters. However, this is a property of the symbol (the way the object is represented), not of the object itself which is being symbolised. In talking about Latin it has always been the custom to refer to words in sense 2 by means of the Nominative Singular of Nouns (e.g. the word '*mensa*', meaning 'table'), and the 1st Singular Present Indicative of Verbs. In talking about French or Italian, however, the accepted usage is to refer to Verbs by the Infinitive instead: the Verb '*aimer*' or the Verb '*amare*' (both 'love' once again). For some other languages, such as Sanskrit, dictionaries are organised by stems or roots (see chapter 4); this is like taking '*am-*' as the heading for the dictionary entry for '*amo*', '*mens-*' for that of '*mensa*', or '*lab-*' for that of '*labor*'. But whichever symbolic convention we adopt, the object which we are talking about will remain the same. If we did happen to refer to French Verbs by the 1st Singular or to Latin Nouns by the root it would not affect their identity, as such, in the slightest.

In order to reinforce this abstract status it will be helpful to make a small change in the way the symbol is written. So far, we have been trying to do this with inverted commas, but they are untidy and the lower case letters still suggest too close a connection with the individual forms in sense 1. From now on we shall therefore follow a convention by which, whenever we need to make clear that we are referring to a word in sense 2, we will write it in small capitals: thus Latin AMO, English LOVE, French AIMER, and so on. It will also be convenient to have a special term for the 'word' in this sense. It is, in particular, a lexical unit and is entered in dictionaries as the fundamental element in the lexicon of a language. We will accordingly call it the **lexeme**. So, to summarise our distinction, we will say that *dies, died, dying* and *die* are forms of the lexeme DIE, that *man* and *men* are the Singular and Plural of MAN, that the lexeme MAN is a Noun but DIE a Verb, likewise in Latin that *amo* and *amat* are both forms of the lexeme AMO, that *mensa* is the Nominative Singular of the Noun MENSA, that AMO 'love' is contrary in meaning to ODI 'hate', and so on.

Having distinguished the lexeme in this sense, we might then reserve the term 'word' for our original sense 1. So, conversely, MAN would have as its forms the two words *man* and *men*, and Latin AMO would subsume the words *amo* 'I love', *amas* 'you love' and so on. But there is still another distinction which is implicit in some of our discussion in chapter 1. In the case of *a trying day*, we remarked that the Adjective '*trying*' is not the same as the other '*trying*' which appears in *They are trying hard*. We will now say that two different lexemes are involved: an Adjective TRYING in the first example but the Verb TRY in the second. However, this is not quite enough, since we still want to say that the first '*trying*' as such is a different word from the second '*trying*', likewise as such. In more technical terms we have two different units (one a form of TRYING, the other of TRY) which are nevertheless **homonymous**. The notion that words may be homonymous will be familiar to most readers. But in what precise terms should homonymy be defined?

Similar identities can be demonstrated for forms of the same lexeme in most languages. In *He came* and *He has come* we distinguish a Past Tense *came* and a Past Participle *come*, both of which belong to the lexeme COME. In *He tried* and *He has tried* the first '*tried*' must again be Past Tense and the second again the Past Participle; for TRY (as for most English Verbs) the two forms are identical both in spelling and in phonetics. The term '**syncretism**' (in origin a term in diachronic linguistics) is often applied synchronically to this situation. In English there is regularly a syncretism between the forms of the Past Tense and the Past Participle. On the other hand, while verbs such as TRY make no distinction at that point, the forms of COME exhibit a much less usual pattern of syncretism in which the Past Participle (the '*come*' of *He has come*) is identical with the Present form (the '*come*' of *They come*). Grammatically, the two words are again as different as *tried* and *try*. In a language such as Latin regular syncretisms leap to the eye in any grammar. The most cited case is in the Nominative and Accusative of Neuters. In Horace's phrase *in omne...aevum* 'for all time' the words *omne* 'all' and *aevum* 'time' are Accusative, this being the construction required by the Preposition *in*. But in other constructions identical forms would appear as the Nominatives of the same lexemes. This applies to all Neuters, the distinction between Nominative and Accusative being **syncretised** throughout that Gender. An alternative term is 'neutralisation': thus, to take another example, the distinction between Singular and Plural is neutralised in a word such as *sheep*.

In these statements it is evident that we are again using the term 'word' in two different senses. Our original 'word in sense 1' was described as an assemblage of syllables and phonemes (or syllables and letters). Accordingly, two such words can be said to differ if and only if their composition differs. *Tries*, *trying* and *tried*, *came* and *come*, etc. all differ in one or more elements, but *tried*, *trying* or *come* are in this sense three words and three words only. Similarly, Latin *omne* is simply a disyllable built up of *om-* and *-ne*, and *aevum* one built up of *ae-* and *-vum*. Homonymy then arises when a single word as it appears on the basis of phonology or spelling (sense 1) nevertheless corresponds to more than one word in another, essentially grammatical, sense. Thus, as we have seen, there are two words in this other sense – sense 3, let us provisionally call it – which correspond to the one written or spoken word *come*. In more technical terms, homonymy is one particular facet of the discrepancies between the two articulations of language (see chapter 1).

This situation can be shown within or across lexemes, as we have seen. But naturally we can have the further case in which the sets of word-forms are homonymous at every point. If we compare the examples *I struck a match* and *I had to strike two matches* with *He won the match* and *He only won two matches* we might distinguish two separate '*match*' lexemes. Dictionaries usually give them separate headings (if only because they have different etymologies!), and following common dictionary notation we can distinguish them as MATCH[1] and MATCH[2]. But each form of MATCH[1] (e.g. Singular *match*) is homonymous with the corresponding form of MATCH[2]. This is the clearest sort of instance in which we would normally speak of lexical homonymy: a reasonable abbreviation is to say that the lexemes themselves are formally identical. But of course there are others, in appearance at least. In many instances our conventions force us to head two dictionary entries with the same 'word', even though, in fact, there are distinctions elsewhere in the paradigms. For example, we also have a Verb which appears in *They match beautifully* – MATCH³ we will have to call it. But we could make a distinction without superscripts if the tradition was to represent Verbs by Participles (MATCHING) instead. Many such instances may be seen more exactly in terms of the homonymy of roots (*match-*) or of lexical stems (see below, chapter 4).

But for the moment we are still concerned with words. This third sense of the term – the word in sense 3 – may also be approached from another angle. One sort of 'word analysis', as we have seen, is in terms of syllables and phonemes. So English [bɪgɒtn] *begotten* may be analysed into three syllables [bɪ], [gɒ], [tn], with stress on the second. The corresponding synthetic statement – a statement of synthesis as opposed to analysis – is that phonemes are 'built up' to form syllables and syllables built up to form the word (in sense 1) as a whole. But words may also be analysed in terms of the primary or grammatical articulation of language. For the student of grammar *begotten* is not a primitive. It has an analysis involving at least two elements, one of which we will now refer to as the lexeme BEGET and the other the element 'Past Participle' which we referred to as a category. What, then, is the corresponding statement of synthesis at this level? As we have seen, the minimal elements of grammar are not identified as combinations of phonological units – the bits, as it were, of the word in sense 1. The unit which is 'built up' of BEGET and 'Past Participle' is a 'word' in another sense, and obviously our sense 3 precisely. In our Western grammatical tradition, this unit would be identified by a verbal formula of the type 'the Past Participle of BEGET': more elaborately, we will say that *begotten* or [bɪgɒtn] (the word in sense 1) 'is' – i.e. is the written or phonetic form taken by – the Past Participle of this lexeme. It is this verbal formula (which we will discuss more precisely in chapter 7) which distinguishes the word in the sense we are now concerned with. Similarly, to go back to our homonyms, we will say that *tried* is either 'the Past Participle of TRY' or 'the Past Tense of TRY' instead. There is at least one other way in which the structure of the word in sense 3 might be expressed, but for the moment this traditional style is perfectly adequate.

The distinction which we have just drawn is naturally neither crucial nor relevant on all occasions. When we are concerned with the syntax of a sentence and we say, for example, that in Horace's *in omne volubilis aevum* 'rolling on for all time' the Preposition *in* governs the 'words' *omne aevum* (these words being in the Accusative and not, as in some other constructions with *in*, in the Ablative), our reference to the Cases 'Accusative' and 'Ablative' makes clear that we are talking of words in sense 3. We must be, since we are analysing the phrase at the grammatical level. But it would be stupid not to represent the words we are talking about by their ordinary written forms. To say that the Preposition IN governs the Accusative Singular Neuter of OMNIS followed by the Accusative Singular of AEVUM (however strictly it derives from our principles) would lead to a cumulatively rather tiresome grammar. It is equally obvious, when we speak of phonemes in 'word-final' position or in the position 'before the word-boundary', that we are talking of words in sense 1. Again, we may say that Horace's line has 'seven words', meaning either words in sense 1 or words in sense 3 (since here – though see later in this chapter – there is no practical consequence of discriminating between them). For this reason, it would be pedantic to impose a distinction of terms – 'word¹' and 'word³', as it were – and insist on following it throughout. The distinction of words in general (senses 1 or 3) and lexemes (sense 2) is the one which has to be maintained most consistently.

Nevertheless, it is useful to be able to make the terminological opposition where we need it. One obvious way of doing so would be to call the word in sense 1 the 'phonological' (or 'ortho-graphic') word, and the word in sense 3 the 'grammatical word'. However, it is perhaps a trifle clumsy to load terms with qualifiers. Furthermore, there is another slightly different sense for which this one may be reserved, as we shall see in a later chapter. A neater alternative is to refer to the word in sense 1, where the distinction is necessary, as the **word-form**. Thus it is the word-form *tried* or [traɪd] which is analysable in terms of letters or phonemes. An additional convenience of this usage, it will be seen, is that we can use the same term 'word-form' whether we are speaking of phonetic forms or of writing. The term **word** may then be reserved, in the strictest usage, for sense 3. Thus the word-form *tried* is the form of the word which we call 'the Past Participle (or the Past Tense) of TRY'. Again, we would say that the first sentence of Yeats's poem has six monosyllabic word-forms (*this*, *is*, *no*, *for*, *old* and *men*) out of seven, the remaining word-form (*country*) being a disyllable. On the other hand, we will not say that word-forms are, as such, Nouns or Verbs or Participles, etc.


## PRACTICAL ILLUSTRATIONS

Some readers may possibly be beginning to feel that, in drawing these distinctions, we are tending to be over-careful. Must we really say, for instance, that in *a trying day* the word-form *trying* corresponds to the word '*trying*' and this happens to be the only word assigned to the lexeme TRYING? Although we have given reasons – comparing this '*trying*' with the other '*trying*' in *They are trying hard* – is it not rather tiresome for this one Adjective in isolation? Readers may also feel that this approach is absolutely typical of theoretical linguistics. In his preface to the latest supplement of the *OED*, the editor grumbles that

> the metalanguages of linguisticians and philosophers have now reached the point where writers of monographs cannot even reach the starting line without regularly defining exactly what they mean by such ordinary (and certainly not new) expressions as *accent*, *sentence*, *utterance*, and *word*. (*OEDS*, IV, p. xi).

I cannot answer for philosophers, but in linguistics at least I doubt very much if it is really the writers of monographs who have been getting under Mr Burchfield's skin. I suspect that the culprits are just such introductory works as this one.

The only reply is that precision is sometimes important and, if we do seem to be multiplying entities, it is not, for all purposes, beyond necessity. The writing of dictionaries is indeed an instance. If a present-day lexicographer does not need to spell out what is meant by 'a word' – to explain why '*trying*' Adjective needs an entry or subentry while '*trying*' Participle does not – it is because the great men who have gone before, including the great lexicographer who first edited the *OED*, have implicitly drawn the distinctions which we are underlining. But there are other fields which lie outside morphology and in which, within living memory, the most elementary blunders have been made. How, for example, do we go about 'counting words' for statistical analysis? When we say that $x$ is a commoner word than $y$ or that in $A$'s writings the word $x$ appears more often than in $B$'s, we are usually implying that $x$ and $y$ are lexemes. But it would be as well to check and make clear that this is so. If we say that English has more monosyllabic words than Latin, or that there are proportionately more such words in Yeats's later poetry than in Chomsky's *Syntactic Structures*, we are instead talking strictly of word-forms. In still other cases we may want to count words in our specifically grammatical sense. Again, it would be important to decide precisely what we were doing.

A concrete illustration may help to bring home the pitfalls. Let us suppose, first of all, that we want to count the number of times that individual Verbs occur in Henry James's novels. We might want to compare the figures with those for some other novelist, or to compare figures for earlier and later works to elucidate the way in which James's style developed. Even cruder 'indices' have been computed for some literary purposes (to prove, as it were, that *The Wings of the Dove* and *The Europeans* cannot possibly have been written by the same man!). Now we will, of course, decide to make our counts by computer. To be precise, we might use a program which will print out a complete list of all the different words which appear in any particular novel (we will call these the word **types**, following a fairly normal usage), and set against each the total number of occurrences in that novel (the total number of **tokens**). We can then look at the list of types and can pick out whichever words (e.g. Verbs) we happen to be interested in.

Well, let us begin by feeding in the first chapter of *The Portrait of a Lady*. What exactly will the computer do? It should be obvious that if this is all we have said it is liable to do some very silly things. Our program will naturally have taken 'words' to mean 'sequences of letters between spaces'. So, for a start, different forms of the same lexeme will be taken as different types; in the dialogue:

> 'Does it mean that...? or does it simply mean that...?'
> 'Whatever else it means, it's pretty sure to mean that, ...?

we would have three tokens of the type *mean* and one of the type *means*. This might not greatly matter; we could just add up the totals at the end. But in two earlier passages we have two other tokens of this second type *means*: 'She chiefly communicates with us by means of telegrams'; 'Because you have – haven't you? – such unlimited means'. We do not want these conflated with the first '*means*', but how can our machine do otherwise? How do we then know, when we get our output, which tokens of *means* were forms of the Verb MEAN and which were not?

A glance through James's text, or through any other text in English for that matter, will show that there are many word-forms that are orthographically homonymous between one part of speech and another. Very often there is a semantic connection: for example, the forms *mind*, *house* [haʊs], *perfect* ['pɜːfɪkt], *close* [kləʊs], *man*, or *mellow* (which are among those appearing as Nouns or Adjectives in the novel's first paragraph) are more or less closely related to the Verb-forms *mind*, *house* [haʊz], *perfect* [pə'fekt], *close* [kləʊz], etc. But there are others (harder to spot!) where there is none. Still in James's first paragraph, the *rest* of 'the rest of the set', the *object* ['ɒbdʒɪkt] of 'the most characteristic object', the *still* of 'still to come', or the *long* of 'the shadows were long upon the...turf' have nothing at all to do with Verbal *rest*, *object* [əb'dʒekt] and so on. To pursue *long* a little further, it appears Adjectivally three times on the first two pages of my copy. After all, it is a pretty common epithet. But the Verb LONG, as in *I always long for silence*, is not so ordinary. Our figures would be meaningless if the two were conflated.

What do we do then? We have got our novel on disk, and we hardly want to waste the investment. Perhaps we will pause and think: what if we can get the computer to label parts of speech automatically? All it needs (we will say) is a few ingenious routines for automatic syntactic analysis, and we will get accuracy at least to a respectable percentage. And so we must embark on a quite new task which has nothing whatever to do with the one we originally had in mind. If we had thought carefully at the outset – and had still decided we wanted to count Verbs in James's novels! – we would have realised that we are concerned with the tokens of lexemes and not of word-forms, and that the simplest ways of identifying forms of verbal lexemes might be either to mark them in the text before it is taped (but then do we need the computer at all?) or to prepare a concordance in which forms of different lexemes can be distinguished from their context.

This may seem a naive little parable. But to any scholar who can recall the first use of computers for literary analysis it will not ring entirely false. Various projects foundered or ran into greater trouble and expense because the investigators did not first respect these seemingly pedantic distinctions. In the case of concordances the earliest experiments were much more successful, and their preparation and publication by computer are now firmly established. But it is again worth asking: what exactly do we mean by an index or concordance of the set of 'words' that a writer employs?

It will be obvious that the WORD-FORM is not the sort of 'word' in which the user of a concordance is most likely to be interested. As in a dictionary, our headings will ideally be LEXEMES; we might like to follow some standard dictionary in determining when lexemes are the same or different. But will the user be interested in WORDS, in the strictly grammatical sense, as well? Perhaps it might be instructive to study which Verbs, let us say, are used most frequently in 'Progressive' or 'Continuous' Tenses (e.g. the Latin or Italian Imperfect) and which in 'Non-Progressive'. Or is it rather that we should show, in general, how the individual LEXEMES are USED grammatically? Certainly, there are general grammatical distinctions which a user might want to take into account. So, for example, in Merguet's set of concordances for Cicero the entries for Verbs distinguish between an Absolute and a Transitive construction, and in the detailed volumes they also note which particular Nouns appear as the Object in individual instances.[1] This was a concordance made by hand by a specialist. But by a well-planned collaboration between man and machine we could in principle get similar results. They might help some

---

[1] H. Merguet, *Lexicon zu den Reden des Cicero*, 4 vols. (Jena, 1877–84); *Lexicon zu den philosophischen Schriften Cicero's*, 3 vols. (Jena, 1887–94).

users much more than a merely mechanical listing with *n* words to the left of each occurrence of the key word and *n* to the right.

The answers will at least bear thinking about. For one particular application let us consider the problem of studying the significant co-occurrences – the collocations, to use a widespread term – of one 'word' with another. Now, of course, the co-occurrent pairs will not always be adjacent in the text; for example in the following imaginary dialogue:

> 'What do you do with potatoes?'
> 'Well, you can just boil them, or you can bake them in the oven, or you can roast them – you know, in a pan with fat – or you can chip them, or sauté them (that means boiling them and then slicing them and frying them), or you can mash them', etc. etc.

a student of cooking vocabulary would be interested in the collocations of FRY and POTATO, MASH and POTATO, SAUTÉ and POTATO, etc., regardless of the distance between them in the text. Since many concordances only show the immediately adjacent forms they would not, perhaps, be the perfect basis for this inquiry. But in general they are an excellent starting-point – even if (as in this example) we might be forced to check back to the original.

Here we have identified the collocations in terms of the lexemes FRY, SAUTÉ, POTATO, etc. But we would need to consider carefully whether this is always the right thing to do. Let us suppose, for example, that we want to investigate the co-occurrence ranges of Adverbs. In *He'll make it very badly* we have the pair *make* and *badly*. In *He made it very badly* we have *made* and *badly* instead. The Tense does not appear to be significant and we will therefore say that in both we have the same collocation of BADLY and the lexeme MAKE. But the Tense is not insignificant in the case of Time Adverbs. If we found an instance of *He made it soon* (full stop: not, e.g., *He made it soon afterwards* or *He soon made it*) it would be just the sort of usage that should engage our attention. As a native speaker, asked out of any context whether the Past Tense with final SOON is 'correct' or not, I find I cannot reasonably give an answer. We would likewise be interested if we found anything of the type *He was making it suddenly* (Note, not

*He was suddenly making it*). In these cases, therefore, we would not want to register collocations of lexeme with lexeme. Indeed, this is a relationship which is not strictly between words either, but between the whole Time-expressions (which will often be phrases, *next week, come the Autumn*, etc.) and the categories of Verb Phrases. If we want to study the lexical patterns by which 'words go together', we had better start by making clear what we mean by 'words'.

This last illustration leads us to the theoretical problems of meaning. It is part of the meaning of SAUTÉ, at least in my non-technical speech, that it collocates with POTATO only. Restrictions on the collocability of SOON or SUDDENLY at least reflect, and are thus important evidence for, the meanings of these lexemes. Here we are concerned with the semantic relationships which words and lexemes can contract within a text or spoken discourse. We have already referred to the problem of semantic relationship within the lexicon itself: the relations between GENERATION (as we will now represent it) and GENERATE, between SENSUAL and SENSE, and so on. There too the analyst of meaning may sometimes have to consider particular members of the paradigm (the Plural form in *the senses*, for example). It is hardly surprising that the terminological distinction between word and lexeme (in our present sense) was first brought to the fore in one of the few studies of the 1960s to achieve a real progress in semantic theory.[2]

## LEXICAL AND INFLECTIONAL MORPHOLOGY

Now that we have drawn these distinctions we can speak more precisely about the different branches of morphology. Of the three that were introduced in chapter 1, two are concerned with relations between lexemes. Take, for instance, the relation between *generate* and *generation*. The latter is more complex: in spelling, *generation = generat(e) + -ion*. But these are not just different forms. By '*generate*' we mean, more precisely, the Verb GENERATE; by '*generation*', the Noun GENERATION. These are different lexemes which will normally have different entries or subentries in a dictionary. Similarly for the Verb '*try*' and the

---

[2] J. Lyons, *Structural Semantics* (Oxford, Blackwell, 1963), p. 11.

Adjective *'trying'*. We have seen that there is a morphological relation: *trying = try + -ing*. But *'try'* is, more precisely, the lexeme TRY, and *'trying'*, if we are talking of the Adjective, is a different lexeme, TRYING.

In this light, **word-formation** is, more strictly, 'lexeme-formation'. We may define it as the branch of morphology which deals with the relations between a **complex lexeme** and a simple(r) lexeme. TRYING is thus a complex lexeme related to the **simple lexeme** TRY. The latter is simple because the form *try* cannot itself be analysed into further morphological elements. Another example we gave was that of *'unageing'* ('monuments of unageing intellect'). This represents a complex lexeme UNAGEING, related to the simpler AGEING. That in turn is itself a complex lexeme, related to the simple AGE.

Similarly, but with one crucial difference, in the case of compounds. *Salmon-falls*, we argued, was related to both *salmon* and *fall*. That is, the lexeme SALMON-FALL (of which *salmon-falls* is the Plural) is related to both SALMON and FALL. *Whatever* was similarly related to *what* and *ever*. But these too are separate lexemes, which might again be strictly written in small capitals (WHATEVER, WHAT, EVER). They have their own entries in dictionaries and, as we pointed out in chapter 1, the compound (WHATEVER) has idiosyncratic uses.

Let us accordingly define **compounding** as the branch of morphology which deals with the relations between a **compound lexeme** and two or more simple(r) lexemes. The compound lexeme SALMON-FALL is related to two simple lexemes SALMON and FALL. A compound lexeme such as WASTEPAPER BASKET, which is in fact more likely to be entered in a dictionary, is again related to two simpler lexemes (WASTEPAPER and BASKET). Of these, one (BASKET) is itself simple; but the other is in turn a compound (WASTE + PAPER).

It will be clear from later chapters that compounding and word-formation have much in common. They can therefore be seen as subfields of a larger field of **lexical morphology**. We may define this, in general, as the study of morphological relations among lexemes. The crucial difference between the subfields is that, in word-formation, a complex lexeme is directly related to at most one simple(r) lexeme. Thus UNAGEING is related, in the first instance, to AGEING. In compounding, the larger unit is related directly to at least two simple(r) lexemes – SALMON-FALL both to SALMON and to FALL.

Our third branch was concerned instead with words and word-forms. Take, for instance, the opposition between *sea* and *seas*. They differ as word-forms: *seas* has an inflection -*s*, while *sea* has no inflection. As words (in our strict sense), they are opposed within what is traditionally called a **paradigm.** That is, they are forms of the same lexeme (SEA), and, in terms of categories, one is the Singular of SEA and the other the Plural of SEA. Within this paradigm:

|  | SEA |
|---|---|
| *Singular* | sea |
| *Plural* | seas |

the inflection -*s* is what we called the marker of Plural. Similarly, it is within the paradigm of Nouns like MAN:

|  | MAN |
|---|---|
| *Singular* | man |
| *Plural* | men |

that Plural is marked differently, by a vowel change. We may define **inflectional morphology** as the branch of morphology that deals with paradigms. It is therefore concerned with two things: on the one hand, with the semantic oppositions among categories; on the other, with the formal means, including inflections, that distinguish them.

But it will help, perhaps, if we refine our notion of a 'category'. The term is used very widely in linguistics, as in ordinary life. A lexeme like MAN belongs to the category 'Noun'; within this, there are categories of Concrete Noun and Abstract Noun; Nouns like GENERATION form a certain category of derived Noun, and so on. The categories that enter into paradigms can be described, more precisely, as **morphosyntactic categories.** The term is chosen because they are directly referred to by specific rules in both morphology and syntax. There is a specific morphological rule in English by which the Plurals of Nouns (exceptions apart) end in -*s*. There is also a syntactic rule by which, if a Noun is Plural and it has as its Determiner a form of the Demonstrative lexemes THIS or THAT, that too must be Plural (*these things*, not *this things*).

A particular tendency of morphosyntactic categories is to form sets of variables. The paradigms of SEA and MAN are of the simplest kind one can imagine: two words opposed on a single dimension. Therefore the point may not be instantly clear. But let us look instead at the paradigm of a Noun in Latin. This too opposes Singular and Plural; but, on another dimension, it opposes six Cases (Nominative, Vocative, Accusative, Genitive, Dative and Ablative), each of which, again, may be marked differently and has its own range of syntactic uses. Thus, in the paradigm of DOMINUS 'lord, master':

DOMINUS

|  | Singular | Plural |
| --- | --- | --- |
| *Nominative* | dominus | domini |
| *Vocative* | domine | domini |
| *Accusative* | dominum | dominos |
| *Genitive* | domini | dominorum |
| *Dative* | domino | dominis |
| *Ablative* | domino | dominis |

eight distinct word-forms – it will be noted that there is considerable homonymy – are assigned to positions in a six-by-two array. The term 'Case' names the vertical dimension, and this can be seen as a variable with the values Nominative, Vocative, Accusative and so on. The horizontal dimension is that of Number. This is a variable with (in Latin as in English) the two values Singular and Plural.

Usage differs, and the term 'category' is widely applied both to the variables in general (Case, Number) and to their particular values. In many contexts this does little harm. We have said hitherto that, in a word like *seas*, *-s* marks the category 'Plural'. That is, it marks the particular value which the variable 'Number' has in this word. That is, it marks the category 'Number'. Such forms of words are well established and cause no confusion. But sometimes we will need to make the distinction, and it will help, for that purpose, if we reserve the term '**morphosyntactic category**' for the larger variable. Case and Number are thus the morphosyntactic categories of the Noun in Latin, Number a morphosyntactic category of the Noun in English. These are therefore properties of the paradigm as a whole. Their individual values are properties or features of particular words within it. When we say, for example, that Latin *dominum* is the Accusative Singular of DOMINUS, we are saying that this word-form (the particular arrangement of phonemes) is the form taken by a word – the word still in our strict sense – characterised (1) by its assignment to DOMINUS and (2) as having the specific properties Accusative and Singular. We will therefore refer to these as **morphosyntactic properties** or **features**. In English *seas, -s* marks (more precisely) the morphosyntactic property Plural.

Inflectional morphology cannot be discussed further at this stage without begging questions. Indeed, I fear that there are teachers of the subject who might think that I have already begged some. But, as we will see, these formulations do allow for strikingly different models.

## RELATED READING

'Lexeme', 'word-form' and 'word' are distinguished as in my *Inflectional Morphology*, pp. 160f. The first two terms are fairly widespread: thus, for example, LYONS, *Semantics*, I, pp. 18f.; BAUER, *Morphology*, p. 7. But a 'word', in my strict sense, is for Bauer and others a 'grammatical word' (BAUER, *Morphology*, p. 9), and for Lyons (I, p. 73) a 'morphosyntactic word'. The topic of syncretism deserves more space than I can give to it: see CARSTAIRS, ch. 4 (on 'Homonymy within paradigms') for an illuminating discussion; also A. Carstairs & J. P. Stemberger, 'A processing constraint on inflectional homonymy', *Linguistics* 26 (1988), pp. 601–17.

'Type' and 'token' (in the James illustration) are terms introduced by C. S. Peirce: for an introductory account see LYONS, *Semantics*, I, pp. 13ff. I cannot leave one of my favourite novelists without mentioning S. Chatman's interesting study, *The Later Style of Henry James* (Oxford, Blackwell, 1972), an early demonstration that a linguist's study of style did not have to be tiresome.

I have used the term 'lexical morphology' as I used it in the first edition. But it has since been adopted by a school of morphologists in the United States who believe, in the extreme case, that all morphology, inflections included, should be treated lexically. For the origins of this view see M. Halle, 'Prolegomena to a theory of word formation', *LIn* 4 (1973), pp. 3–16; for criticism, ANDERSON, 'Where's morphology?'. Before this, many Americans had seen the lexicon as little more than, in Bloomfield's words, 'a stock of morphemes' (BLOOMFIELD, p. 162): thus CHOMSKY, *Structures* (lexical rules p. 26 and elsewhere). Lexical morphology (in our sense) had therefore to belong to grammar: thus, in particular, LEES. The return to a traditional view began in 1970 with CHOMSKY, 'Nominalization'.

For detached surveys of what we may best call 'lexicalist morphology' see R. Coates, 'Lexical morphology', in J. Lyons, R. Coates, M. Deuchar & G. Gazdar (eds.), *New Horizons in Linguistics*, II (Harmondsworth, Penguin, 1987), pp. 103–21; BAUER, *Morphology*, ch. 9.

I have reserved the term 'word-formation' for what most authors call 'derivational morphology': see chapter 4 for my reluctance to follow them. Morphosyntactic categories and properties are distinguished as in my *Inflectional Morphology*, pp. 161ff. Another solution might be to distinguish 'categories' (e.g. Singular or Accusative) from 'categorial dimensions' (Number dimension or Case dimension): compare WURZEL, §4.3, which speaks (though without explicit definition) of 'categorial complexes'.

# 3
# Inflections and word-formation

Similarity between fields: formatives.
*Why the distinction?* Division of dictionary and grammar; but why is that justified? Word-formation as change of part of speech: criterion not satisfactory. Inflections as syntactically determined (Italian *-o/-a* in Nouns vs Adjectives); criterion natural but not sufficient (Number of Nouns, Comparatives, English *-ion*). Test whether complex word can be replaced by simple. Criterion of regularity: gaps in word-formation; regularity and irregularity of meaning. No single criterion adequate in all cases.
*Change and indeterminacy.* Changes in the status of formatives (Latin/Italian *-sc-*); hence synchronic blurring (Participles and Participial Adjectives). Likewise for derived and simple lexemes: effect of learned borrowing (French Adjectives in *-al*).

In the last chapter we underlined the technical distinction between relations within paradigms (inflectional morphology) and relations among lexemes (lexical morphology). In the case of compounding its justification is sufficiently obvious. Forms like *what* and *ever* or *salmon* and *fall* represent distinct lexemes (WHAT, EVER, SALMON, FALL), and forms which combine them, if not syntactic, must also be lexemes (WHATEVER, SALMON-FALL). In the history of languages compounds of this type do not usually develop into inflectional formations, and there is little or no indeterminacy. But the distinction between inflections and word-formation is more difficult. In the form *generation* the ending *-ion* is not a word, just as *-s* is not a word in *generations*. On the face of it, both are simply formative elements or, as we will call them, **formatives**. Moreover, the same ending may be both inflectional and lexical: *-ing* in the Verb-form *trying* (Present Participle of TRY) and in the homonymous Adjective *trying* (TRYING). Now there are reasons for drawing the distinction, which were implied, in part, in our brief discussion in chapter 1. But it is not instantly recognisable, and most scholars have stressed that there are boundary cases. There are also some who have denied that it exists. We must therefore look more carefully at the justification for it, and try to clarify the arguments by which forms are assigned to one type or the other.

## WHY THE DISTINCTION?

The explicit grounds on which we have distinguished word-formation are that, in some cases, two or more related words have different entries in a dictionary. We expect, and find, that pairs such as *generate* and *generation*, or larger series such as *age*, *ageing* and *unageing*, are defined individually. In other cases, they are subsumed by the same entry. Thus we expect, and find, that a single definition covers not just *beget*, but also *begets*, *begat*, *begotten* and *begetting*. Putting it the other way round, we expect that a grammar will treat the last five words as members of the same paradigm. *Generate* and *generation* we expect to find in different paradigms.

But our established dictionaries and grammars have not been handed to us on tablets of stone. Why do we not say, instead, that there is a single lexeme under which both 'GENERATION' and 'GENERATE' are subsumed? *Generations*, let us say, would be its 'Nominal Plural' as opposed to 'Nominal Singular' *generation*, *generated* its 'Verbal Past Tense' or 'Past Participle', and so on. Similarly, for another such pair, we would say that *automation* was the 'Nominal Singular' and *automate* the 'Verbal Present Tense' (excluding '3rd Singular') of a single lexeme which subsumes both 'AUTOMATE' and 'AUTOMATION'. Alternatively, why not say that *beget*, *begets* and so on are five separate lexemes (BEGET, BEGETS, BEGAT, BEGOTTEN, BEGETTING)? In this way our distinction could be done away with. Either all morphology, bar compounding, would be 'inflectional', or all morphology would be 'lexical'.

In the case of *generate* and *generation*, an initial answer might be that the words belong to different 'parts of speech'. The first is a Verb and has a grammar like other Verbs such as *create* or *make*; the second is a Noun and goes with other Nouns such as *nature* or *life*. But a moment's reflection will show that this criterion is not adequate. Firstly, our traditional parts of speech have not been handed to us on tablets of stone either. If Nouns and Verbs have a different syntax so, for example, do Finite Verbs like *begat* and

Participles like *begotten*. The former do not appear after the Auxiliary BE:

> Whatever is begat, bore, and dies

nor as Modifiers:

> Or beauty bore out of its own despair

Equally the latter cannot appear as Main Verbs:

> And Jacob begotten Joseph

We must therefore ask why the distinction between Noun and Verb should be put on a special plane. The point is brought out more clearly if we consider the history of the classification of parts of speech. In the English grammar by QUIRK *et al.*, the major or 'open' classes are said to be Nouns, Adjectives, Full Verbs and Adverbs. But, until the later Middle Ages, the words in Latin which we now call Adjectives were seen as one of many subclasses of Nouns. Accordingly, a simple word like *stultus* 'stupid' belonged to the same 'part of speech' as the complex word *stultitia* 'stupidity'. The ancient grammarians also separated Finite Verbs and Participles. Thus, in Latin, the Participle in *natus e Maria virgine* 'born of the Virgin Mary' (*natus* 'born') would not have been assigned to the same part of speech as, for example, the Present *nascitur* 'is being born'. But in ancient rules for the inflections, Finite forms and Participles were commonly taken together.

A second difficulty is that words which are given separately in dictionaries are often syntactically similar. On any analysis, *duke* has a syntax like that of *duchess*: *the Duchess of Malfi* or *the Duke of Malfi*, *the White Duchess* or *the White Duke*, *Everyone loves a duke* or *Everyone loves a duchess*. So do *waiter* and *waitress*, *actor* and *actress*, and so on. Yet dictionaries treat these as separate lexemes (DUKE, DUCHESS, ...). In an Italian dictionary, ZIO 'uncle' will have one entry and ZIA 'aunt' another; so too might, for example, CUGINO 'male cousin' and CUGINA 'female cousin'. But for any grammarian all these words belong to the same part of speech. Now syntax is relevant to our distinction, as we will see. But an appeal to parts of speech is in itself neither sufficient nor clear.

Why then do we not say that, for example, *cugino* and *cugina* ('cousin' Masculine and 'cousin' Feminine) are forms of the same lexeme? In Italian, Nouns and Adjectives have similar inflections. For Adjectives, one pattern has a formal distinction between Singular and Plural only. This can be illustrated with the paradigm of FELICE 'fortunate' or 'happy':

| | |
|---|---|
| *Singular* | felice |
| *Plural* | felici |

with the Singular ending -*e* and Plural ending -*i*. But the same pattern is also found in many Nouns, for example MONTE 'mountain':

| | |
|---|---|
| *Singular* | monte |
| *Plural* | monti |

If we consider just the inflections, MONTE and FELICE are in exactly the same class.

In two other classes of Nouns we find the same distinction between Singular and Plural, but two different pairs of endings. These may be illustrated with the Masculine LIBRO 'book' and the Feminine TAVOLA 'table':[1]

| | 'book' | 'table' |
|---|---|---|
| *Singular* | libro | tavola |
| *Plural* | libri | tavole |

– Singular -*o* and Plural -*i*, Singular -*a* and Plural -*e*. But when we return to the Adjectives, these last four endings form paradigms which distinguish Masculine and Feminine as well as Singular and Plural. An example is that of NUOVO 'new':

| | *Masculine* | *Feminine* |
|---|---|---|
| *Singular* | nuovo | nuova |
| *Plural* | nuovi | nuove |

where the pairs of endings which distinguish different Nouns such as LIBRO and TAVOLA now mark different Genders of the same lexeme.

How do forms such as *cugino* and *cugina* fit into these patterns? The range of endings is identical with that of NUOVO. Since they

---

[1] Also Masculine TAVOLO (see below); but let us take the leading dictionary form to start with.

are also parallel in meaning, we could apparently set up an isomorphic paradigm:

|  | *'Masculine'* | *'Feminine'* |
|---|---|---|
| *Singular* | cugino | cugina |
| *Plural* | cugini | cugine |

in which the Masculines and Feminines are again distinguished by the Singular -*o* and -*a*, the Plural -*i* and -*e*. If we argued in this way, CUGINO/A 'cousin' would indeed be one lexeme. So would ZIO/A 'sibling of parent': 'Masculine' Singular *zio* 'uncle', Plural 'zii 'uncles'; 'Feminine' Singular *zia* 'aunt', Plural *zie* 'aunts'. For good measure, we might argue that the traditional division between Nouns and Adjectives is itself spurious. An alternative division, if we again consider nothing but the inflections, would be between lexemes whose paradigms distinguish Singular and Plural only and those which also distinguish Masculine and Feminine. The former would include traditional Adjectives such as FELICE, as well as Nouns like MONTE, LIBRO and TAVOLA. The latter would include what are traditionally pairs of Nouns, such as CUGINO/A, as well as Adjectives such as NUOVO.

Of course, we will not in fact say anything so silly. But to explain why, we must look at the syntactic relations which these words enter into, and not just at their endings. In the phrase *un libro nuovo* 'a new book', the Adjective, as one may see, is Masculine; in *una tavola nuova* 'a new table', it is Feminine. But in such a construction the choice between *nuovo* and *nuova* is entirely determined or predictable. One could not say either *un libro nuova* (substituting -*a* in the first example) or *una tavola nuovo* (substituting -*o* in the second). No more, indeed, could one switch the Articles (*un* and *una*) and say *una libro nuovo* or *un tavola nuova*; there is a rule requiring that both Adjective and Article should agree in Gender with the Masculine *libro* or the Feminine *tavola*.[2] It follows that the difference between *nuovo* and *nuova* cannot in itself bear any difference in meaning. To distinguish the phrases from one another we need merely point to the choice of Nouns: LIBRO versus TAVOLA. To distinguish them

[2] The general rule has exceptions, as my colleague Giulio Lepschy reminds me, in metonymic compounds of the type [*una*] *terz'anno* '[a] third-year [female] student'. The syntactic peculiarity points, of course, to the compositional nature of the construction.

from other phrases we need merely add that the Nouns are in the Singular (not Plural), that there is an Indefinite Article (not Definite, Demonstrative, etc.), and that the specific lexeme NUOVO acts as Modifier. Everything else (the Number and Gender of the Adjective, the Number and Gender of the Article) follows automatically.

The Gender of the Nouns LIBRO and TAVOLA is, however, a quite different matter. The phrase *una libra nuova* would not be a mistake, as it were, for *un libro nuovo*; there is no rule of grammar which it contravenes. It simply contains a different Noun (LIBRA 'balance') and accordingly means something different. Nor is *un tavolo nuovo* a 'mistake' for *una tavola nuova*. Rather it is an alternative way of saying the same thing; according to my information, the general meaning 'table' may be expressed as readily by the Masculine 'TAVOLO' (more strictly by the paradigm forms *tavolo* Singular and *tavoli* Plural) as it may by the Feminine 'TAVOLA' which we have considered hitherto. In neither case, therefore, is there a general rule by which the choice of Gender is determined. In one it is simply part and parcel of the choice of lexeme (LIBRO 'book' rather than LIBRA 'balance', MONTE 'mountain' and so on), and in the other the lexeme itself varies freely between one paradigm class ('TAVOLA') and the other ('TAVOLO'). All this will be familiar to students of Italian or of most other European languages. For the Nouns, Gender is in principle inherent in the individual lexeme: LIBRO is Masculine whatever the construction it happens to appear in, and in TAVOLO/A it is the individual Noun itself that varies. The same point may be made for the paradigms in *-e* and *-i*: the Noun MONTE 'mountain' is inherently Masculine (hence the Masculine Article and Adjective in *un monte bello* 'a beautiful mountain'), whereas SIEPE 'hedge' is inherently Feminine (*una siepe bella* 'a beautiful hedge'). All this must be given in the dictionary. For the Adjectives, however, the Gender is determined by grammatical or otherwise by general rule. If '*monte*' is Masculine and '*siepe*' Feminine then which, one might foolishly be tempted to ask, is '*felice*'? For an Adjective the question is meaningless: sometimes it stands in a construction with a Masculine (*un uomo felice* 'a happy man'), and sometimes the opposite (*una donna felice* 'a happy woman').

We now have a better classification in which, regardless of the paradigms of endings, lexemes such as BUONO and FELICE have one sort of characteristic and lexemes such as LIBRO, MONTE, TAVOLA or TAVOLO another. How then do the words for 'cousin', 'uncle' or 'aunt', etc. fit into this pattern? The answer is again supplied by the syntax of the phrases. In *un mio cugino* 'a cousin [specifically "male cousin"] of mine' the Gender of *un* 'a' and *mio* 'my, of mine' are determined by the same grammatical rule that we have considered already; the only additional point is that the Possessive Adjective normally precedes the Noun, whereas in our earlier examples the Descriptive Adjectives *nuovo* and *nuova* followed. So, one could no more say *una mia cugino* than one could say *una mia libro* for 'a book of mine'. Conversely, one could not say *un mio cugina* instead of *una mia cugina* 'a female cousin of mine' – any more than one could say *un mio tavola*, with the Feminine form for 'table'. But there is no further rule which, in turn, can determine the Gender of *cugino* and *cugina*: the difference between *un mio cugino* and *una mia cugina* lies precisely in the choice of either a Masculine in -*o* or Feminine in -*a* to serve as the determining element for the remainder. The same observation holds for every construction in the language: although it is puzzling if one says, for example, *Giovanni è una mia cugina* 'John [i.e. a man's name] is a female cousin of mine', nevertheless there is no rule of grammar requiring the Gender of Subject and Complement to agree. Masculine and Feminine throughout inhere, once again, in the forms '*cugino*' and '*cugina*' themselves.

For this reason the 'cousin' words are traditionally and rightly grouped with LIBRO or TAVOLA and not, as in the designedly spurious argument outlined earlier, with NUOVO, MIO and so on. It does not matter that the roots *cugin-* and *nuov-* are accompanied by the same formal range of endings; syntactically, their status is not the same. By the same token the 'cousin' words belong to the class of Nouns, and by the same token again their forms are divided between two different lexemes: a Masculine CUGINO in the subclass of LIBRO and a Feminine CUGINA in that of TAVOLA. Both the part of speech assignment (Noun not Adjective) and the morphological status of the Gender (lexical not inflectional) justify themselves within the framework of the same syntactic analysis. By contrast, NUOVO or MIO is a single Adjective, and the

Gender difference between *nuovo* and *nuova*, *nuovi* and *nuove* has an inflectional status. A sufficient criterion, we surmise, is that *a* and *b* are in an inflectional opposition if (in at least some instances) the choice between them is determined by a general grammatical rule.

This is a criterion entirely appropriate to the theoretical distinction. To say that an opposition is 'lexical' means that the difference is stated in the lexicon or dictionary; it is therefore 'non-lexical' if, instead, its terms are in general selected by the grammar. Unfortunately, the converse is not a sufficient criterion for lexical or 'non-inflectional' status; for a grammatical opposition, too, the choice may sometimes be just as free. In the sentence *I miei cugini sono arrivati* 'My cousins have arrived' the Number of the Noun (*cugini* '[male] cousins' as opposed to *cugino* '[male] cousin') is no more determinable than its Gender. Both merely determine, in turn, the Gender and Number of *i* and *miei*, the Number of the Auxiliary *sono* (compare Singular *è*), and the Gender and Number of *arrivati* 'arrived'. Yet we will say that the Number of Nouns is inflectional (*cugini* being the 'Plural of CUGINO'), whereas their Gender is lexical (CUGINO being a different lexeme from CUGINA). Why so? For the Gender the supporting argument will perhaps be obvious enough. Its rôle in the construction (Noun with Modifying Adjective, Possessive, etc.) is paralleled by words which cannot but be independent lexemes: LIBRO and TAVOLA, MONTE and SIEPE. These last are overwhelmingly more numerous, and so establish a pattern into which CUGINO and CUGINA fit. Number, by contrast, is chosen freely for one element after another: *libro* versus *libri*, *tavola* versus *tavole*, and so on. Although there are a few for which it is normally fixed (Plural *cesoie* 'scissors' just like English *scissors*), they are not sufficient to disturb the pattern. Hence it MAY be inflectional. But we cannot say that it IS inflectional unless we introduce some criterion other than that of determinability.

For another example, we may turn to the opposition of Positive and Comparative in English. In the sentence *It's getting hot* we could also substitute the Comparative: *It's getting hotter*. There is again no grammatical rule which determines the choice of one word or the other. Do we say, then, that HOT and HOTTER are two different lexemes? According to some analyses we might; the category of Grade (Positive, Comparative and Superlative) has often been cited as a borderline instance. But that would be contrary to the normal practice of lexicographers. In the *OED* there are entries for '*hotter*' (Sc. and north dial. 'to move up and down with vibration'), but not qua Comparative of '*hot*'; that is instead given under the 'forms of "*hot*"', just as the Plural *men* is given under the 'forms of "*man*"', the Past Tense *left* under the 'forms of "*leave*"', and so on.

By what criterion might this practice be justified? If we examine the grammar further we will find other constructions in which the Positive and Comparative are not freely substitutable: one says *They are hotter than the others* but not *They are hot than the others*. Similarly, there are constructions in which neither the Positive nor the Comparative can appear in place of the Superlative: *the hottest of the lot* but neither *the hot of the lot* nor *the hotter of the lot*. Although the choices are not determined by other specific words in the construction (as the Masculine Plural *miei* was determined specifically by the Plural of the Masculine *cugini*, we might be tempted to argue that they are determined by the nature of the construction itself. But then there is a snag with earlier examples such as GENERATE and GENERATION. In a 'Gerundial' phrase (*generating electricity, automating our work-processes*) the construction requires a form in -*ing*: one without -*ing* could not be substituted in the same sentence contexts (*They disapprove of automate factories*, and so on). Hence, we would say, the opposition between *generate* and *generating, automate* and *automating* is inflectional rather than lexical. But equally the corresponding Nominal construction (*the generation of electricity, the automation of our work-processes*) appears to require the form in -*ion*. Again we cannot substitute the simple form (*the automate of factories*) while remaining within the rules of syntax. If we pursue this line of argument, we will be forced to conclude that *automate* and *automation, generate* and *generation* are also forms of single lexemes.

Why then is it right to separate them? One important point is words in -*ion* can always be replaced by simple words. In *the generation of electricity* we can substitute *cost* to yield *the cost of electricity*, in addition to saying that *Automation is a good thing* we could also say that *War is a good thing*, and so on. In that sense the

*-ion* is not properly to be considered part of the construction. It is merely part of the make-up of a certain class of Noun-forms (*generation* but not *cost*, *automation* but not *war*) which can function at a certain position within it. On the other hand, there is no indisputably simple form that can be substituted for *hotter* in *It's hotter than the others*. In this construction the only alternatives are more complex phrases: for example, *more* or *less beautiful* in *She's more/less beautiful than you*. The Comparative is therefore an essential part of the grammatical statement. To distinguish the construction properly one has to say that *than* is preceded either by an Adjective with *less* or (as the case may be) by an Adjective with *-er* or *more*.

Such is the case seen, as it were, from the grammarian's viewpoint. But dictionary writers will have their own complementary arguments. It will not be enough simply to say that there are Verbs in *-te* and Nouns in *-tion*. For one thing, not all Verbs in fact have such a Noun corresponding: one can say *He dilutes his whisky* and *the dilution of whisky*, but not *The salution of officers is compulsory* as an alternative to *One must salute officers*. There are also a few Nouns in *-ion* without a corresponding Verb. *Elocution* seems to belong to this formation and indeed one could understand *She's elocuting marvellously*; but I do not think I would say it unless I was being facetious. In such cases speakers can sometimes be in doubt. I have been asking myself for the last quarter of an hour whether there is a word '*militation*'. If one found it anywhere it might be in bad social–scientific English (*the militation of other factors against the underlying trends in the economy*). But I cannot quite convince myself that this phrase would be used (instead of *the way that other factors militate*...).[3] There are further cases where the Noun is normal, but the Verb seems doubtful. For example, is there a Verb '*halate*' to match the photographer's term *halation*? The latter was coined as such from the base *halo*; the source (from 1859) is cited in the *OED*. In the intervening century a Verb or Participle could plausibly have arisen (e.g. *These negatives are badly halated*). But it is not recorded in the supplement of the *OED* or in *Webster's Third International*. One doubts whether it has been used.

---

[3] In the first edition I used the example *pontification*. But, just by using it, I have completely confused my intuitions.

There would thus be a lack of regularity (to put it at its crudest) in any set of paradigms that took *automate* and *automation* as its model. One would include a 'Verbal' *salute* but not a 'Nominal' *salution*, another *elocution* but not *elocute*, another *function* but not *funct*, and so on. These gaps are not predictable by general rule. There is no reason at all why there should not be a Verb HALATE except that, apparently, there isn't. The lexicographer must therefore show, in individual cases, whether both forms exist or not. Moreover, we are also faced with semantic problems. A *delegation* is a collection of people who have been 'delegated', and a *selection* (of goods or what-not) will have been 'selected'. But an *election* is not a collection of people who have been 'elected', nor would one speak of a *diversion* or a *direction* of parcels (compare *an assignment of parcels*) arriving. ELECTION, DIVERSION and DIRECTION lack what one might call the 'Passive' sense. There are also a few which lack the converse 'Active' sense (that of *the generation of electricity* or *his delegation of the responsibility*). For example, one can say *He opted for apple-pie* but not *his option for* (meaning 'his decision to choose') *apple-pie*. Do our 'paradigms' have homonymous 'Active' and 'Passive' terms? If so, there are yet more gaps for certain of our putative 'lexemes'.

But that would still be far too crude. The 'Active'/'Passive' distinction is at best an overall criterion of classification, which must then be qualified and supplemented in numerous individual cases. Perhaps, the reader may say, our example OPTION does have a quasi-Active sense: for instance, *his option for* (meaning 'his option to purchase') *three tons of apple-pie*. But this is a quite specific business usage, which cannot be predicted from the general meanings of OPT as such. For our earlier example SALUTE one might be tempted to bring in the Noun SALUTATION; although there is no *-ion* form at least there is one in *-ation* instead. But again the senses of Verb and Noun do not precisely correspond: one could not say *the salutation of officers* either. Similar points can be made for most of the pairs which we have cited: DIRECTION has a largely unpredictable sense (vis à vis DIRECT) in the normal collocation *He was going in the other direction*, GENERATION in *three generations ago* and so on. It does not follow that Noun and Verb are semantically unrelated. But one cannot establish an overall correlation ('*option*' is to '*opt*' as '*direction*' is to '*direct*', as '*generation*' is to '*generate*' and so on), and simply leave it at that. The same point can be illustrated for other patterns of word-formation. The Noun OVERSIGHT, for example, is related to the Verb OVERSEE; and in a recent radio interview I heard a businessman use it in a sense exactly predictable from its morphological analysis. He wanted to work, he said, 'without the persistent oversight of government bodies'.[4] But the example immediately reminds us that the normal sense is not predictable. When a government body makes an oversight it is, if anything, a failure in 'overseeing'. Therefore a dictionary writer has to make a separate statement about its meaning. Likewise a dictionary has to have special entries, often with several related but different senses, for Nouns such as GENERATION, OPTION and DIRECTION.

Such, then, is the case as seen from the complementary viewpoint of the lexicographer. By contrast, a dictionary will have nothing special to say about the oppositions between Italian Singulars and Plurals or English Comparatives or Positives. Semantically, *cugino* is indeed to *cugini* as *monte* is to *monti* or *libro* to *libri*. Similarly, *hot* is to *hotter* as *cold* is to *colder*, as *pretty* is to *prettier*, and so on. Where this rule has to be qualified it will only be in larger collocations such as compounds or idioms (*a hot-spot*, or *It's getting too hot for me here*). It can therefore be left to the grammarian to explain how Italian Plurals, in general, differ semantically from the corresponding Singulars; and how English Comparatives, in general, are used differently from the corresponding Positives.

Now in linguistics no single criterion should be applied in absolute terms to individual instances. Alongside the normal form *cesoie* 'scissors' which we cited earlier, the *Cambridge Italian Dictionary*[5] also gives the Singular *cesoia* with the translation 'shears' and the rubric 'eng[ineering]'. Here a correlation which is apparently inflectional does, nevertheless, require an occasional lexical qualification. Occasionally, too, an inflectional paradigm will show an unexpected gap. Still in Italian, one would expect SOCCOMBERE 'succumb' to have a Participle *soccombuto* (and, indeed, it is explicit or implicit in dictionaries); nevertheless, I

---

[4] BBC, Radio 4, 23 March 1986.
[5] Barbara Reynolds (ed.), *The Cambridge Italian Dictionary*, vol. 1: *Italian–English* (Cambridge, Cambridge University Press, 1962).

have been told that speakers are not happy with it. This might perhaps be compared with the case of *militation*. Conversely, there are scientific terms in *-ate* and *-ation* which stand in virtually mechanical relationships. I do not know whether I met the Verb *chelate* (in, say, *a chelating agent*) before or after the Noun *chelation*. But once the sense of either is explained, one does not need further explanation, or further recourse to a dictionary, to understand the other. In such cases, what is in other instances a clearly lexical pattern can, nevertheless, be semantically regular. It is therefore vital that we should keep in mind all relevant criteria, both lexicographical and syntactic, and that we should look in general at the range of words exhibiting a particular pattern. In syntax, CHELATION behaves no differently from simple Nouns. In morphology, it has a formation in *-ion* which, in many other cases, such as *generation* from *generate* or *delegation* from *delegate*, is not semantically regular. In principle, we can imagine that it too might in future branch out independently of *chelate*, especially if it were to acquire non-scientific uses. Accordingly the Noun and Verb are distinct lexemes (CHELATION, CHELATE), even though their relationship is at present predictable. By contrast, *cesoia* and *cesoie* are exceptions to a pattern which in general can be seen as regular and grammatical.

## CHANGE AND INDETERMINACY

In this discussion we have considered the problem synchronically and have assumed, moreover, that the boundary is sufficiently determinate in all cases. But in the history of languages the status of a formative may naturally vary between one stage and another. The Latin form *maturescit* 'it ripens' has a stem formed with the Inchoative element *-sc-* ('becomes, begins to, begins to become'). This is classed as a lexical formation, the Verb MATURESCO 'ripen' being a different lexeme from the Adjective MATURUS 'ripe'. Looking forwards in time, the same element (etymologically) appears in modern Italian *fini-sc-e* (phonetically [fiˈniʃʃe]) '[he] finishes' or *appari-sc-o* [appaˈrisko] 'I appear'. Looking backwards, one may equally reconstruct an Indo-European *-sk-*, which is reflected most obviously by the comparison between Greek *gi-gnɔ́ː-sk-ɔː* (γιγνώσκω) 'I come to know' and the Latin *co-gno-sc-o*. But the rôle of this '*-sc-*' does not remain the same from one language period to the next. In Indo-European one can argue, at least, for an inflectional status: forms in *-sk-* (or *-ē-sk-*) were characteristic not of a separate set of lexemes, but rather of a separate 'Inchoative' section in the range of Present forms of Verbs.[6] In Latin the formative was lexical, as we have said. In Italian it has become part of the paradigm entirely. *Finisce* and *apparisco* are ordinary forms of the lexemes FINIRE 'finish' and APPARIRE 'appear', the *-sc-* appearing only in certain forms of the Imperative, Present Indicative and Present Subjunctive, and then, moreover, for just a subclass of one of the major conjugations. Over the millennia, the same element has changed from probable inflectional to certain lexical status, and later back (so far as that distinction goes) to inflectional again.

Since rôles can shift historically, it is not surprising that the boundary can in fact be blurred at one particular stage. In the phrase *a crowded room*, CROWDED may reasonably be classed as a derived 'Participial Adjective' (and is so classed in the latest supplement to the *OED*). A common test is that it may be modified by *very*: *a very crowded room*. By contrast, *heated* in *a well heated room* remains the Past Participle of the Verb HEAT, among other reasons because one does not say *a very heated room*. Here (as in the case of the two forms '*trying*') an identical range of formatives (*-ed*, *-en*, etc.) has at present both an inflectional and a lexical rôle. Where, then, do we draw the boundary in individual cases? In *a written confession*, for example, is *written* a form of WRITE or of a separate lexeme WRITTEN? We cannot say *a very written confession* (but, of course, there are Adjectives which cannot be modified by *very* for semantic reasons). Nor is a putative WRITTEN quite established in the Predicative construction: *if his confession had been written* is likely to be understood as a Passive (compare *if his confession had been finished*) rather than as the equivalent of *if his confession had been a written one*. Such tests might point to a continuing Verbal status. But against this a putative Participle would have restricted collocations in the Attributive construction: one does not talk of *a written book* nor, really, of *a written letter* (though one does say *He wrote a letter* or

---

[6] For discussion of this formative see C. Watkins, 'Hittite and Indo-European studies: the denominative statives in *-ē-*', *TPhS* 1971, pp. 51–93.

*He wrote a book*). Nor can *a written confession* be readily detached from a *hand-written* (or *typewritten*, or *unwritten*) *confession*, where there are certainly no Verbs HAND-WRITE, TYPEWRITE or (in the relevant sense) UNWRITE. These points suggest that we should recognise an Adjective. Diachronically, 'WRITTEN' (like others of its kind) is in the process of emerging from its Verbal origin. But synchronically, the decision is bound to be partly arbitrary.

In other cases, we may be sure that a Participial Adjective exists; but it is less certain which specific uses should be assigned to it. There is without doubt an Adjective BENT: for example, in *a bent policeman*. In this collocation its meaning is not predictable from that of the Verb BEND, and indeed one does not normally talk of policemen 'being bent by' criminals. But the same form has other senses in other contexts. In *He was bent on doing it* we may again identify an Adjective: whereas the sense of *bent* requires a construction with *on*, there is no corresponding construction with the verb (*We bent him on doing it, Something bent him on doing it*). The argument is far less clear, however, in Milton's sonnet 'On his Blindness':

> though my soul more bent
> To serve therewith my Maker,

especially if we try to think in terms of Milton's English and not that of a modern reader. Beside these metaphorical uses, there is also a literal sense in, for example, *a bent pin*. Now a bent pin is certainly a pin that has been bent, just as a broken arm is an arm that has been broken, a smashed windscreen a windscreen that has been smashed, and so on. On grounds of regularity we might claim that *bent* is now a Participle. But a bent pin might instead be seen as a pin that has a certain shape, like, for example, a bent stick or a crooked stick. Moreover it is a form of instrument, and the collocation is in that sense more cohesive than in, say, *a bent screw*. In such cases it is easy to see how the slide from Participle to Adjective takes place. It is not lost, for example, on writers of glossaries and other indexes to texts, who may find it very difficult to decide which part of speech a particular form belongs to.

Participial Adjectives are a notorious instance of indeterminacy, and not just in English. But in dealing with languages one should never forget that they are historically fluid, and that the changes tend to flow in particular directions. We remarked at the beginning of this chapter that the difference between inflections and compounding is easily determined; this goes hand in hand with the observation that the development of an inflection from an element in a compound, or vice versa, is historically unusual. But fluidity between inflections and word-formation is not rare and neither is indeterminacy. It is perhaps a pointless challenge to say which observation explains which. On the one hand, it is because change is not always sudden that there is indeterminacy; on the other hand, it is because there is indeterminacy that change can be easy.

There is a similar indeterminacy, which we touched on in a preliminary way in chapter 1, between complex lexemes, or lexemes derived by processes of word-formation, and simple lexemes. Take, for example, the Noun WEALTH. There are certainly Nouns in -*th*, as TRUTH from TRUE; and, etymologically, WEALTH from WELL or WEAL is one of them. Synchronically, the form still ends in this consonant, and it pointedly rhymes with *health* in the phrase *health and wealth*. The problem, of course, is that it has effectively drifted apart from its historical base. For no speaker of English is there still a connection with WELL, and for most speakers WEAL scarcely exists even in idioms. If one wanted to pursue this analysis one would have to say that *weal-* [wel] was a 'partially independent' element which can only appear with -*th* following.

Similar problems arise repeatedly from the historical borrowing of learned formations. The Noun formation in -*ion* is well established (as we have shown earlier). But does NATION, for example, belong to it? Its source (via Old French) is the Latin NATIO 'race, nation', which was related synchronically to NATIVUS 'native', NATURA 'nature' and others on the base of the Verb NASCOR 'be born' (Past Participle *natus*). Many educated speakers of English know this perfectly well, and in English itself there is at least a semantic connection between NATIVE and NATION, at least a morphological connection between NATIVE and NATIVITY (in *The Nativity*), and at least a semantic connection again between the latter and NATAL. In that case are they simply *nat-ion*, *nat-ive*, *nat-iv-ity*, *nat-al* – all being derived from the 'partially independent' base *nate(e)-*? Different scholars will judge differently. But the case is at least a great deal stronger than for CYNIC and DOG in chapter 1.

The most awkward cases are when languages borrow from their own earlier stages. French, like English, has a pattern by which Adjectives are formed in -*al* (or -*el*); thus *national* from *nation* 'nation', *original* from *origine* 'origin', or *personnel* 'personal' from *personne*. In both languages this began as a Latinising formation, the forms being either borrowed as wholes from Latin Adjectives in -*alis* (for example, Late Latin *originalis* from a form of ORIGO 'origin') or formed from Nouns, such as that of NATION, which were themselves of a sufficiently learned shape. But in French the Latin Noun will often have a natural reflex also. For example, alongside the Adjective-form *mensuel* 'monthly' (which is a nineteenth-century adaptation of Latin *mensualis*) we also have the Noun-form *mois* 'month', which has developed from Latin *mensis* by the normal processes of sound-change.[7] Similarly, *paternel* 'paternal' and *maternel* 'maternal' exist alongside *père* 'father' and *mère* 'mother', *monacal* 'monastic' and *clérical* 'clerical' alongside *moine* 'monk' and *clerc* 'clerk, cleric', and so on. Do these Adjectives all belong to the same synchronic formation? Are *moine* [mwan] and *mois* [mwa] in some sense the same root as *monac-* [mɔnak] and *mensu-* [mãsɥ]?[8] Without retracing the history, it would be hard to account for their phonetic differences. Moreover, there are also doublets among the Adjectives themselves: from *matin* 'morning' there is the regular *matinal* '[taking place] in the morning', but we are also faced with the Latinate *matutinal* (from a form of Latin MATUTINUS). Is *matutin-*, at least, a 'partially independent' base whose derivative bears only a semantic relationship to MATIN?

In extreme cases the Adjectives seem clearly independent. *Mental* 'mental' ultimately has a Latin base (that of MENS 'mind') which, on its own, has no French reflex either learned or popular; nor can *vernal* 'vernal, of the spring' be matched with anything but the Latin VER 'spring' and the derived Adjective VERNALIS. Again, in the case of *radical* 'radical' the etymologically related

[7] The date, and other factual statements, are from E. Gamillscheg, *Etymologisches Wörterbuch der französischen Sprache* (Heidelberg, Winter, 1928).

[8] Transcriptions of French follow the rather conservative system used in dictionaries: thus, for instance, *Harrap's New Standard French and English Dictionary* (London, Harrap, 1980).

Noun (*racine* 'root') is too far removed in both form and meaning. At this extreme one can say with confidence that there is no synchronic connection, just as at the other extreme (that of *national* or *matinal*) one can be quite sure that there is. But between the extremes there is no firm criterion by which one can draw the line. Are *clerc* and *clérical* morphologically related or not – compare English *clerk* and *clerical*? There is no certain answer, and, given the historical circumstances, it is hardly to be expected that there should be. The decision is a matter of analytic convenience – and, as we hinted in chapter 1, it is often hard to decide when the morphological analyst should pack it in.

## RELATED READING

For recent treatments of this topic see BAUER, *Morphology*, ch. 6; WURZEL, §2.2; SCALISE, pp. 102–15; BYBEE, ch. 4. Readers who know German will find PLANK, ch. 2, original and provocative. For earlier accounts see BLOOMFIELD, pp. 222ff.; ROBINS, *Linguistics*, pp. 240ff.; also A. A. Hill, *Introduction to Linguistic Structures* (New York, Harcourt Brace, 1958), pp. 119ff., on English 'postbases' vs 'suffixes'. Note again that where I speak of word-formation others will commonly speak of derivation or derivational morphology; also that some writers, such as Hill, have seen the problem as one of separating types of morpheme, rather than of rules, formations or processes.

For the view that there is no 'principled distinction' between inflection and word-formation see, for example, W. Zwanenburg in ALINEI, pp. 352ff.; Zwanenburg argues specifically against my contribution to the same exchange of papers (ALINEI, pp. 85–92). It is naturally quite common among the 'lexical' or 'lexicalist' school (see the references for chapter 2); but compare S. Scalise, 'Inflection and derivation', *Linguistics* 26 (1988), pp. 561–81, for the proposal that a distinction should be made within the lexicon. For inflection and derivation as a continuum see again BYBEE, ch. 4.

The Gender of Nouns and Adjectives is discussed with clarity by A. Martinet, *A Functional View of Language* (Oxford, Clarendon Press, 1962), pp. 15ff., in the context of French; also by SAPIR, pp. 95f. But the wrong approach is not wholly a figment: compare F. B. Agard & R. J. Di Pietro, *The Grammatical Structures of English and Italian* (Chicago, University of Chicago Press, 1965), pp. 20ff. The replacement of a complex by a simple form is an old test: thus MARTINET, §4.35; SAPIR, pp. 84f. (on *farmer* and *duckling*). But note that it does not strictly work unless suppletive inflections (like *were* as a replacement for *seemed*) are identified as complex. The problem with Grade has also been recognised for decades: see, for example, A. A. Hill, *Introduction to Linguistic Structures*, pp. 168ff., arguing that English *-er* and *-est* are lexical. On the importance of syntax in identifying inflections compare, in general, ANDERSON, 'Where's morphology?', pp. 587ff.

See chapter 4 for further discussion of gaps and irregularities in word-formation. CHOMSKY, 'Nominalization' takes them as the main ground for abandoning a transformational account of word-formation, which had sought to integrate it with the syntax. On the 'rigid parallelism' of inflectional paradigms see already BLOOMFIELD, pp. 223f. On the general problem of discrepancies between criteria in linguistic analysis see C. E. Bazell, 'The correspondence fallacy in structural linguistics', reprinted *RiL 11*, pp. 271–98. First published in Istanbul in 1952, this would have been a classic article if it had appeared less obscurely.

On English Participles and Participial Adjectives see QUIRK *et al.*, pp. 413–16; also SCALISE, pp. 127–31, on the search for a solution within lexicalist morphology. On the problem of learned derivatives see CORBIN, part 2, § 3.1; on their role in general, the brief discussion by ULLMAN, pp. 108ff. (also 145ff.). At the end of the 1960s generative phonologists made a determined attempt to reduce them to synchronic rule: for French in particular see S. A. Schane, *French Phonology and Morphology* (Cambridge, Mass., MIT Press, 1968). For the movement of which this formed part see again LASS, ch. 9; BAUER, *Morphology*, pp. 116ff.

# 4
# Lexical derivation

What we have called word-formation is usually called 'derivational morphology'. The formation of *election* or *generation* is thus a derivational formation, by which nouns are derived from verbs. By the same token, *-ion* is a derivational formative or derivational morpheme. I have avoided this terminology for two reasons. Firstly, there are lexical relations in which it is not obvious that one word is derived from the other. Let us return, for example, to the oppositions in Italian between ZIO 'uncle' and ZIA 'aunt' or CUGINO 'male cousin' and CUGINA 'female cousin'. They too belong to lexical morphology, for the reasons which we have explored in chapter 3. But there is no strong reason for saying either that the Feminines ZIA and CUGINA are derived from the Masculines, or vice versa. In meaning, their oppositions are like those of the morphologically unrelated PADRE 'father' and MADRE 'mother' or FRATELLO 'brother' and SORELLA 'sister'. In form, neither is more complex than the other: each pair has a common element (*zi-*, *cugin-*) followed in one case by a Masculine ending (Singular *-o*) and in the other by a Feminine ending (Singular *-a*). On the face of it, all four Nouns are simple or all four are complex; neither the Masculines nor the Feminines have priority.

The second reason is that we can talk, and will talk, of inflectional derivations. Formally, as *generation* can be derived from *generate* by adding the lexical ending *-ion*, so the Plural *generations* can be derived from *generation* by adding the inflectional ending *-s*. If, say, the Feminine *cugina* is derived from the Masculine, then equally the Plurals *cugini* (Masculine) and *cugine* (Feminine) might be derived from the Singulars. We might instead see both *cugino* and *cugina* as derived from their common element *cugin-*. But equally, in the paradigm of the Adjective NUOVO 'new', both *nuovo* and *nuova* might be derived from *nuov-*. A model of morphology which is formally derivational applies to words in general and not just to relations between lexemes.

Nevertheless, the term 'derivational' expresses an important insight. For words like *generation* or *imputation* are not only derived in dictionaries from simpler words like *generate* or *impute*; they can also be created, consciously or unconsciously, by speakers. Take, for example, the form *capsization*. I have not found it in dictionaries, and for the 'act of capsizing', given time to reflect, I would myself prefer *capsizal*. But I have heard it used quite naturally by someone interviewed in a news programme ('a massive capsization in a few minutes').[1] Now it is conceivable that the speaker had either heard or used this word before. But it is more probable that he had not; or, if he had, that it was simply reinvented, following the model of such nouns as STABILISATION from STABILISE or STERILISATION from STERILISE, in the course of that utterance. In this case, the invention or reinvention is unconscious, and there is no evidence that the implied lexeme ('CAPSIZATION') is becoming established. But in many others the coining becomes permanent. To take an example from linguistics, the terms 'disambiguate' and 'disambiguation' are first attested from the early 1960s (*OEDS*). I recall encountering them, in papers by the philosopher of language Jerrold Katz, and thinking how unnecessary and ugly they were. But they were rapidly accepted; and, although I still find them inelegant, I cannot swear that I have not used them in my own classes. In this case it is hard to say whether the word was created consciously or unconsciously. But in other fields technical terminology is invented deliberately and according to explicit principles. Take, for example, the naming of enzymes in *-ase* (*dehydrogenase*, for an enzyme that

---

[1] BBC, Radio 4, *World at One*, 8 March 1987, with reference to the sinking of the ferry *Herald of Free Enterprise*.

transfers hydrogen, *ribonuclease*, for one involved in the hydrolysis of ribonucleic acid, and so on).

In 'derivational morphology' we are therefore concerned not only with grammatical processes of derivation (for example, that by which a Verbal Noun in -(*at*)*ion* is formed from a simpler element), but also with the creative derivation of new words that follow existing patterns. Let us take the formal processes first and the problems of creativity second.

## FORMATIONS

The derivation of *generation* from *generate* or *diversion* from *divert* illustrates a **formation** in which, in general, Noun-forms are derived from Verb-forms by the addition of -*ion*. In phonetic terms, ['dʒenəreɪt] + ´[jən] = [dʒenə'reɪʃn], [daɪ'vɜːt] + ´[jən] = [daɪ'vɜːʃn], where the acute accent before [jən] (´[jən]) indicates that the accent is also moved, where necessary, to the syllable before it. Since this ending -*ion* is part of a formation, it has already been referred to as a **formative**; and, since the formation is lexical, it is more precisely a **lexical formative**. On that basis, we might represent the process diagrammatically as follows:

$$[X]_V \rightarrow [X + ´[jən]]_N$$

In this notation, '*X*' is a variable with the potential values ['dʒenəreɪt], [daɪ'vɜːt] and so on. To the left of the arrow the subscript 'V', for Verb, shows its part of speech: this is a useful notation which originates in work on generative grammars, and is known technically as a 'labelled bracketing'. Similarly, the subscript 'N' which labels the brackets to the right of the arrow indicates that, when ´[jən] is added to some value of *X*, the result will be a Noun. The arrow itself symbolises an operation. In words, then, there is an operation by which Nouns may be derived by adding ´[jən] or -*ion* to the end of a Verb.

As a preliminary formulation this does perfectly well, and something like it is implied by any traditional account of the process. However, it calls for a few additions and clarifications. One important point is that we are concerned not only with the derivation of forms from forms (*generate* → *generation* or ['dʒenəreɪt] → [dʒenə'reɪʃn]), but also with that of lexemes from lexemes (GENERATE → GENERATION). For a language like English, this may still seem a trifle pedantic: the forms related by the operation are both word-forms and are both entered as words in a dictionary. But let us consider the problem in, for example, Latin. The Adjective LUCIDUS 'shining' is related by a process of word-formation to the Verb LUCEO 'shine'; similarly, MADIDUS 'wet' to MADEO 'be wet' or STUPIDUS 'stupefied, stupid' to STUPEO 'be stupefied'. But what exactly is the formal operation? Like other Adjectives, LUCIDUS has a paradigm: Nominative Singular Masculine *lucidus*, Nominative Singular Feminine *lucida* and so on. The Verb too has a paradigm, which includes forms such as *luceo* 'I am shining' or *lucebit* '[it] will shine'. But when we analyse such forms it is clear that the process of word-formation does not derive *lucidus* from *luceo*, or *lucida* from *lucebit*, or any member of one paradigm from any member of the other, but simply *lucid-* (*luc-* + *-id-*) from *luc-*. These are not words or word-forms, and become parts of word-forms only when inflectional endings, such as *-a* in *lucid-a* or *-ebit* in *luc-ebit*, are added to them. In such a case, the point is not pedantic. If processes of word-formation are said to form 'words' from 'words', these words are lexemes and have to be distinguished from the phonetic or written forms that undergo, or result from, the relevant operation.

A form such as *luc-* is traditionally called a **root**. This is a form that underlies at least one paradigm or partial paradigm, and is itself morphologically simple. Thus *luc-* underlies the paradigms of both LUCEO and LUCIDUS: by the addition of appropriate formatives (lexical *-id-*, inflectional *-a* in *liquida*, and so on) the complete forms of each can be derived from it. Moreover, it cannot be analysed further, except etymologically. A form such as *lucid-* is in turn a **stem**. This too is a form that underlies at least one paradigm or partial paradigm; but it is itself morphologically complex. Thus *lucid-* underlies the paradigm of LUCIDUS, but can be further analysed into *luc-* and *-id-*. In general, then, the formal processes of lexical morphology derive a stem which is associated with a lexeme (as *lucid-* is associated with LUCIDUS) from a simpler form associated with another lexeme. In the example before us, the stem is derived from a root (*luc-*, associated with LUCEO). But it too may be a stem. From the Adjective LUCIDUS there is in turn a Noun LUCIDITAS (compare English LUCIDITY). The associated stem has the form *luciditat-* (Genitive Singular *luciditatis*) and is in turn derived from *lucid-*.

This formulation will also cover the example from English. At the risk again of seeming tiresome, we can say that a stem *diversion* underlies the Singular and Plural forms of DIVERSION and a root *divert* the varying forms of DIVERT. However, there are still some processes, some marginal and some central in particular languages, that do not quite fall under the pattern. Take once more the case in Italian of CUGINO 'male cousin' and CUGINA 'female cousin'. By definition, there is a root *cugin-*, which is associated with both lexemes. But no stem is derived from it: normally, one lexeme adds the Masculine endings (Singular *cugin-o*, Plural *cugin-i*) and the other adds the Feminine endings (Singular *cugin-a*, Plural *cugin-e*), in each case to the same root. For an example in English, consider the relationship between the Verb FISH, in *He was fishing for mackerel*, and the Noun FISH. This is a relation of **conversion**, the form *fish*, which is basically a Noun, being converted, by what is also called a process of 'zero-derivation', into a Verb. The pattern is common in English, and in many cases, such as this, it is clear enough which lexeme is derived from which: $FISH_N \rightarrow FISH_V$. But the form *fish-* in *fishing* is not itself more complex than *fish* as a Noun. Both paradigms (of $FISH_N$ and of $FISH_V$) share the same form. Basically, it is the root of $FISH_N$; in the derivation of $FISH_V$ it is not changed, but merely converted to a new role.

A different case, which by its nature will always be marginal, is where a root or stem is found only in a derived form. We were hesitant to say that *butcher*, for example, was derived from *butch-*. But what of a form like *jubilation* or *trepidation*? There are no established Verb-forms *jubilate* and *trepidate*; therefore one might argue that, despite the apparent ending *-ion*, both Nouns are simple. However, we must always bear in mind the possibility of what historians of language call a **back-formation**. Suppose someone were to say 'I shouldn't start jubilating too soon.' It is immediately intelligible; more so than, say, 'He made his money butching.' For the nonce at least, speaker and hearer will together assume an analysis of *jubilation* on the lines of forms like *celebration* from *celebrate*. In the case of *trepidation*, we must also

65

consider the Adjective *intrepid*. If this were an isolated form it might raise similar problems. There is a Negative formation in *in-* (*decent → indecent, credible → incredible*) and, although there is no Positive form '*trepid*', the meaning of *intrepid* ('without fear', 'not to be deterred') may also be construed as Negative. A back-formation might be facetious ('a trepid explorer'), but could perhaps be understood. Similarly, *delible* ('a delible marker') is a possible back-formation from *indelible*, while, for comparison, *tact* from *intact* ('a tact skeleton') is incomprehensible. If *intrepid* and *trepidation* are taken together, we can reasonably argue that, although there is no lexeme TREPID, the form *trepid* is a source from which both are derived.

It will be clear that *trepid* must, by definition, be a root; the only difference between it and other roots is that no simple lexeme is directly associated with it. *Intrepid* is then derived in just the same way as *indecent*, and is the stem or uninflected form of INTREPID. Hence the tendency to interpret it as Negative. From the same root we may derive a Verbal stem *trepidate*; again the only difference between this and other stems is that there is no directly associated lexeme TREPIDATE. That in turn is the source for both the form *trepidation* and the lexeme TREPIDATION. By the same process *jubilation* and JUBILATION, if the case is accepted, can be derived from *jubilate*. This is arguably a root. Alternatively, if *jubilee* is seen as morphologically related, it is itself a stem derived from a root *jubil-*.

These qualifications all concern the forms that enter into lexical relations: *luc-* and *lucid-*, *cugin-*, *trepid* and so on. But a further point is that formations, as such, have meanings. Take, for example, the process by which *indecent* is derived from *decent*:

$$[X]_A \rightarrow [[\text{ɪn}] + X]_A$$

One aspect of its meaning is shown by the part of speech labels: by it, complex forms that are Adjectival (A) are derived from simpler forms that are themselves Adjectival. Similarly, the operation adding *-ion* or ´[jən] derives forms of Nouns (*generation*, *diversion*) from forms of Verbs (*generate*, *divert*). Syntactically, the words behave like other Nouns: they can take Articles and other Determiners (*a diversion*, *three generations*) and so on. But they are specifically Verbal (or Deverbal) Nouns, and in phrases like *the generation of electricity* the relation of the Noun to its Complement (*of electricity*) is also, in part, like that of the underlying Verb to its Object (*They generate electricity*).

But clearly that is not all. In addition, the formation in *in-* is Negative, INDECENT meaning, in general, 'not decent', INCREDIBLE 'not credible' and so on. This is a feature that it shares with other formations: in *un-* (*kind → unkind, suitable → unsuitable*); in *non-* (*toxic → non-toxic, standard → non-standard*); in *dis-* (*loyal → disloyal, engaged → disengaged*); in [æ] (*symmetrical → asymmetrical*) or in [eɪ] (*periodic → aperiodic, moral → amoral*). The formation in *-ion* also has a meaning which, in this case, we may demonstrate by contrast. From GENERATE, for example, we can derive both GENERATION and GENERATOR; likewise from INCINERATE both INCINERATION and INCINERATOR; and from ACT both ACTION and ACTOR. But the two formations have different semantic effects. Nouns in *-or*, or more generally [ə], are Agent Nouns. An actor, though the sense is specialised, is a person who acts; likewise a speculator is someone who speculates, an elector someone who elects, a preacher ([ə] written *-er*) someone who preaches. A generator, in the normal sense, is not a person; nor is an incinerator. Nevertheless, they too perform the act of generating or incinerating. In contrast, a Noun in *-ion* is typically an Action Noun, denoting not a performer or instrument or agent but the act or process itself. That is the sense of GENERATION in *the generation of electricity*, of ACTION in *his generous action*, of INCINERATION in *I ordered its incineration*, of SPECULATION in *Speculation would be foolish* and so on.

Now in all this we should not forget that lexemes can bear unpredictable senses. The meaning of INSUBORDINATE, in *his insubordinate attitude*, does not simply negate that of SUBORDINATE; nor that of SAVOURY, in *an unsavoury character*, or UNHOLY, in *an unholy mess*, those of SAVOURY and HOLY. Of the Nouns in *-ion*, GENERATION has a special sense in *three generations ago*; similarly DIRECTION in *He went in the opposite direction*, or ACTION in *They brought an action against us*. In chapter 3 we laid particular stress on senses of this kind, since their prevalence is a major reason for distinguishing lexical or derivational formations from inflections. But in giving irregularity its due we must recognise that there is also regularity. In learning the language, speakers will repeatedly produce, hear and read new complex forms that they have neither met nor said before: new Negatives in *un-* or *in-*, new Action Nouns in *-(at)ion* and so on. It is because they know the sense of the formation, and not just those of individual lexemes that have been learned already, that such forms can be used and understood correctly. For the same reason, lexemes which have special senses often bear more literal senses too. Sometimes both are established: compare again the use of GENERATION in *the generation of electricity*, or of DIRECTION in *her direction of the economy*. In other cases a more literal sense can be forced by the context. In a dictionary definition an incinerator is again a furnace or some other apparatus for incinerating, and a reactor, though the word has various technical senses, is not simply a person who reacts. But suppose someone were to say 'He was a quite unscrupulous incinerator of papers', or 'She is basically a reactor rather than an initiator.' Even if such usages seem forced or unfamiliar, the sentences are easily understood. That is again because we know the meaning of the formation, as well as those of individual lexemes.

In brief, the meaning of derived words is in part synthetic and in part analytic. It is synthetic in that many words have meanings that cannot entirely be determined from their parts. If we know, for example, the meanings of GAOL and PRISON and we also know that of the process

$$X \rightarrow [X + [\partial]]_N$$

we still cannot know that a gaoler is someone who keeps people in prison while a prisoner is someone who is kept there. The difference can only be described synthetically, for GAOLER and PRISONER as wholes. Yet even in cases such as this the meanings are also, in part, analytic. As forms in *-er*, both GAOLER and PRISONER are Agentive rather than Action Nouns or other Abstracts. Nor are their senses unconnected with those of GAOL and PRISON, just as that of GENERATION, even when it does not denote an action, cannot be detached from GENERATE. At the other extreme, there are complex lexemes whose meanings are wholly analytic. That of RESUSCITATION ('the act or achievement of resuscitating') follows directly from that of RESUSCITATE; likewise that of an earlier example, AUTOMATION, from that of AUTOMATE, and so on. That is, they follow given the meaning of the formation. We have implied that this is a single meaning, characteristic of the process as a whole. Alternatively, a formation may have two or more related meanings, or a general meaning with two or more subsenses. Whatever its nature, it too must be described.

Finally, our account of formations must also say something about their **productivity**. In chapter 3 we laid stress on the prevalence of gaps in word-formation: HALATION but apparently no corresponding Verb 'HALATE'; a Verb MILITATE but a question-mark over 'MILITATION'. Similarly, there is no established lexical Negative of, say, RARE or BRAVE. Of the relevant formations, neither that in *in-* (*inrare*, *inbrave*), nor that in *un-* (*unrare*, *unbrave*), nor that in *non-* (*non-rare*, *non-brave*), is fully productive. That is, there are values of $X$, under the sole condition that $X$ is an Adjective, for which the derived form is at best not usual. This was again one reason for distinguishing lexical formations from inflections.

But we have also noted that new forms (*capsization*, *disambiguation*) can be created. Even if there are no established lexemes UNRARE or UNBRAVE, one might not be so surprised if someone were to talk of, say, 'a not exactly unrare situation' or, perhaps, 'their relatively unbrave conduct'. If such formations are not automatically productive, they are at least **semi-productive**. Forms that are new to the speaker can be created or re-created, can be understood and can in principle become established, but not with total freedom. This raises theoretical difficulties, which bear on our concept of language and of a language, and will require a separate section.

## PRODUCTIVITY

One basic problem is that productivity appears to vary. Formation *a*, taken as a whole, may be more productive than formation *b*; in addition, a single formation may be more productive in some circumstances than in others. Another problem is that different formations may have similar meanings. When that is so they tend to compete; hence, in particular, a more productive process may be in competition with a less productive.

At one extreme, we find single formations that can approach full productivity. An example in English is that of Adjectives in *-able*: *computable* from *compute*, *get-at-able*, or better perhaps the Negative *unget-at-able*, from the Prepositional Verb *get at*. Another is the formation of Nouns in *-ness*. From *unget-at-able* might one not, in turn, derive *unget-at-ableness*? We may not expect to find it in a dictionary. But it is of the nature of creativity that it will always run ahead of what is in dictionaries. Can one similarly derive *computableness* from *computable*? One difficulty is that its apparent sense is already covered by *computability*: with Adjectives in *-able*, the formation of Nouns in *-ity* is also highly productive. But it is hard to be certain that *computableness* might not be heard.

At the other extreme, there are formations that are virtually **unproductive**. Take, for example, the formation of Nouns in *-th*. We assumed in an earlier chapter that *truth* was derived from *true*; similarly, *warmth* and *growth* are related to *warm* and *grow*, and, if we allow for further phonological changes, *width* to *wide*, *length* to *long* and so on. But it is not a formation that readily yields new lexemes. An instructive illustration is the form *coolth*, which appears in dictionaries, and for which the *OED* records a long succession of literary uses. Despite these and its transparent analogy with *warmth*, it has never become established as a lexeme which could seriously compete with COOLNESS (or, with a simple conversion, COOL). Still less is it tending to supplant them. Other conceivable forms, like '*thickth*' for *thickness*, are likely only as a verbal joke. Now the fact that we can understand both *coolth* and *thickth* confirms that the formation exists. It would be wrong to treat these Nouns as if they were simple. But the process is one by which an established set of forms is analysed; new ones can be synthesised at best unnaturally.

The difference between *-th* and *-ness* is particularly striking. Both form Nouns from Adjectives, and in that sense they compete. But the competition is almost wholly an encroachment of the productive formation on the domain of the unproductive. Take the form *trueness*. With some senses of TRUE it is still excluded by *truth*: one would not normally talk of the 'trueness' of a story, and still less would a logician, or a linguist infected by formal logic, refer to 'trueness tables' or 'trueness conditions'.

But in other senses it is already established ('the trueness of his aim', or 'the trueness of a line'). *Warmness* is in dictionaries and can easily usurp the sense of *warmth* ('the warmness of his reception'). *Longness* is in general not, and might seem to be excluded by *length*. But it does seem possible with peripheral senses of LONG (the 'longness', say, of a drink?).

For a more complex instance of competition let us take a more detailed look at the formations of Negative Adjectives. We have identified five: in *in-* (*indecent*), in *un-* (*unkind*), in *non-* (*non-toxic*), in *dis-* (*disloyal*) and in [æ] or [eɪ] (*asymmetrical, aperiodic*). At first sight, all five have straightforward meanings ('not decent', 'not kind', 'not toxic', 'not loyal', 'not symmetrical', 'not periodic'). But, even at first glance, they are not equally productive. Take first the formation in *dis-*. It is hard to know whether, for all speakers, *dis-* is separate from *dys-* (in, for example, *dysfunctional*). It also appears in a Verbal formation (*mount → dismount*) and possibly, through this, there might develop a new Participial Adjective. *Disinterested* (from the early seventeenth century) was originally the Past Participle of a Verb *disinterest*. But, with these qualifications, the process seems unproductive. It came in, with Adjectives like *disloyal*, from Mediaeval French. But new ones are now hard to find and are not easily established. '*Dishuman*', which the *OEDS* records once from D. H. Lawrence, is a revealing failure.

Now let us take the formation in *in-*. Adjectives in *in-* are typically Latinate: *indecent*, for instance, corresponds in form to Latin INDECENS. But they are common, and in earlier centuries *in-* tended to form doublets with *un-*. *Inalienable* and *unalienable* are both cited from the seventeenth century (*OED*); *incomprehensible* and *uncomprehensible* from the fourteenth; *indemonstrable* and *undemonstrable* from the late sixteenth; *insanitary* and *unsanitary* from the late nineteenth. Within limits, therefore, it was once productive. But its present status is questionable. *Numerate* and its Negative *innumerate* are both coinings of the late 1950s (*OEDS*), evidently parallel to *literate* and *illiterate*. Since *innumerate* has become established, it would be hard to say that the formation is wholly unproductive. But other examples are not easily found. By contrast, the formation in *un-* has never been limited to Latinate words, and is so productive that dictionaries can hardly be expected to keep up with it. When one meets what might be a new form ('the unbowdlerised text of Shakespeare', or 'a refreshingly un-Northern-Irish attitude'), it scarcely matters whether it is new or not.

The competition between *in-* and *un-* can also have a semantic dimension. Compare, for example, *immeasurable* and *unmeasurable*. The former has the Latinate prefix, with a borrowed assimilation of *in-* to *im-*; the latter the native alternative. Otherwise, from what we have said so far, we might expect them to be synonymous. But *unmeasurable* means, literally, 'not measurable', while *immeasurable* carries much more readily the special implication 'of vast size'. The text of Shakespeare includes many doublets, which are not in general systematic. For example, there seems little reason why he, or his printers, should have used *unproper* in *Othello* 4.1.68:

> That nightly lie in those unproper beds

and *improper* in *Lear* 5.3.221f.:

> and did him service
> Improper for a slave.

But a modern reader might be tempted to feel that, if anything, these should be the other way round. *Improper*, in collocations like *improper conduct*, implies moral criticism; that is clearly the sense in *Othello*. *Unproper*, if it can be used at all, seems more appropriate as a simple negation of *proper*. Another pair are *insubstantial*:

> And, like this insubstantial pageant faded (*Tempest* 4.1.155)

and *unsubstantial*:

> Thou unsubstantial air that I embrace (*Lear* 4.1.7)

My own instinct, perhaps influenced by a clearer memory of the *The Tempest*, leads me to expect *insubstantial* in both. I could certainly use the form in *un-*; but it might perhaps negate what is now the more ordinary sense of *substantial* (as in 'an unsubstantial breakfast').

With these nuances in mind, we can bring in the formation in *non-*. This too is productive and there are many competing pairs:

*irreligious* and *non-religious, insensitive* and *non-sensitive; unnatural* and *non-natural, unrenewable* and *non-renewable*. But the differences in meaning are much clearer. To call someone insensitive is to criticise them; *non-sensitive* (in, say, 'non-sensitive material') simply negates *sensitive*. *Insubordinate* has a special sense, as we have noted. One cannot use it neutrally, in (say) 'I would like to move to an insubordinate position.' But in that sense *non-subordinate* would be possible. *Incorrupt* is also special (as applied, say, to the corpse of St Cuthbert). For the more usual sense of CORRUPT ('a corrupt official'), only *non-corrupt* seems likely. *Irreligious* is again evaluative, *non-religious* not.

With *un-* and *non-* the contrasts are more systematic. Compare, for example, *unsocial* and *non-social*, or *un-American* and *non-American*. The forms in *non-* are again literal negatives ('not social', 'not American'). To talk, say, of a species of wasp as a 'non-social insect' is simply to make a neutral description. But the forms in *un-* both carry the sense of a departure from the norm. It is normal for people to be social: to say of someone that they are 'unsocial' is to point to a trait that stands out and would usually be viewed unfavourably. 'Un-American behaviour' is, similarly, behaviour that is not typical or not expected (for example, by conformist opinion within the United States) of Americans. With Adjectives of nationality *un-* appears to be fully productive. '*Un-Northern-Irish*' is an example given earlier; '*un-Welsh*', '*un-South-African*', '*un-Israeli*' all seem equally possible. The sense is also regular, apart from contingent overtones. 'A refreshingly un-Israeli attitude' implies departure from a norm which one deplores. Others might talk instead of 'a regrettably un-Israeli attitude'. But the feature of 'departure from a norm' is constant.

With other Adjectives the pattern is less consistent, and there are certainly Negatives in *un-* which do mean simply 'not X'. But it has often been noted that *un-* more easily negates a positive quality. One talks normally, for example, of people who are unkind or unhappy or unintelligent, but not of them being 'unbeastly', 'unsad', 'unugly' or 'unstupid'. The norm, as one sees it, is what is good, not what is bad. For the same reason, the Negatives of *toxic* or *poisonous* are the neutral *non-toxic* or *non-poisonous* rather than the evaluative *untoxic* or *unpoisonous*. The

latter might suggest that toxicity is the norm and to be preferred.
There is a slightly different repercussion in the case of Participial
Adjectives. Here what is negated is the sense of the Verb: to be
un-X-ed (unpainted, unpolished, unblemished, unmarred) is,
basically, 'not to have been X-ed'. That may, in principle, be a
good thing (*unblemished* versus *blemished* or *uncluttered* versus
*cluttered*) or a bad thing. But whichever it is, such forms will tend
to be evaluative. By contrast, forms like *non-aligned* or *non-
commissioned* are scrupulously objective. *Unaligned* might suggest
that being aligned was more desirable; *uncommissioned* might be
taken to imply 'not yet commissioned' or 'inferior to being
commissioned'.

This leaves the formation in *a(n)-*. It had a boost some
generations ago: *amoral* got (as a nonce-word) into the original
*OED*, and *apolitical, alogical, atonal, asocial* and *anormal* are all
cited at least once in *OEDS*. Their fortunes have varied: for
'*alogical*' or '*anormal*' I would certainly prefer *non-logical* and
*non-normal*. But *amoral*, in opposition to *immoral*, is still in
educated usage. Other new or relatively new forms are in the
field of scientific terminology. We have already cited *aperiodic*
(phonologically [eɪ]-); others we might expect to find in a good
dictionary are *aplacental* (COLLINS[2] gives either [eɪ]- or [æ]-),
*athematic* (usually [æ]- but also [eɪ]-), *anechoic* or *anhydrous*
(*an-* is only [æn]-), *aneuploid* (with the *an-* accented ['æn],
*aplanogamete* ([æ]- according to *OEDS*). Doubtless there are
more known only to specialists. The formative is of Greek origin,
and in such forms it is narrowly academic. But in that domain it
is productive.

Much more could be said about Negative formations. But let us
draw some general lessons. We have seen that formations as
wholes may vary in productivity. Those in *non-* and *un-*, for
example, are more productive than those in *dis-* and *in-*. We have
also seen that the productivity of a formation may be higher in a
particular domain. *Un-*, though generally productive, is not fully
so except in a domain like that of Adjectives of nationality. *In-*
may be used to coin a form like *innumerate*, but this belongs to a
domain that is clearly Latinate. *A(n)-* is particularly a formative
of scientific terminology. In other cases, the domain may be
morphological: *-ity*, which is in general a Latinate competitor of

-*ness*, is especially productive in conjunction with -*able* (*saleable* → *saleability*, *recycleable* → *recycleability* and so on). In others, there are subtle tendencies of meaning: *un-*, as we have seen, is more productive in negating positively valued properties.

These factors are all part of the general description of these formations. But when we talk of creativity we are talking not of a process in the abstract but of the creation of individual words with individual uses. This may also be affected by factors which are external to the formation.

The most obvious perhaps is that a word is usually not created if the sense that it would have is not needed. In the first century BC, the Roman scholar Varro remarked that Latin had a word for a female lion (*leaena* 'lioness'), but no distinct word for female crows. The reason, he explained, is that we rarely need to refer specifically to them.[2] Similarly, English has such forms as *countess* and *waitress*, or *lioness* and *tigress*; but not, for example, '*bishopess*' or '*bearess*'. The reasons again might be that our churches have not historically had female bishops and our society is not one in which we ordinarily need to distinguish bears by sex. Conditions might change. If women were to play an equal rôle in the church hierarchy, '*bishopess*' might be used and might become as familiar as *deaconess*, *priestess* or *mayoress*. But at present it sounds at best facetious.

Another factor is that words tend not to be created if the sense that they would have is supplied by ones that already exist. Take, for example, '*dog-ess*' or '*horse-ess*'. The problem here is not that we have historically had no occasion to distinguish females from males. Dogs and horses are domestic animals and there has been a clear interest in breeding them. But the senses are already covered by *bitch* and *mare*. In this example, creation is blocked or inhibited by simple lexemes. But it may also be inhibited by existing complex forms. One has no reason not to refer to the state of being embarrassed, and, if all else were equal, a form in -*ness* ('*embarrassedness*') would suit. But it is not normal, since it is blocked by *embarrassment*. Similarly, there is no obvious reason why one should not talk of someone being 'unsane', except that there is an established form *insane*.

[2] *De Lingua latina*, 9.56.

These inhibiting factors are peculiar to the lexicon. In syntax, there is no bar to the phrase *a female bishop* ('I was attending the enthronement of a female bishop') or, for example, to a Negative with *not* ('He was not sane'). Creativity in syntax is in that sense unrestricted. But lexical processes can be inhibited. They tend, as we said earlier, to be semiproductive. Is it possible, now, to give a more precise account of this notion?

Some of our findings might easily suggest that semiproductivity can be explained away. Let us begin by drawing a distinction between **established lexemes** and **potential lexemes**. A potential lexeme is one that could be created by a productive process. For example, the formation of Adjectives in *un-* is productive; therefore, among many others, there is a potential lexeme '*unsane*'. An established lexeme is one that is actually part of a speaker's vocabulary. For example, there is an established lexeme INSANE. Let us then propose that formations are simply either productive or unproductive. That of Nouns in *-th* is unproductive. That means that there is a set of established lexemes that exhibit it (TRUTH, WARMTH and so on); but, unless its status changes, no new ones can be created. That of Nouns in *-ness* is productive. There is again a set of established lexemes (HAPPINESS and so on). But, unless and until its status changes, any form *X-ness*, where *X* meets the appropriate condition, is a potential lexeme. In other cases, a formation may be productive under one condition and unproductive under another. For example, the formation of Nouns in *-ion* (FUSION, REJECTION and so on) is unproductive except in combination with *-ate*. Established lexemes such as FUSION are in the lexicon, as are lexemes such as AUTOMATION (← AUTOMATE) or COMPUTATION (← COMPUTE). But, beyond that, only forms in *-ation* represent potential lexemes.

To say that a lexeme is potential is to say that it may, in principle, be used and may, in principle, become established. But it may then be blocked in either of the ways that we have illustrated. '*Unsane*' could in principle be used, but it happens to be blocked by INSANE. '*Bishopess*' is in fact attested in print (*OED*, s.v., quotations from Thackeray and *Macmillan's Magazine* for 1880). That is evidence for the productivity of the formation. But it is not established since there is no serious need for it. Now a formation is fully productive, or is fully productive in a particular domain, if, as it happens, no potential lexeme is blocked. For example, *un-X* may be fully productive in the domain of Adjectives of nationality, since its sense is appropriate for any *X* and there are no established lexemes that exactly have it. To say that a formation is 'semiproductive' is simply to say that some potential lexemes ARE blocked.

This is a neat account and explains many of the facts. But once it is spelled out we can see that it is inadequate. Take, for example, the competition between *warmth* and *warmness*. Both have been in the language for a long time (see *OED*), but, in present usage, *warmth* is the established form. Why then can one also use *warmness*? One possible answer is that it too is established, though less firmly. Another is that the formation in *-ness* is so productive that the inhibiting influence of *warmth* is overridden. But neither explanation is in accordance with our theory. We have talked of lexemes being established, but not of one being established more firmly than another. Nor have we said anything about a blocking factor being overridden. The second explanation suggests that this may happen if a formation is especially productive. But our theory says nothing about degrees of productivity.

There are plenty of examples which confirm that blocking is not absolute. As *insane* negates *sane*, so, for example, *inconsiderate* and *insufferable* are established Negatives of *considerate* and *sufferable*. But what of '*unconsiderate*' and '*unsufferable*'? They may not be usual, but they are much better than '*horse-ess*' for *mare*. A likely explanation is that the productiveness of *in-* has sharply declined. Therefore *un-*, which remains highly productive, is tending to replace it. A contributory factor may be that *inconsiderate* and *insufferable* are not themselves such common words. Therefore the inhibiting effect is weaker. As *-ness* encroaches on *-th*, so it encroaches on the larger, and in part productive, formation in *-ity*. *Stupidity* and *profundity* are established; but they do not exclude *stupidness* and *profoundness*. So too is *productivity*, both as a term in economics and, as we have used it, with the general meaning 'property of being productive'. But in this sense one can also use *productiveness*: will many readers have wanted to correct me when I wrote it earlier in this paragraph? Now *-ity*, like *in-*, is Latinate: forms like *stupidity* from *stúpid* or *productívity* from *prodúctive* reflect the Latin accentuation, and as a class they tend to be bookish. The formation in *-ness* is native and its domain is correspondingly wider. If there was an Adjective '*glud*', one would automatically form '*gludness*' not '*gluddity*'. Therefore existing forms in *-ity* may not block it, even though new ones (on the pattern of *-able* → *-ability*) can still be created.

In this light, it is not enough to say merely that formations are blocked by existing lexemes. In the case of '*horse-ess*', another factor is that *mare* is an ordinary word and firmly established. Another is that the formation in *-ess* is productive over a fairly narrow domain. The case of '*embarrassedness*' for *embarrassment* might be compared to that of, say, '*advertisation*' for *advertisement*. Here too the formation is productive (*computerisation, containerisation* and so on). Earlier on we had the nonce example '*capsization*'. But *embarrassment* and *advertisement* are common words: the latter, in particular, in almost everyday use. *Capsizal*, which would inhibit '*capsization*', is not.

It seems, then, that a practical account will have to acknowledge that there are degrees of productivity; also that there is a gradation between established forms and those not established. But the theoretical problems are deeper, and have to do with the Saussurean distinction (SAUSSURE, pt 1, ch. 3), between synchrony and diachrony. The coining and adoption of new words are historical phenomena. When *containerisation*, for example, became part of our vocabulary, the language to that extent changed. Yet we are trying to explain them on the basis of a stable system. This will include a rule for Verbs in *-ise*, and another for Nouns in *-ation*. So, for any $X$ (where $X$ meets certain initial conditions), $X \rightarrow X\text{-}ise \rightarrow X\text{-}isation$. It is of no concern to these rules which forms are actually used. Over a certain period, *containerisation* came into use. But the system did not change; all that changed is that one lexeme, which was potential before, became established. Nor will it change if other forms ('*parcelisation*', say, or '*basketisation*') are introduced in the future. The language is in that sense constant, even though the details of its vocabulary are not.

Such accounts are typical of linguistics in the Saussurean tradition. 'La langue' is stable; changes are individual and at another level. But let us return to the example of '*coolth*'. We can easily explain why it has not been generally accepted. The formation is unproductive; therefore it allows no forms beyond the limited set that are established. But in that case why has '*coolth*' been used? If it is not a potential lexeme, how was its creation possible at all?

The obvious answer is that, even when a formation is unproductive, new forms can be created by analogy. *Cool* is the antonym of warm, and there is thus a close relationship between them. *Warmth* is firmly established; so, as *warmth* is formed from *warm*, '*coolth*' is also formed from *cool*. But this is apparently a different kind of explanation. Previously we have said that new forms can arise because they are already potential lexemes. Their creation is explained, in part, by a rule. But now we are saying that a form can be created even though no rule allows for it. It arises simply because it is similar to existing forms.

Are these explanations truly separate? The view implied by many theorists is that they must be. Rules are synchronic: they lay down what is possible and excluded in a language at a specific time. Analogy is diachronic: it explains why what was once excluded can become possible. Take, for example, the rule for the Past Tense. I might apply it tomorrow to a Verb I have never used before: say, 'I disexculpated him.' But the rule itself will not change: it is open-ended and applies to any Verb not known to be an exception. It would be different if, let us say, I started to use *sung* instead of *sang* ('He sung it beautifully'). We might explain this analogically (compare *flung* or *spun*). But if the usage becomes established, the rule for SING will have changed.

In the case of inflections, such distinctions seem quite easy. But let us return to the creation of, for example, *innumerate*. One factor is that the formation is large: there were many Negatives in *in-* already in the language. Another is that they are typically Latinate, and *numerate*, with the root of Latin NUMERUS 'number', was itself formed on a strictly Latinate pattern. This might suggest that what we have here is the application of a rule. Given *numerate*, *innumerate* was a potential lexeme. So were (and are) *unnumerate* and *non-numerate*; but in this instance, though the formations in *un-* and *non-* are generally far more productive, that in *in-* prevailed. Another factor, however, is the parallel between *innumerate* and *illiterate*. The Positive, *numerate*, is parallel in form to *literate* (the latter with the root of Latin LITERA 'letter'). Its sense was also parallel: 'having the skill of using numbers', like 'having the skill to read and write'. This might suggest that *innumerate* is like '*coolth*'. The formation itself was unproductive and it was not a potential lexeme. Instead it was formed by a specific analogy: *numerate → innumerate = literate → illiterate*.

Which account is correct? The question might amuse the people who invented these words, who, for all I know, are still alive. For surely all these factors were involved. There clearly was a specific analogy; however, the form was easy to accept because, in any speaker's experience, the formation does not seem closed. Here the creation was conscious and deliberate. But take, for example, *computerisation* or *containerisation*. Did these come into use because there is a process deriving Nouns in *-isation*? Or were they formed by analogy with earlier creations – such as *maximisation, standardisation* or *miniaturisation*? The answers are Yes and Yes; the choice implied is unreal.

This is plainly part of a much wider argument, as to whether the distinction between synchrony and diachrony, useful though it may be in practice, is conceptually sound. But however it is resolved, what is commonly called 'derivational' morphology is central to it.


RELATED READING

GUILBERT places word-formation and composition within a wider theory of lexical creativity: see part 1, ch. 2, for his general typology. I have not found a similar study in English. Among general textbooks, Bolinger's gives a good account of the creative rôle of 'derivational' morphology: see D. L. Bolinger, *Aspects of Language* (2nd edn, New York, Harcourt Brace Jovanovich, 1975), pp. 107ff. On a process that I would see as marginal to morphology see L. J. Calvet, *Les Sigles*, in the 'Que sais-je?' series (Paris, Presses Universitaires de France, 1980).

My account of formations is influenced by ARONOFF ('word-formation rules'). But this has the limitations that might be expected in a study of English, and suffers (as I see it) from a blurring of the distinction between word-forms and lexemes. For a commentary and subsequent developments see SCALISE, chs. 3 and 5. Compare too CORBIN's recent and good study of word-formation in French. 'Root' and 'stem' are from the tradition of Indo-European philology: definitions in *OED* (s.vv. *root*, sb[1], §15; *stem* sb[1], §5.b); also e.g. ROBINS,

*Linguistics*, pp. 196f. (root vs affix), 244. Note that the root in morphology (e.g. *royal* in *royalty*) is not the same as the root in etymology (*\*reg-* > Latin *reg-* 'king' and so on). For the latter see C. Watkins's fascinating *American Heritage Dictionary of Indo-European Roots* (Boston, Houghton Mifflin, 1985). On conversion in English see MARCHAND, ch. 5 ('Derivation by a zero-morpheme'). For a rare discussion of the criteria by which it is established, see G. Sanders, 'Zero derivation and the overt analogue criterion', in HAMMOND & NOONAN, pp. 155–75.

See ALINEI for a range of opinions on the problem of meaning: note that where I ascribe meaning to formations, many others will ascribe it to 'derivational morphemes'. On synthetic and analytic meaning see especially PLANK, pp. 24ff. *Gaoler* vs *prisoner* are from L. Zgusta, *Manual of Lexicography* (Prague, Academia, 1971), p. 128.

The literature on productivity is quite large. ARONOFF (ch. 3 especially) is brief but seminal; PLANK is particularly valuable; so also is J. Van Marle, *On the Paradigmatic Dimension of Morphological Creativity* (Dordrecht, Foris, 1985). For another introductory treatment see BAUER, *Morphology*, ch. 5. 'Semi-productivity' is from an early paper by S. C. Dik, 'Some critical remarks on the treatment of morphological structure in transformational generative grammar', *Lingua* 18 (1967), pp. 352–83. For a simple distinction between 'available' and 'non-available' processes ('disponibles'/'non disponibles') see CORBIN, p. 177. On word-formation in English see MARCHAND; ADAMS; QUIRK *et al.*, appendix 1; BAUER, *Word-formation*: note again Bauer's doctrine on productivity (ch. 4). On Negatives see K. E. Zimmer, *Affixal Negation in English and Other Languages* (Supplement to *Word*, New York, 1964), which was also important for theory. On the productiveness of *-ity* after *-able* see A. Cutler, 'Degrees of transparency in word formation', *Canadian Journal of Linguistics* 26 (1981), pp. 73–7.

For the lexicon as a blocking device see SCALISE, ch. 2; the idea originated (I think) in work by R. P. Botha, *The Function of the Lexicon in Transformational Generative Grammar* (The Hague, Mouton, 1968), on compounding. A subtler solution is to see established lexemes as a norm distinct from the Saussurean system. For the general concept of a norm see E. Coseriu, *Teoría del lenguaje y lingüística general* (Madrid, Gredos, 1962), pp. 94ff.: unfortunately, Coseriu rarely publishes in English. On analogy see ANTTILA; also R. Anttila, *Analogy* (The Hague, Mouton, 1977). For a theory of analogy replacing that of rules see R. Skousen, *Analogical Modelling of Language* (Dordrecht, Kluwer, 1989); but this is gratuitously schematic and not easy to read. A study of PAUL (ch. 5 especially) might well be more profitable.

On word-formation as a problem for the classic concept of a generative grammar see my *Generative Grammar and Linguistic Competence* (London, Allen and Unwin, 1979), pp. 25ff. The best discussion of the interplay of grammar and lexicon is that of LYONS, *Semantics*, II, pp. 528ff. (on Adjectives in *-able*).

# 5
# Compounds

Compounding as the derivation of compound lexemes. Parallels with
word-formation: meanings of compounds; semiproductivity. Difference
between compounds and word-formation.
*The syntax of compounds.* Parallels with syntax: layering; semantic
relations within compounds. Can compounding be part of syntax?
Transformational account of compounds; and criticisms of it.
Compounding as a lexical process: how far should formations be
distinguished? 'Minimalist' and 'maximalist' solutions. Any
generalisation limited: by idiosyncratic meanings; by indeterminacy.
*Compounds and non-compounds.* Change and indeterminacy: of compounds
vs simple lexemes; of compounds vs word-formation. Also of compounds
vs syntax. Morphological criteria: compounds inflected as wholes.
Semantic criteria; compounds vs idioms. Phonological criteria: position
of stress in English. Syntactic criteria: tmesis; compounds as syntactic
wholes. No single test decisive.

Compounding is a process by which a **compound lexeme** is
derived from two or more simpler lexemes. For example,
BLACKBIRD is a compound Noun whose form, *blackbird*, combines
those of BLACK and BIRD. Its formation may be sketched as
follows:

$$[X]_A + [Y]_N \rightarrow [\acute{X} + Y]_N$$

where the acute accent $(\acute{X})$ shows that the combined form is
accented on its first member (*bláckbird*). As in earlier formulae, $X$
and $Y$ are variables, the first ranging over Adjectives (A) and the
second over Nouns (N); their combination is in turn a Noun.
Thus, by the same process, $[greyhound]_N$ is derived from $[grey]_A$
and $[hound]_N$, *blackthorn* from *black* and *thorn*, and so on.

Compounding is a lexical process: it derives lexemes from
lexemes (BLACK + BIRD → BLACKBIRD), not simply forms from
forms (*black + bird → blackbird*). The reasons largely parallel those
given earlier for distinguishing word-formation from inflection.
In syntax compound words behave like simple words: *There is a
dead bird on the doorstep* or, substituting BLACKBIRD, *There is a
dead blackbird on the doorstep*. There are in general no constructions in which the compound *blackbird* can appear but not

82

the simple *bird*; nor vice versa. For grammarians compounds are interesting because they have an internal structure. But that is the end of it. As wholes they are units like any other, like simple lexemes (BIRD) or complex lexemes (WARBLER).

We also found that derived lexemes tended to have idiosyncratic meanings. GENERATION and DIRECTION, for example, had senses not wholly predictable from those of GENERATE and DIRECT. Similarly, a blackbird is not predictably any bird that is black; a raven, for example, or a coot. It is a bird of one particular species, and indeed the female is not black but brown. A greyhound ['greɪhaʊnd] likewise is not literally a grey hound ['greɪ 'haʊnd]. Many meanings are still less explicable. Another bird name, *nuthatch*, has the phonology of a compound: there are no simple forms with the medial cluster t + h ['nʌthætʃ]. But it is hard to connect it with either *nut* or *hatch*. A whinchat is perhaps a little more transparently a chat (a bird of the genus *saxicola*) associated with gorse (dialectal *whins*). But in my speech the word for gorse is *gorse*, and although *chat* appears at one point in my field guide (plate headed 'Wheatears, Chats, etc.'), I knew the compound long before I bothered to inquire about its elements. One source of opaque compounds is the process known as 'popular etymology'. *Asparagus*, for example, has been widely reinterpreted as *sparrowgrass* (often abbreviated by market traders to *grass*). *Cockroach*, which is compounded inexplicably from *cock* and *roach*, is in origin a loan from Spanish *cucaracha*.

Such meanings are one reason why, in practice, compounds must be entered in dictionaries. Another is that compounding, like word-formation, is not fully productive. BLACKBIRD and BLUEBIRD, BLACKTHORN and WHITETHORN are lexemes, but '*whitebird*' and '*redbird*', '*greenthorn*' and '*pinkthorn*' are not. In this case it is obvious which forms a dictionary has to list. But in other cases we again encounter problems of semiproductivity. One is familiar, for example, with the risks of overeating and overreacting; so, there are verbs OVEREAT and OVERREACT. '*Overdrink*' will seem less natural to many speakers ('Overdrinking is a common failing in hot climates'). '*Overtalk*' or '*oversing*' will perhaps seem even worse. But in the right context they could be understood: 'Just as that woman overacts on stage, so she overtalks all the time she is off it'; 'Oversinging Mozart is even worse than overacting Shakespeare.' They are not established, but one hesitates to say that they are impossible.

Another formation, in part compositional and in part derivational, is the following:

$$[X]_N + [Y]_V \rightarrow [X + [Y + er]]_N$$

(witness *meat-eater, lady-killer, whisky-drinker*). With some Verbs this is more productive than normal dictionaries can be expected to acknowledge. If we start with *drink* we can have [*a heavy*] *whisky-drinker, wine-drinker, gin-drinker*, and why not, for example, *Beaujolais-drinker, Crême-de-Menthe-drinker*, and so on? *Smoke* yields *cigar-smoker, cigarette-smoker, pipe-smoker* – and why not, say, *cheroot-smoker* or *Gauloise-smoker*? But there are other combinations that give more reason to pause. *Woman-hater* and *lady-killer* are established; *schoolgirl-hater* or *nun-killer* have to be forced ('I am not a woman-hater, just a schoolgirl-hater'). Or take *eat*. One can say of someone that they are *a great cheese-eater* or *meat-eater*, but *butter-eater* seems less secure and *egg-eater* even more so. Why so, given that some people do indeed eat striking quantities of eggs? There seems no simple answer, except that *cheese-eater* has acquired clearer status as a unit. But possibly not all readers will agree with these judgments. It is of the essence of semiproductivity that one cannot be sure.

In these respects compounding resembles word-formation. The formal difference is that one involves an operation on a single lexeme (GENERATE → GENERATION), while the other involves two. But there is also an important semantic difference. In word-formation the meaning of the derived word, in so far as it is analytic, reflects those (1) of the base lexeme (GENERATE), (2) of the operation (add *-ion*). But in compounding we are concerned with (1) the meanings of the lexemes and (2) the relationship between them. Compare, for example, *boathouse* and *houseboat*. The base lexemes are the same, BOAT and HOUSE. The formation

$$[X]_N + [Y]_N \rightarrow [X + Y]_N$$

is also the same. But as the elements appear in different orders ($X = boat$, $Y = house$; $X = house$, $Y = boat$), so the semantic dependency, of *boat* on *house* in one case, of *house* on *boat* in the other, is different too.

This may seem an obvious enough point. But what is not obvious is how, or in what detail, the semantic relations should be specified. Let us address this problem first, and then move on to others.

## THE SYNTAX OF COMPOUNDS

The title of this section may seem contradictory: and, in a sense, it is. For have we not said that, from the viewpoint of syntax, a compound is a single unit? Nevertheless, compound words have structures that are syntax-like in two respects.

Firstly, there are layers of compounds, which are like layers of syntactic construction. *Fruit-juice carton* (main accent on *fruit*) is a Noun compounded of *fruit-juice* and *carton* (compare *wíne-bottle, béer barrel*). But *frúit-juice* is in turn compounded of *fruit* and *juice*. The smaller compound is included within the larger:

[[fruit juice] carton]

just as, in syntax, phrases are included within phrases:

[the juice of [the fruit]]

To speak in terms which have long been familiar in syntactic theory, any compound may, in principle, be an immediate constituent of a further compound.

The second resemblance lies in the semantic relations between members. Take, for example, the sentence *She is a good book-keeper*. In meaning this is like *She is good at keeping the books*; *book* is understood in relation to *keeper* in the same way as, in the syntactic construction, it is understood in relation to *keeping*. The formation is productive, as we have remarked. If someone were to use a new form ('I must say you are a very good dráinpipe decorator'), it would be intelligible because the hearer knows that the first member is to be construed as if it was, in syntactic terms, the Object of the second. The formation of *blackbird* or *whitethorn* is perhaps unproductive. But suppose a child asks a parent: 'Daddy, why is that brown bird called a blackbird?' The child is puzzled because the construal of *black* with *bird* is like that of an Adjective and a Noun within a syntactic Noun Phrase.

These resemblances, considered simply as resemblances, seem indisputable. But scholars are not agreed as to the conclusions that should be drawn. One view is that compounding is itself part of syntax. *Book-keeper* has a compound construction; *She keeps the books* has a clause or sentence construction; but the relation of Verb to Direct Object, between forms of the Verb KEEP and the Noun BOOK, is identical. In both *the bláckbird* and *the bláck bird* the Adjective *black* is the syntactic Modifier of *bird*; the only grammatical difference is that in one case they have been collapsed into a constituent with a single accent. In *She emptied the fruit-juice carton* there is a single hierarchy of constituents:

[she [emptied [the [[fruit juice] carton]]]]

in which, contrary to what we said earlier, the elements of the compound, *fruit*, *juice* and *carton*, are themselves syntactic units. Their accentuation is again irrelevant.

The other view, which is implied in the introduction to this chapter, is that the resemblances are simply resemblances. The semantic relations within some compounds (such as *book-keeper* and *blackbird*) are like those in specific syntactic constructions. But they are not identical, and are to be described separately. Some compounds (such as *fruit-juice carton*) are formed by layers of constituents. But they are not part of the syntactic layering.

One argument for the first view – the 'syntactic view' as we will call it – is that it simplifies the design of a grammar. A single component covers compounding as well as other constructions. There is no need for another, quasi-syntactic component which will handle it under lexical morphology. The grammar will also unite meanings which are similar. Take again *book-keeper*. The syntax will relate its construction to that of *keeps books*; and, by the same process, other compounds (*woolgatherer*, *screwdriver*, *bookmaker*) will be related to other constructions with Verbs (*gathers wool*, *drives screws*, *makes books*). The meaning of one structure will follow automatically from that of the other. As *keeps books* has the general meaning of a Verb plus Object, so *book-keeper*, leaving aside what is idiosyncratic, has the general meaning of an Object plus Agentive. If we take what may be called the 'lexical' view, we are obliged to describe the meaning twice, once in syntax (for the construction of *keeps books*) and again in morphology.

If these arguments are convincing, the best formulation is in terms of a **transformational** syntax. In the transformational model, sentences or other forms with similar meanings are related formally by rules which derive one structure from another. For example, the meaning of *It is a black bird* is like that of *It is a bird which is black*; accordingly, we postulate a **transformational rule** by which Relative clauses with an Adjectival Predicate (such as the Predicate *is black*) are reduced to single Adjectives before the Noun (*black bird*). The meaning of *It is a blackbird*, idiosyncratic aspects apart, is similar. Accordingly we postulate a further transformational rule by which Adjective plus Noun (*black bird*) may be collapsed into one word (*blackbird*). In the same way, *book-keeper* can be derived transformationally from *keeper of books*, which in turn can be derived from *person who keeps books*. In the end, all transformations lead back to a **deep structure** which underlies everything derived from it. The same deep structure will underlie both *She is a good book-keeper* and *She is a person who keeps the books well*, and it is this that determines what is common in their meaning. A common deep structure will similarly underlie *It is a bird which is black, It is a black bird* and *It is a blackbird*.

This model of syntax was very popular throughout the 1960s and the first half of the 1970s, and a transformational description of compounds was at that time widely accepted. But it was accepted in the face of serious criticism. What, for example, is the deep structure of a compound with two Nouns? *Windmill*, to take one which is sufficiently transparent, might be related transformationally to *mill which is powered by wind*. That seems to explain its meaning perfectly. But a flourmill is not, at least in normal usage, a mill that is powered by flour. Should we therefore derive *flourmill* by a separate transformation from *mill which produces flour*? Or should we say that it is potentially ambiguous, and so derivable either from that or from *mill which is powered by flour*? If so, is *windmill* to be derived alternatively from *mill which produces wind*? Differences like this are legion. A tiepin, for example, is a pin used to secure or adorn a tie; a safety pin (phonetically [ˈseɪftɪpɪn]) is not, in the same sense, a pin that secures safety. A meathook is a hook on which one hangs meat; but a boathook is not similarly a hook on which one hangs boats. For each of these there is a problem. Is *boathook*, for example, variously derivable from *hook which is used in a boat*, *hook to which one attaches a boat* (thus potentially meaning what it does not in fact mean), *hook which adorns a boat*, *hook for making a boat* (compare *pástry hook*), and perhaps others? It seems that underlying sources can be multiplied without end. We simply take a dictionary definition of each compound, dream up every additional definition that it might have if it meant something else, and make deep structures out of them.

The problem with these compounds is not just that they have established idiosyncratic meanings. So do *blackbird* and, for example, *bookmaker*; nevertheless, there are syntactic phrases that parallel them. But for compounds with two Nouns we can posit no consistent transformation. They have in common that the first Noun qualifies the second. Windmills and flourmills are both kinds of mill; meathooks, boathooks and pastry hooks are all kinds of hook. In that respect they are like *blackbird* or *whitethorn*. But when we try to trace their structure to syntactic sources, the distinction between what is common and what is idiosyncratic is lost in uncertainty.

These are relatively transparent compounds: if one had not heard, say, of a hatpin one could have a stab at guessing what it was. When they are less transparent the difficulties are worse. Take again the bird name *nuthatch*. This does not conform to the semantic pattern of a Noun plus Noun, nor readily to any other. All we can say is that the word has meaning as a whole and, within it, *nut* and *hatch* appear to be juxtaposed. *Linchpin* and *tholepin* are more regular, but their first elements are fossils. In other compounds the parts bear a clearer relation to the whole, but appropriate underlying structures, if we must devise them, are ad hoc and even comic. Readers might like to amuse themselves by working out a transformational derivation for, say, *carhop* or *striptease*, *cuptie* and *offside*, *slap-up* (in *a slap-up dinner*) or *snarl-up* (in *a traffic snarl-up*).

If we adopt the lexical view, these difficulties disappear. *Nuthatch* represents a lexeme (NUTHATCH) with its own entry in a dictionary, and semantically, if not formally, that is all there is to say. *Linchpin* and *tholepin* fit the pattern of a Modifier plus Head; hence a speaker who does not know what they denote may again make a partial guess. But their meanings too are given completely in their dictionary entries. It will be no different in the case of *windmill* and *flourmill, tiepin* and *safety pin* and so on. These too can be construed in general as a Modifier (*wind, flour* and so on) plus a Head. So, if a speaker happened to use a new word of this type, hearers would not be totally at a loss. Suppose, for example, that he talked of a 'handkerchief pin'. In the light of the general structure one can divine that this is a kind of pin and that, specifically, it has something to do with handkerchieves. Beyond that, hearers might be stuck. Or they might be more imaginative: perhaps, for example, it is a jeweller's gimmick which is meant to fasten the handkerchief in a man's top pocket. But they would arrive at this meaning not because there is a syntactic rule deriving a potential compound from *pin which adorns a handkerchief*. They simply guess that this is one way that the collocation might make sense. Alternatively, one might understand it by specific analogy with *tiepin* or *hatpin*. They too have meanings that are given in their separate dictionary entries.

If compounds as such form a class, consistency dictates that other types, like those of *book-keeper* or *blackbird*, should be treated similarly. *Blackbird* has again the lexical pattern of a Modifier plus Head. It is accordingly taken in the same way as a syntactic Adjective plus Head (*black bird*), just as *flourmill* is taken, if one thinks about it, in the same way as the syntactic collocation in *mill which produces flour*. But again the relations are not grammatically identical. Likewise for *book-keeper*. Its lexical structure may be merely 'N + [V + Agentive]'; but its meaning can be understood as like that of the syntactic phrase *keeps the books* ('Verb plus Object') or *keeper of the books*.

So far, if we accept the lexical view, so good. But there will still be problems in deciding how far different formations should be separated. So far we have distinguished compounds formed from different parts of speech. For example, we have assumed that the type 'Adjective + Noun' (*blackbird, whitethorn*) is different from 'Noun + Noun' (*flourmill, tiepin*). We have also distinguished compounds whose parts have different semantic functions. For example, the type 'Modifier + Head' (*blackbird* or *flourmill*) is implicitly distinct from compounds with no Head (*striptease, mishmash*) or from those with Objects (*book-keeper,* or *pickpocket*). But it is not obvious how far either kind of distinction should be pushed. Take, for example, the compounds with a Head Noun. Its Modifier may be an Adjective or another Noun, as we have seen. It may also be a Verbal form in *-ing* (*wálking stick, knítting needle, lóving cup*); a plain Verb (*playschool, walkway, slíp road*); a Preposition (*outpatient, in-group*). Are these indeed five different formations: Modifying Adjective + Head Noun, Modifying Noun + Head Noun, and so on? Or are they just one? Suppose that some unestablished form is used: say, *sóldering needle* or *walkroad*. We recognise that its first element is a Modifier; we identify it as the *-ing* form of SOLDER or the root of WALK; we interpret the whole by analogy with established forms like *soldering iron* or *walkway*. To explain how speakers are able to do this, it does not seem necessary to divide the formation further.

Now let us look more closely at the case of Adjectives plus Nouns. *Blackbird*, as we said, denotes a kind of bird, and *whitethorn* a kind of thorn. But *greybeard*, for example, does not denote a beard, nor *whitethroat* a throat, nor *bigmouth* a mouth. In a syntactic account, these might be derived by another transformation: say, from *man who has a grey beard, warbler which has a white throat, person who has a big mouth*. But a lexical account could also separate them. According to BLOOMFIELD, pp. 235f., *blackbird* is an 'endocentric' compound. It is so because, in any sentence where it might appear, its Head Noun, *bird*, would make equal sense. *Whitethroat* or *bigmouth* are 'exocentric'. In some contexts they make sense (*a whitethroat's nest, He is a bigmouth*) and their second members do not (*a throat's nest, He is a mouth*). We too could make a distinction. Although the parts of speech are the same, and the relation of the Adjective to the Noun is the same, we could say that the function of the Noun is different.

But should we? The 'exocentric' pattern is in part productive: *Blackshirt* and *Brówn shirt* are examples that were accepted readily between the wars, and if some organisation were to dress its thugs in blue shirts or in round hats, *blueshirt* or *roundhat* might be created similarly. That may be thought to prove that it is a distinct formation. But there is an alternative explanation. *Roundhat*, for example, might be created and understood by specific analogy with existing forms: *roundhead* among others. Others are formed individually by other analogies. *Brown shirt* (from 1932 in *OEDS*) already has the model *Blackshirt* (from

1922), and that in turn had models such as *Redcoat*. If that is correct there is no need to distinguish separate formations, any more than, in the 'Noun + Noun' type, we need posit a distinct formation covering *windmill, watermill* or *windpump*, as opposed to *flourmill, físh farm* or *chéese factory*.

There is no easy way to discriminate between such explanations. In lexical morphology analogies undoubtedly operate; and, undoubtedly, there are general processes. But we have already noted, at the end of the last chapter, that they are hard to separate. We have neither precise rules, nor nothing that can be called a rule at all, but broad tendencies. How many currents has the ocean? We can isolate some large ones, like the Gulf Stream; and, on our time scale, they are permanent. Others are too small and too transitory. But what exactly should we show on a map, or include in a model?

In practice, most grammarians seek a middle way between what we may call the 'minimalist' and 'maximalist' solutions. A minimalist treatment will distinguish formations only when there is the clearest structural difference. Thus, in English, it would distinguish Noun plus Agentive (*book-keeper, screwdriver*) from Verb plus Noun (*pickpocket, holdall, stopcock*) and from Noun plus plain Verb (*daybreak, moonshine*). But it would not make finer distinctions, between *book-keeper* (Object + Agentive) and *office-worker* (Locative + Agentive), or between *daybreak* (Subject + Verb) and *spacewalk*. It would establish one formation for a Modifier plus a Head Noun, not separate formations for Adjective plus Noun (*blackbird*), Verb plus Noun (*playschool*) and so on. Still less would it distinguish (as do QUIRK *et al.*, pp. 1570ff.) between *dáncing girl* (*girl* understood as Subject) and *knítting needle* (*needle* understood as Instrumental), or between *slipway* (*way* as Locative) and *crybaby*. These differences would be explained by the individual collocations.

A maximalist solution would distinguish not only these, but every other type for which some form of generalisation can be made. Take, for instance, the general type of Verb plus Preposition (*washout, lie-in, playback*). This is, in general, productive: *tailback* (from 1975 in *OEDS*), *fallout* (from 1950) and *stopover* are among those which were not familiar when I was a child. But in the late 1960s Verb + *in* became especially productive. The starting-point was *sit-in* ('occupation of a building by protesters who sit in it and refuse to move'); and, for a few years, combinations on this model (*love-in, talk-in, sleep-in, laugh-in*) could be coined very freely. At this distance, it is hard to remember which were used and which not. The fashion did not last. But, at its height, Verb + *in* was more productive than Verb + Preposition in general; and, to bring that out, a maximalist might have treated it as a distinct formation.

Between such extremes there is more than one compromise. But, whichever way we incline, it is likely that our criteria will be in part explanatory and in part purely taxonomic. We must also accept that any set of generalisations will be limited in three ways.

Firstly, the meanings of many compounds do not follow from the formation to which they are assigned. Nothing in that of *yellow-belly* will tell us that this is a word for a coward. Nothing in that of *bluebottle*, whether it is the same or different, tells us that it denotes a fly and not, say, a bird or a fish. This is an obvious point which we assumed at the beginning. Some compound lexemes, like some complex lexemes, have predictable meanings. Many do not, and a grammarian's classification must be complemented by a dictionary.

But secondly, and more seriously, it may not be clear how a particular compound should be classed. Suppose that we distinguish – as again do QUIRK *et al.* – between the type of *sightseeing* (*sight* as Object) and that of *sunbathing* (*sun* as Adverbial). Which then is *horseriding*? QUIRK *et al.*, p. 1572, interpret *horse* as Adverbial ('on a horse'). But the syntax of RIDE would equally allow it to be taken as an Object. Broader patterns may also merge. In *crybaby* the first element is a Verb, in *girlfriend* it is a Noun. But Verbs and Nouns are often related by conversion: which then is, for example, *love* in *lóve child*? Suppose that we accept the common distinction between *blackbird* ('endocentric') and *whitethroat* ('exocentric'). The first type will include some similes: a silverfish is not a fish, nor a ladybird (even in some folk taxonomy) a bird. So may the second. Then to which type belong *bluebottle* or *yellowhammer*? Does the latter denote a finch which resembles a yellow hammer, or do we understand that it has a head which is like one? Both make equally bad sense. Is the whole fly like a blue bottle, or its abdomen?

Finally, there are compounds so opaque that it is pointless to assign them to any formation at all. Are *nuthatch* and *cuptie* Modifier plus Noun, or Complement plus Verb, or what? We might answer if we had to; but we would say nothing about their meaning that is not already in their dictionary entries. We could also force ourselves to classify the forms in the last paragraph. But there is little value in pigeon-holing for pigeon-holing's sake.

## COMPOUNDS AND NON-COMPOUNDS

As languages change, a compound can develop into a simple lexeme. *Lord* and *lady* both derive from compounds in Old English: *hlāford* < *hlāfweard* 'loaf keeper', *hlǣfdīge* 'loaf kneader'. It can also develop into a derivational formation. The *-heit* of German *Freiheit* 'freedom' or *Gesundheit* 'health' is now a simple formative, with etymological cognates in other Germanic languages (for example, *-hood* in English *boyhood* or *manhood*). But originally it was an independent lexeme entering into a compounding formation. Indeed, it is recorded as a word in certain dialectal phrases.[1]

The present status of these forms is clear. But we have learned already that where there is a tendency to change there may also be synchronic indeterminacy. *Magpie*, for example, is historically from *Mag* (short for *Margaret*) and Old French *pie*, from its Latin name *pica*. It has a sequence of consonants, $g + p$, not found in native words that are indubitably simple. Phonologically we may argue that it is still a compound; but semantically it is yet more opaque than our earlier example *nuthatch*. If there were no word '*pie*' at all we might argue that it was simple. *Pullover* is less than a century old (from 1907 in *OEDS*). If it is a compound it is transparently of the type Verb plus Preposition. But is it? GIMSON gives the pronunciation ['pʊlˌəʊvə]; and this accentual pattern, with a secondary stress on *over*, is normal for a form like *stopover*. But for many speakers *pullover* is often closer to ['pʊləvə], with the accent of, for example, *Gulliver*. In phonology it is already developing into a simple form.

There can also be indeterminacy between compounds and

---

[1] Cf. F. Kluge, *Etymologisches Wörterbuch der deutschen Sprache* (20th edn, revised by W. Mitzka, Berlin, De Gruyter 1967), s.v. *-heit*.

word-formation. *Policeman* and *postman* originate, at least, in compounds with the second member MAN. But phonetically they have lost the full vowel: [pə'liːsmən] not -[mæn]. Moreover, there is another class of forms which do have [mæn], such as *insurance man* or (in my speech) *gas man*. Has the -[mən] then broken away from MAN, becoming a lexical formative on its own? There are two possible objections. Firstly, the Plural (also [mən]) would be slightly puzzling. As a reduced form of *men* it is what one expects; but if it has no synchronic connection with *men*, why do we not find regular Plurals (*'policemans'*, etc.) beginning to develop? One might hear such forms from children (along with *singed* for *sang* and other hyper-regularities), but they do not become established. The second and more important objection lies in the opposition between POLICEMAN and POLICEWOMAN. In meaning, one is to the other as MAN is to WOMAN, and the latter is a more recent form which takes the former as a model. Nor would POSTWOMAN be unexpected, provided that 'postwomen' existed. The form in -*woman* suggests that those in -[mən] also retain their character as compounds. But the case has to be argued.

In a language such as English there are also serious problems in determining the boundary between compounds and syntactic constructions. The definition itself is clear: a compound (such as *madman*) is 'one word', and a construction (such as [*a*] *mad man*) two or more separate 'words'. But in practice what are the criteria for distinguishing them? GIRL-FRIEND, for example, could be written in any of three ways: as two words (*girl friend*), as one word hyphenated (*girl-friend*), or unhyphenated. We have used other examples, like *fish farm* or *safety pin*, which are usually, if not always, written as two words. Clearly, we cannot take the spelling conventions as our guide. Any printer or typist knows that they are not consistent. But by what criterion have we in fact decided that these and other forms are one lexeme and not two?

Criteria may be sought at every level: from morphology and semantics, from phonology and syntax. Where a morphological criterion is available it may, of course, be decisive. *Socio-economic* is certainly a compound, because its first member is a stem or stem-variant plus suffix (compare *soci-al*, *soci-o-logy*, etc.) which cannot form a word on its own. The same is true of the type *Anglo-American*, *Franco-Chinese*, *Italo-Celtic*, etc. On the other hand, *heir apparent* is not a compound, because in the Plural (*heirs apparent*) HEIR is still inflected as a separate unit. Such tests are largely sufficient in languages where most words are inflected. Take, for example, the Latin Verb LIQUEFACIO 'make liquid'. This has a compound stem whose first member, *lique*, is in turn a bare stem of the simple LIQUET 'be liquid'. BENEDICO ('bless' in Church Latin) is a compound whose first member is the Adverb BENE 'well'. This cannot be replaced by its Comparative or Superlative (say, OPTIMEDICO 'bless especially'). But in English there is generally no positive test. *Social Democratic* MAY be a compound, in that *Social* is not inflected separately; but then how could it be? Equally, it may NOT be a compound, in that *Social* can appear independently; but then so can *mad* in *madman*, *girl* in *girlfriend* and so on. The types which do allow positive results (*socio-economic* or *heir apparent*) are only the extreme cases. The test for *heir apparent* will also reveal uncertainties. In *solicitor general*, the first member is not usually inflected (e.g. *the solicitor generals in the last three governments*). But perhaps a pedant will insist that it should be, and there are certainly styles in which *solicitors general* would be more normal. Turning to a more ordinary situation, could three people in a restaurant order *three prunes and custards* or *three tournedo Rossini's*? For the author, at least, both are more acceptable than *three apple-pie and creams* or *three sole bonne-femme's*. There are several factors at work, and it is not easy to be sure of the facts.

Semantic criteria have often been emphasised. The phrases *a black bird* and *a blue jay* have meanings predictable from the individual words and their construction: the former refers to any 'bird' which is 'black' (e.g. a rook), and the latter to a 'jay' which is 'blue' (whatever that means, a European reader may say!). But the compounds *blackbird* and *bluejay* have meanings which are not predictable; the latter too is the name of a particular (North American) species. Other compounds, as we have seen, have meanings that are even less transparent.

But this criterion will not do on its own. Take, for example, the collocation 'PULL (one's) SOCKS UP'. A sentence like *He pulled his socks up* could have a meaning predictable from those of PULL, SOCK and so on. (Literally, he took his socks and pulled them up his legs.) But it also has what is generally called an idiomatic meaning (compare the equally idiomatic *He pulled himself together*). There is a similar collocation in *I've made my mind up*. This scarcely has a literal meaning, as we can rapidly discover if we replace *my* with an Article (*I have made a mind up*). Like many compounds, collocations such as these have idiosyncratic senses; and, ideally, they are given in a dictionary. There are, for example, several special 'Dictionaries of English Idioms', particularly to assist foreign learners.

But from a grammarian's viewpoint there are good reasons for saying that these are NOT compounds. In *He pulled his socks up* the form *pulled* is still the Past Tense of the Verb PULL, and as such contrasts with other Verbal forms (*He must pull his socks up, He's showing signs of pulling his socks up*, etc.) regardless of whether the idiomatic or literal sense is intended. Again, *his* is specifically the Possessive form of HE, replaceable by a form of THEY in *They pulled their socks up*, by a form of another Pronoun SHE in *She'll have to pull her socks up* and so on. Of course, there are restrictions: *socks* cannot be replaced by the Singular *sock* (*He must pull his sock up* can only be understood literally), and there must be agreement between the Subject of PULL and the Possessive (I cannot say of my pupil that *I shall have to pull his socks up for him*). But all this is stated in terms of the lexeme PULL, a particular form of the lexeme SOCK, of particular members in a construction of Verb + Possessive + Object and so on, and not in terms of a unitary element. Unlike a compound such as *blackbird*, these must be analysed syntactically.

We can make the same point in a language like Latin. The Roman *tribunus militaris* (to cite the Nominative Singular) was an officer of a specific military rank: the precise meaning cannot be deduced from those of TRIBUNUS 'tribune' and MILITARIS 'military' any more than that of BLACKBIRD can be deduced from those of BLACK and BIRD. A dictionary should therefore explain this, under TRIBUNUS or in its own entry. But for the grammarian it is still two words: if we turn it into the Plural (*tribuni militares* 'military tribunes') or the Accusative (*tribunum militarem*) the endings of both the Noun *tribunus* and its modifying Adjective *militaris* have to be altered in accordance with a regular syntactic rule of agreement. Collocations such as this are sometimes described as 'compounds' in the earlier tradition. But they are not like our Verbs LIQUEFACIO or BENEDICO ('make liquid', 'bless'), which are again inflected once, like simple Verbs.

An idiomatic collocation, like TRIBUNUS MILITARIS or English PULL (*one's*) SOCKS UP, can be described more briefly as an **idiom**. In principle, such idioms are distinct from morphological compounds. But in a language like English the distinction is not, in practice, easy. Take, for example, *mental hospital*. This does not literally denote a hospital that is mental, and we might argue, on that ground, that it is at least an idiom. But is it a compound? There is no morphological test, since MENTAL is in any case invariable. A topless bar is similarly not a bar which is topless, nor a refrigerated butcher a butcher who has been refrigerated. If we followed the semantic criterion alone these too might be classed as compounds. One objection is that other words can be inserted in the middle: one could presumably talk of a 'refrigerated pork butcher' or a 'topless sandwich bar'. But perhaps these could be compounds too, with the constituency structure [[*refrigerated pork*] *butcher*], [*topless* [*sandwich bar*]].

At this point many scholars will appeal to phonological criteria. English compounds (they will argue) are stressed on their first member: ['blækbɜːd] (*blackbird*), or, with a secondary stress, ['jeləʊˌhæmə] (*yellowhammer*). *Méntal hospital*, though written as two words, has similarly a primary stress on *men-*, not *hos-*. Therefore it too is a compound. But *topless bar* and *refrigerated butcher* have their main stress on *bar* and *butcher*. Therefore they are not compounds. *Mádman* is a compound even though, if we apply the semantic criterion, its meaning is predictable. So is *wild flower*; in Sir John Betjeman's parody of the Harvest Hymn:

> We spray the fields and scatter
> The poison on the ground,
> So that no wicked wild flowers
> Upon our farm be found.

it is the rhythmic counterpart of *scatter*.[2] For its stress compare *wild ánimal*; for that of *madman*, the pub name *The Gréen Mán*, for example. But a place name like *Torquay* is not a compound. Although it is always written as one word, and its meaning is unique, it is phonetically [ˌtɔːˈkiː], not ['tɔːkiː].

---

[2] *Collected Poems* (3rd edn, London, John Murray, 1970), p. 350.

The examples given earlier in this chapter were all compounds by this test, and when they were written as two words the accent was marked. But if we used this test alone we would make divisions that in other respects seem very arbitrary. We referred earlier to forms like *socio-economic* and *Anglo-American*. By this criterion they would not be compounds (*socio-económic*, *Anglo-Américan*). Adjectives like *séasick* or *báttle-tested* ('sick AT sea', 'tested IN battle') would be included; but not, for example, *snow-whíte* or *sea-gréen* ('white AS snow', 'green AS the sea'). We might be tempted to restrict the test to Nouns. But then consider forms like *red ádmiral* or *purple émperor*. These are semantically 'exocentric'. Just as a ladybird is not a 'bird', so they denote species of butterflies and have nothing to do with 'admirals' or 'emperors'; are they constructions merely because their stresses are like *a tall admiral* rather than, say, *a reár-admiral*? Even more arguable are those which are semantically of the type of *Blackshirt* or *Redcoat*: for example, *Red Beret* (paratrooper) or *black belt* (judo expert entitled to wear such a belt). These too have phrase-like stress, but in meaning they are not phrasal constructions with BERET and BELT as Head. Are they compounds, or merely fixed instances of metonymy (figures of speech in which an attribute or adjunct stands for the whole)?

Furthermore, this is another criterion whose results are subject to variation. One reason is that the distinction may often be obliterated by sentence stress and intonation. A compound like *óak-tree* CAN have its second member prominent: e.g. *I'd say that's an oak búsh rather than an oak trée*. Conversely, a phrase may lack stress on its Head: e.g. *It's a funny sort of bláck bird* (not, say, a brown one) may be identical to *a funny sort of blackbird* (not, say, a starling). Some forms vary freely. In my own speech, ICE-CREAM used to be [ˌaɪsˈkriːm], which is the pronunciation given by GIMSON. But it is now variably either that or [ˈaɪskriːm]. I am not at all sure whether I say, for example, *milk sháke* or *mílk shake*, *office párty* or *óffice party*, *teddy béar* or *téddy bear*. American usage is often different from British, and this can cause confusion. I remember the reaction when, some twenty years ago, I asked for a 'hót dóg' in Los Angeles.

Finally, we turn or return to criteria drawn from syntax. One obvious test is that the members of a compound should not be

separable. For example, in *I put out the fire* the collocation PUT
OUT has a meaning ('extinguish') which is not predictable from
that of PUT and OUT. But one can also say *I put the fire out*;
therefore this is what is usually called a 'Phrasal Verb' and not a
compound. In German, the Infinitive *ausmachen* (literally 'make
out') has the same meaning; and, since it is written as one word,
and has one accent (*áusmachen*), it is traditionally a compound
Verb. But in other forms its elements are separated: *Ich* ('I')
*machte* ('made') *das Feuer* ('the fire') *aus* ('out'). In the tradition
of Greek grammar, a sporadic splitting of compound Verbs is
referred to by the term '**tmesis**' (literally 'cutting'). But if we
follow the syntactic test, a 'compound' which can be split is not
a compound at all.

We might also test whether a modifying or dependent member
can enter into its own construction. One could talk of *reed and
corn buntings* or *a flock of white and red admirals*; therefore, it
might be argued, *red admiral, corn bunting*, etc. cannot be
compounds. Again, the members would be separated in *a hospital
– mental, isn't it?* or *parties, cocktail and otherwise*; therefore
*mental hospital* and *cocktail party* would not be compounds either.
But in fact this is more a reflection of transparency and possible
semantic contrast. One does not talk of *sick- and death- beds* or of
*birds, black and otherwise* (meaning 'blackbirds') – the latter
because it would only be understood non-idiomatically. But one
type of collocation allows co-ordination without difficulty (e.g.
*macro- and micro-economic studies*), and many others are not
objectionable: e.g. *missel- and song-thrushes*. The last two are
compounds phonologically (*míssel-thrush, sóng-thrush*), as are *réed
bunting* and *córn bunting*. It seems arbitrary to exclude them by the
syntactic test alone. A further problem is that a writer may analyse
a compound quite facetiously: '[historians] do not sit open-
mouthed waiting for something to fall into it' (from *The Times
Literary Supplement*), with *mouth* picked up by *it*; similarly, and
perhaps less improbably, 'He's a lady-killer because he likes them
so much'.

This discussion could continue, and we could find other special
tests of various sorts in other languages. But the problem is by
now clear. On the one hand, no criterion is irrelevant. It is to be
expected of compounds that they should be single units

inflectionally, phonologically and so on. In that sense there is no test which is THE criterion par excellence. On the other hand, no two tests give results that wholly agree. A Verb like German AUSMACHEN is a compound in every respect, except that its elements are separable in syntax. English *wild flower* and *wild animal* are parallel, except that one has 'compound stress' and the other not. The elements of *heir apparent* are syntactically inseparable; but it is not a compound inflectionally. We have also found that some tests give results that vary between speakers, or for one speaker.

A wise scholar will not be perplexed. In the history of a language, collocations and figures of speech may often be **institutionalised** (as clichés or idioms) without also being **lexicalised** as single units: this is true of, for example, *a sick joke*, where *sick* can still have its own Modifier (*a very sick joke*). Alternatively, lexicalisation may follow (either at once, as for *dishwasher*, or later, as for *son of a bitch*) and this may lead to the fossilisation of at least one member (e.g. *whinchat*), to a purely derivational formation (e.g. *childhood*) or to virtual morphological unity (e.g. *chaffinch* [tʃæfintʃ]). For a language like English, it would be simple-minded to expect that a single feature – be it a stress pattern or whatever – should mark the boundary between what is lexicalised and what is merely institutionalised. This is not to say that the distinction is spurious; it is often the mark of a genuine unit, like the lexeme, that we have trouble with it! But a grammarian will have to work with varying and partly fluid criteria.

RELATED READING

Compare BAUER, *Morphology*, pp. 33–8, 100–4; in the latter section Bauer suggests that compounding has more in common with syntax than with word-formation. On compounds in English see MARCHAND, ch. 2; BAUER, *Word-formation*, pp. 201–16; ADAMS, chs. 5–9; QUIRK *et al.*, pp. 1567–80.

The transformational account of compounds was developed by LEES; earliest criticism in reviews by P. Schachter, *International Journal of American Linguistics* 28 (1962), pp. 134–46, and by me, 'Transformational grammar', *Archivum Linguisticum* 13 (1961), pp. 196–209. For its eventual rejection within the Chomskyan school see SCALISE, pp. 8ff. For a later and more nuanced syntactic account see J. N. Levi, *The Syntax and Semantics of Complex Nominals* (New York, Academic Press, 1978); but Levi's 'complex nominals' include phrases as well as compounds, and all exocentric forms, for example, are excluded. For 'deep' and 'surface' it may be helpful to look at older introductions to transformational grammar: for example, R. D. Huddleston, *An Introduction to English Transformational Syntax* (London, Longman, 1976). What survives of these notions would no longer allow the operations that Lees, or Levi, proposed.

The opposite view is adopted to varying degrees in 'lexical' or 'lexicalist' morphology. For a survey and critique of several contributions see R. P. Botha, *Morphological Mechanisms : Lexicalist Analysis of Synthetic Compounds* (Oxford, Pergamon Press, 1984); Botha himself concludes that 'synthetic compounds' (those, like *book-keeper*, which correspond to a Verbal construction) cannot be detached from syntax, while 'root' or 'primary' compounds (*windmill*, for example) can.

For experiments which support a minimalist view of Noun–Noun compounds see P. Downing, 'On the creation and use of English compound nouns', *Lg* 53 (1977), pp. 810–42.

'Endocentric' and 'exocentric' are from BLOOMFIELD, pp. 235f., and relate to his use of these terms in syntax (p. 194). For a later and better account, of this distinction and of the syntactic types of nominal compounds generally, see E. Benveniste, 'Fondements syntaxiques de la composition nominale', reprinted in BENVENISTE, pp. 145–62.

On the boundary between composition and derivation see W. von Wartburg & S. Ullmann, *Problèmes et méthodes de la linguistique* (Paris, Presses Universitaires de France, 1969), §2.4; *policeman* is briefly discussed by QUIRK *et al.*, pp. 1520f. For compounds vs phrases one might still begin with BLOOMFIELD, pp. 227ff. See, in particular, BLOOMFIELD, pp. 229ff., on morphological criteria. The French equivalents of English *socio-*, *Franco-* and so on are discussed at length by GUILBERT, pp. 225ff. ('composition allogène').

For a reliance on semantic criteria see O. Jespersen, *A Modern English Grammar*, VI (Copenhagen, Munksgaard, 1942), ch. 8. LYONS, *Semantics*, II, pp. 535ff., proposes a distinction between 'compound lexemes' (compounds whose meanings are in part idiosyncratic) and 'syntactic compounds', whose meanings 'can be accounted for in terms of the productive rules of the language-system'. This cuts across a further distinction between 'word-compounds' and 'phrasal compounds', drawn (in English) by stress. For the criterion of stress in English see BLOOMFIELD, p. 228; CHOMSKY & HALLE, pp. 16f. and elsewhere (the 'compound rule'): many textbook treatments simply follow one or the other. It depends very much on the received American view of English accentuation: for criticism (of CHOMSKY & HALLE's version) see D. L. Bolinger, 'Accent is predictable (if you're a mind reader)', *Lg* 48 (1972), pp. 633–44, one of many by the same author.

# 6
# Morphemes and allomorphs

Lexical and inflectional morphemes; words as sequences of morphemes.
The morpheme as a syntactic primitive; as a unit of distribution; as
'same of form and meaning'. Alternations: complementary and
contrastive distribution. Morphemes as abstract units; allomorphy.
*An agglutinating system.* The Noun in Turkish: Case and Plural
morphemes. Vowel alternations: Front vs Back; Rounded vs Unrounded;
vowel harmony. Possessive and Agentive morphemes. Consonant
alternations: 'soft *g*'; alternations of voiced and voiceless.
*Types of alternation.* Recurrent and non-recurrent alternations.
Morphemic conditioning, lexical and grammatical. Phonological
conditioning: morphemically restricted vs automatic. Alternations of Past
Participle in English.

We can now return to inflectional morphology. As we noted in
chapter 1, there are alternative models, and in practice different
types of language tend to be described differently.

The simplest model is one based on the morpheme. In a line
from Yeats which we cited:

And therefore I have sailed the seas and come

both *sailed* and *seas* were divided into two units. The first
identifies the lexeme, and can be called a **lexical morpheme**.
Following the convention for lexemes established in chapter 2, we
can refer to these, in small capitals, as the morphemes SAIL and
SEA. The second unit is an **inflectional morpheme**. In *sailed* the
ending -*ed* marks Past Participle; let us therefore say, more
precisely, that it represents a morpheme 'Past Participle'. In *seas*
the ending is a Plural marker, and we will accordingly say that it
represents the morpheme 'Plural'. In each word the morphemes
form a sequence. So, their grammatical make-up – that of the
'word' as opposed to the 'word-form' – can be shown thus:

> SAIL + Past Participle
> SEA + Plural

One attraction of this analysis is that inflectional morphology
can be integrated with syntax. In the line from Yeats, *have sailed*

(or the sequence of morphemes HAVE + SAIL + Past Participle) is syntactically a Predicator with *the seas* (THE + SEA + Plural) as Object. We might display the structure like this:

| Predicator | Object |
|---|---|
| [HAVE + SAIL + Past Participle] | [THE + SEA + Plural] |

Similarly, within the phrase *have sailed*, an Auxiliary (the single morpheme HAVE) is related to a Main Verb (SAIL + Past Participle):

| Auxiliary | Main Verb |
|---|---|
| HAVE | [SAIL + Past Participle] |

In just the same way, we can say that *sailed* is syntactically a Root (SAIL) plus an inflection:

| ROOT | INFLECTION |
|---|---|
| SAIL | Past Participle |

In this analysis, the word (*sailed*) remains a syntactic unit. But in others it might not: in the Chomskyan account which was summarised in chapter 1, *have sailed* would be, at a deeper level, [HAVE + Past Participle] + SAIL. But in none would it be fundamental. The primitive unit of syntax, the smallest unit that can bear meaning, the ultimate basis for our entire description of the primary articulation of language, is the morpheme.

This is perhaps the most powerful argument for the morphemic model. But in the American school of the 1940s it was common to approach the unit from a phonological angle. In describing a language a linguist states the possible distribution of each of its elements. (Of course we do other things as well, but that was seen as at least the central problem.) One such element is the phoneme. We establish, for example, that English has a phoneme /v/ whose distribution includes the possibility of occurrence initially (as in /vəʊlz/ *voles*), but excludes, among others, that of occurrence after initial /k/ (see chapter 1 on *quab* and [kvɒb]). The evidence is the character and distribution of the phonetic features themselves: labiodental articulation, varying degrees of voicing plus relatively short duration, distributional contrast with the longer and voiceless [f] of *foals* and so on. But then one finds that larger fragments of an utterance also seem to recur as distributional units. In the phonemic transcriptions of *I have been sailing*, *I sailed the Channel*, *He sails his own yacht*, etc. we find a single

*[handwritten margin note: ✓✓ morpheme — the smallest unit that can bear meaning.]*

piece /seɪl/ which can contrast with other pieces such as /swɪm/ in *I have been swimming*, /rəʊ/ in *I rowed the Channel*, or /stɪə/ in *He steers his own yacht*. We must therefore set up a second unit, the morpheme, to account for these recurrences in turn. Thus the morpheme SAIL has a distribution which allows /seɪl/ to appear in each of these environments but not, for example, to substitute for /strɒŋ/ *strong-* in *He is stronger than me*. Naturally, SAIL is not identical with /seɪl/ as such, any more than the phoneme /v/ is identical with the phonetic fragment [v]. But again it is the recurrence of /seɪl/, and its contrasts with other fragments such as /swɪm/, which form the essential evidence.

In many theoretical discussions only the utterance as a whole (e.g. the phonemically written /aɪvbiːnseɪlɪŋ/) was taken for granted. Furthermore, the units were to be established on strictly distributional evidence – i.e. without using evidence of meaning or syntactic function. This is particularly true of Harris's important *Methods in Structural Linguistics* (HARRIS). But a similar analysis may be based on the study of proportions within paradigms. In the following array of Verb-forms:

| sail  | sailing  | sails [seɪlz]      | sailed [seɪld]    |
|-------|----------|--------------------|-------------------|
| row   | rowing   | rows [rəʊz]        | rowed [rəʊd]      |
| fish  | fishing  | fishes [fɪʃɪz]     | fished [fɪʃt]     |
| cross | crossing | crosses [krɒsɪz]   | crossed [krɒst]   |

the words in each column have an equivalent range of grammatical functions, and those in each row have a common range of lexical meaning. We may therefore establish proportions by which *sail* is to *sailing* as *row* to *rowing*, *sail* to *row* as *sailing* to *rowing*, and so on. At the same time, each form in the second, third and fourth columns consists of the form in the first ($R$, let us say) with another fragment following. The second has the structure $R + ing$; we may accordingly say that the presence or absence of *-ing* is parallel to the grammatical difference between each of the pairs *sailing*:*sail*, *rowing*:*row*, etc. The third has the structure $R + [z]$ or $R + [ɪz]$; the presence of [z] or [ɪz] accordingly parallels whatever is grammatically in common here. Likewise in the fourth column the presence of [d] or [t] matches the grammatical or semantic feature which is common to *sailed*, *rowed*, *fished* and *crossed*.

By the same token, the value of $R$ is constant for any of the four individual rows. We may accordingly say that the value $R = sail$ or [seɪl] is parallel to the semantic features which are in common to the first row, the value $R = row$ or [rəʊ] to those for the second and so on. To sum up, the array as a whole may be said to display an abstract structure as follows:

| A | A X | A Y | A Z |
|---|-----|-----|-----|
| B | B X | B Y | B Z |
| C | C X | C Y | C Z |
| D | D X | D Y | D Z |

in which A, B, X, etc., may be understood to refer EITHER to the features of meaning or grammatical function on the one hand, OR to the forms [seɪl], [rəʊ], [ɪŋ] etc., on the other. Thus Y is indifferently interpretable either as the form in the third column which varies between [z] and [ɪz], or as the features of meaning and grammar which all of *sails, rows,* etc., have in common. In this sense each of A, B, X, Y, etc., stands for a corresponding 'same of form and meaning'. Furthermore, they are MINIMAL 'sames of form and meaning'; we cannot group the words into other proportions in such a way that even smaller forms will be seen to parallel more detailed features of grammar and semantics.

In Bloomfield's theory the morpheme is defined in just such a  sense. The fundamental assumption of linguistics (if we may briefly summarise his argument) is that form and meaning are in some way in correspondence. If a sentence is uttered on Tuesday and then uttered again on Wednesday, it has the same form and is employed with a meaning which we take to be the same also. This then is one 'same of form and meaning' which, as such, is either minimal or non-minimal as the case may be. If minimal, the whole utterance is itself one morpheme. If non-minimal, it is composed of smaller fragments which themselves are morphemes. But there is an obvious difficulty if the morpheme in this sense is to be reconciled with the morpheme qua minimal syntactic unit. In other forms which were discussed in chapter 1:

| | |
|---|---|
| catch [kætʃ] | caught [kɔːt] |
| beget [bɪget] | begotten [bɪgɒtn] |
| bear [bɛə] | born [bɔːn] |

the proportions are impeccable on grounds of meaning and syntactic function. But formally there are alternations. We cannot say that the ending -[t], in *caught* or in *crossed* and *fished*, is the 'same form' as the -[n] of *begotten* or *born*. Nor, for the lexical morphemes, can we say that [kætʃ] is the same as [kɔː], [bɪget] the same as [bɪgɒt], or [bɛə] the same as [bɔː]. Formal features alternate while semantic properties remain constant.

In Bloomfield's formulation forms like [kætʃ] and [kɔː] were one morpheme, the latter derived from the former by a process of 'phonetic modification'; -[t] and -[n] would be different morphemes, but related to units of meaning ('sememes') that were the same. But his successors adopted a different solution. In phonology, they pointed out, a single distributional unit can subsume a set of quite distinct phonetic fragments. For example, in many dialects of Spanish [s] and [h] (second and third consonants in ['kasah] 'houses') are variants or 'allophones' of the same phoneme /s/. So, this word is phonemically /'kasas/, as in the spelling *casas*. A necessary test – though not in itself sufficient – was to determine whether the fragments or 'phones' in question are in **contrastive** or in **complementary distribution**. If Spanish had a word-form with [s] in such a position that, by substituting [h], one would obtain a different word-form (either actual or possible), the phones would thereby contrast. Therefore they would represent two different phonemes, /s/ and /h/. But in fact that is not so: [s] appears only in positions or environments where [h] does not appear, and vice versa. Their distributions complement each other and, on this and other evidence, they are one phoneme /s/. A phoneme, in American phonologies of the period, was seen as a class of allophones in complementary distribution. Spanish /s/ is thus the class [s], [h] and so on.

The same distributional test was then applied to the morpheme. Let us start once more from the ending -[t] (*caugh-t, fish-ed*). This differs from -[n]; but again they are in complementary distribution. A [t] appears only in environments in which [n] does not appear (e.g. there is no word *caugh-n*), and [n] only in environments where [t] does not appear. We can therefore establish a single distributional unit of which [t] and [n] are variants. This is the unit that we have already labelled 'Past Participle'. Then take *catch* and *caugh-*. These too are complementary: the latter appears only before -[t], the former everywhere else. Therefore they too are variants of a single distributional unit, which we will label 'CATCH'. These abstract units were again defined as classes. Thus, to continue, 'BEGET' will label a class with the members [bɪget], [bɪgæt] (in the Past Tense) and [bɪgɒt]-. BEAR will be a class with the members [bɛə] and [bɔ:].

In the terminology of this period, the formal variants were called '**morphs**'. *Caught* will thus consist of two morphs [kɔ:] and [t], *begotten* of the morphs [bɪgɒt] and [n], *beget* of the single morph [bɪget], and so on. The term '**morpheme**' was reserved for the abstract unit. So, in terms of morphemes, our entire proportion will be represented like this:

| | |
|---|---|
| CATCH | CATCH + Past Participle |
| BEGET | BEGET + Past Participle |
| BEAR | BEAR + Past Participle |

just as it would have been in terms of the syntactic approach to the morpheme which we illustrated earlier. Finally, the relation between morphs and morphemes is that of **allomorphy**. If morph $x$ is a member of morpheme $y$ it is an **allomorph** of that morpheme. Thus both [t] and [n] are allomorphs of Past Participle; so too are the [d] of *sailed* and the [ɪd] of *wait-ed*. Among lexical morphemes, CATCH has the allomorphs [kætʃ] and [kɔ:].

Some of this belongs to history. The term 'morpheme' has always been used independently of the model, as we ourselves have used it in chapter 1. Its definition as a class of allomorphs in complementary distribution has largely been abandoned. But the general picture of word-structure is still valid; and, before we expound and assess it further, it is as well to have looked at its origins.

## AN AGGLUTINATING SYSTEM

It will also help to look at a more extended illustration. In English there are problems with the model as it stands, and they will be the starting point for the next chapter. But there are other languages for which it is very appropriate, and it is to one of these that we must now turn.

Of the languages of Europe, Turkish is by far the best suited:

it is of the type that nineteenth-century scholars called agglutinating, and, since it is also rich in alternations, it will illustrate that aspect of the model well. We may add that Lewis's *Turkish Grammar*, which we will refer to (LEWIS), is an accessible work which can be enjoyably studied further. Let us begin with the lexical unit meaning 'village', part of whose paradigm runs as follows (LEWIS, p. 29):

|  | *Singular* | *Plural* |
|---|---|---|
| *Absolute* | köy | köyler |
| *Accusative* | köyü | köyleri |
| *Genitive* | köyün | köylerin |
| *Dative* | köye | köylere |
| *Locative* | köyde | köylerde |
| *Ablative* | köyden | köylerden |

From the viewpoint of syntax and semantics this introduces two of the relevant sets of categories, that of Number (Singular and Plural) and that of Case, whose different terms Absolute (for a Subject or an Indefinite Object), Accusative (for a Definite Object 'the village') and so on serve here to distinguish the various syntactic and semantic functions of the Nominal phrase. At the same time, the forms themselves may be analysed into a minimal word-form *köy* (classified in itself as Absolute Singular) which may be followed either by one or by two further elements. Throughout the second column it is followed immediately by *-ler*; we may therefore posit a Plural morpheme with this as (so far) its only allomorph. In the first column there is no form – nothing that we might posit as a 'Singular' allomorph – corresponding. Turning to the rows, there is again no further morpheme which we may posit in the first row *köy* and *köyler*. But in the remainder each of these forms is followed by a further form which may be assigned to a Case morpheme Accusative, Genitive and so on. In the fourth, fifth and sixth rows the morphemes Dative, Locative and Ablative each have one allomorph only: respectively, *-e*, *-de* and *-den*. In the second and third, however, the form can be seen to vary between an allomorph with an *ü* vowel in the first column (Accusative *-ü*, Genitive *-ün*) and one with an *i* in the second (Accusative *-i*, Genitive *-in*). For 'allomorph' it is also common to say 'alternant'. In Turkish, therefore, we have so far established two allomorphs or alternants of the Accusative morpheme, namely -*ü* and -*i*. Similarly, there is an alternation between -*ün* and -*in* as allomorphs of Genitive.

On the basis of this analysis the general structure of these dozen forms may be summed up by the following formula:

KÖY (Plural) (Case)

meaning that the morpheme which we will represent as KÖY 'village' may be followed by the morpheme Plural alone, or by Plural followed in turn by a Case morpheme, by a Case morpheme alone, or by neither. The brackets round 'Plural' and 'Case' in the formula mean that these elements may be independently present or absent depending on the particular instance. If we then turn to the corresponding forms for a further lexical unit meaning 'end' (LEWIS, p. 30), we will find that the same general structure is maintained:

|  | *Singular* | *Plural* |
|---|---|---|
| *Absolute* | son | sonlar |
| *Accusative* | sonu | sonları |
| *Genitive* | sonun | sonların |
| *Dative* | sona | sonlara |
| *Locative* | sonda | sonlarda |
| *Ablative* | sondan | sonlardan |

and indeed it will be maintained for any other Noun we look at.

At the same time, the forms for 'end' introduce a fresh set of allomorphs for each of the morphemes which we have posited. In *köyler* Plural had the allomorph -*ler*; in *sonlar* etc. the corresponding form is -*lar*. In *köye, köyde* and *köyden* Dative, Locative and Ablative were marked by -*e*, -*de* and -*den*; in *sona, sonda* and *sondan* they are marked by -*a*, -*da* and -*dan*. For all four morphemes we can accordingly posit a further variation or alternation between a set of forms with *e* in one paradigm (-*ler, e,* -*de* and -*den*) and a set with *a* in the other (-*lar, -a, -da* and -*dan*). Finally, the paradigm for 'end' establishes two further allomorphs both for the Accusative and for the Genitive. In the forms for 'village' the alternations lay between a form in *ü* and a form in *i*; here they lie between forms in *u* (-*u* or -*un*) and in *ı* (-*ı* or -*ın*). Each of these morphemes will accordingly subsume at least four phonologically distinct variants.

If we were trying to discover the structure of Turkish from scratch (an unnecessary task, but in learning linguistics it is helpful to put oneself in this kind of position), we would rapidly suspect that the alternations of allomorphs which we have posited have some fairly general rationale. They seem to form a regular feature of the system – not, as it were, a set of isolated peculiarities of individual morphemes. Otherwise why do the same vowel variations keep recurring, in our present exposition for up to four units already? In fact the general rules are well known, and are of a type which is found in many other languages. Vowels, first of all, may be classified as phonologically Front or Back. Those which appear in the 'village' paradigm (broadly [ɛ] *e*, [œ] *ö*, [i] *i* and [y] *ü*) form the Front class and those in the 'end' paradigm (broadly [ɑ] *a*, [ɔ] *o*, [ɯ] *ı* and [u] *u*[1]) are the corresponding members of the Back class. In the phonology of any native word-form, all the vowels must belong either to one class or to the other. This is a rule of phonology, regardless of morphological structure (LEWIS, pp. 15f.), but since the Plural and Case allomorphs form part of the phonological word, it follows that they must conform to it. In the first paradigm *köy* has a Front vowel; accordingly, all the following allomorphs -*ler*, -*ü*, -*ün*, -*e*, etc. have Front vowels to match. In the second *son* has a Back vowel; accordingly, -*lar*, -*u*, etc. are also Back.

In addition to the Front/Back oppositions, vowels may be divided into Close (*i, ü, ı, u*) versus Open (*e, ö, a, o*) and on another dimension into Unrounded (*i, ı, e, a*) and Rounded (*ü, u, ö, o*). The total system may accordingly be displayed as follows:

|  | Front | | Back | |
|---|---|---|---|---|
|  | Unrounded | Rounded | Unrounded | Rounded |
| Close | i | ü | ı | u |
| Open | e | ö | a | o |

(compare LEWIS, p. 13), where the two-way alternations for one set of morphemes (Ablative -*den*/-*dan*, Plural -*ler*/-*lar*, etc.) can be seen to involve the two vowels that are both Open and Unrounded, and the four-way alternations in the Accusative and

---

[1] But I do not wish to give the impression that the phonetics of vowels in Turkish is dead easy. In practical classes, students often have difficulty both in transcription and in working the system out.

Genitive (e.g. Accusative -*i*/-*ü*/-*ı*/-*u*) to involve the entire set of Close vowels, both Front and Back (as explained already) and also Rounded and Unrounded. Again, this can be explained by purely phonological restrictions (LEWIS, pp. 15–16, 18) on Rounded and Unrounded Close syllables. In *köyün* or *sonun* the allomorph of Genitive is Rounded (-*ün* or -*un*) because the preceding syllable has the Rounded *ö* or *o*; in *köylerin* or *sonların* it is Unrounded (-*in* or -*ın*) because in these forms the preceding syllable has an Unrounded *e* or *a* instead. It follows that a Noun morpheme whose own allomorph has an Unrounded vowel will be followed by Unrounded allomorphs of Accusative and Genitive in the Singular paradigm also. Thus for the Absolute *el* 'hand' (with Front vowel *e*) we may predict the Accusative *eli* and Genitive *elin* (note: with Front vowels in the Case allomorph, following the first rule), and for the Absolute *akşam* [akʃam] 'evening' (with Back vowel *a*) we may predict the corresponding forms *akşamı* and *akşamın* (LEWIS, pp. 29, 30).

These rules for vowel or syllable sequences (rules of **vowel harmony**, as they are generally called) are confirmed for morpheme after morpheme in the remainder of the paradigms. One way of marking personal 'possession' ('my village', 'our village' and so on) is by a Person morpheme coming between the Plural and Case morphemes if any. With the 1st Singular 'my' the paradigm for 'village' may be illustrated as follows:

|  | Singular | Plural |
|---|---|---|
| *Absolute* | köyüm | köylerim |
| *Accusative* | köyümü | köylerimi |
| *Dative* | köyüme | köylerime |

(compare LEWIS, pp. 39–41), where the intervening morpheme – which we may abbreviate as '1st Sg.' – has allomorphs alternating between the Front Rounded -*üm* after *köy* in the first column and the Front Unrounded -*im* after -*ler* in the second. Likewise the corresponding forms for 1st Plural 'our' show an alternation between -*ümüz* and -*imiz*:

|  | Singular | Plural |
|---|---|---|
| *Absolute* | köyümüz | köylerimiz |
| *Accusative* | köyümüzü | köylerimizi |
| *Dative* | köyümüze | köylerimize |

– and so on for other Person morphemes. If we turn to a Noun with Close Back harmony instead we find, as we would expect, that the 1st Sg. morpheme alternates between -*um* and -*ım* and the 1st Pl. 'our' morpheme between -*umuz* and -*ımız*. Examples are the Absolute Singular and Plural *çocuğum* 'my child' and *çocuklarım* 'my children', and the corresponding forms *çocuğumuz* 'our child' *çocuklarımız* 'our children'. Note that the allomorphs of the Noun morpheme, ÇOCUK 'child', alternate between *çocuk* (phonetically [tʃɔdʒuk]) in some contexts and *çocuğ*- (see below) in others.

Nor are the effects confined to inflections. The Noun whose Absolute form is *dişçi* 'dentist' is formed from *diş* [diʃ] 'tooth' by the addition of an element which in this context takes the form -*çi* [tʃi] (LEWIS, p. 59). But in *sütçü* 'milkman' (from the Front Rounded *süt* 'milk') it has an *ü* vowel, and in other cases it will have an *u* or an *ı*. In such forms we would recognise a further morpheme – let us call it Agentive – whose allomorphs behave according to the same rules as the Case and other morphemes which we have considered earlier. So, for example, we would predict that the form for 'of my dentists' could be represented as a sequence of morphemes as follows:

DIŞ    Agentive    Plural    1st Sg    Genitive

where the last four elements will all be subject to rules of vowel harmony dictated, ultimately, by the first. The resulting word-form will be analysed into the sequence of smaller forms *diş-çi-ler-im-in*.

We need hardly add that similar two-fold and four-fold alternations (forms in *e* alternating with forms in *a*, allomorphs with Close vowels varying between *i*, *ü*, *ı* and *u*) are also shown by the majority of morphemes which accompany Verbs (LEWIS, pp. 96ff.). But in the course of the grammar we will also find a number of other systematic variations. The morpheme ÇOCUK 'child' enters into one such pattern. As we have seen, it ends in *k* in some contexts: namely, when it is final (*çocuk*) or before a consonant (*çocuklar* 'children'). But when it is followed by a vowel there is phonetically no velar consonant; instead the preceding *u* lengthens and 'swallows up' (LEWIS, p. 5) the vowel in question. It is this effect which is marked in writing by the letter *ğ* (the 'soft *g'*) in *çocuğum* [tʃɔdʒuːm] or *çocuğumuz* [tʃɔdʒuːmuz]. A similar alternation is found in the forms of other morphemes: for example, Absolute *ekmek* 'bread' but Accusative *ekmeği* [ɛkmɛː]. More widely, it may also be related to variations of other consonants in the same environments. For example, the morphemes KITAP 'book' (from Arabic) and TAÇ 'crown' (from Persian) have the allomorphs *kitap* and *taç* [tatʃ] in one case but in the other *kitab* and *tac* [tadʒ] (e.g. Accusative *kitabı, tacı*). It must be noted, however, that a pattern of this kind does not hold for all morphemes with allomorphs ending in one or other of these consonants. In part, at least, it is necessary for individual cases to be distinguished (examples later in this chapter).

There are other consonant variations which do hold regularly. In Nouns such as *yolcu* 'traveller' from *yol* 'road', *eskici* 'old-clothes man' from *eski* 'old', *toptancı* 'wholesaler' from *toptan* 'wholesale', and *tütüncü* 'tobacconist' from *tütün* 'tobacco', we may establish the same morpheme Agentive that accounted for -*çi* in *dişçi* 'dentist' (LEWIS, p. 59). But the allomorphs that appear in these forms begin with a voiced consonant (-*cu* [dʒu], -*ci* [dʒi], -*cı* [dʒɯ] and -*cü* [dʒy]), whereas those in our earlier examples began with a voiceless *ç* [tʃ]. In this case we are concerned with a general pattern (LEWIS, p. 12) by which any morpheme whose alternant begins with *c, d* or *g* in one set of contexts (e.g. after the *l* of *yol* in *yolcu* or the vowel of *eski* in *eskici*) will have as its alternant a corresponding form in *ç, t* or *k* whenever it is preceded, within a word, by a form whose final consonant is itself voiceless (e.g. the *diş* or *süt* of the forms *dişçi* and *sütçü* which we cited above). This one morpheme Agentive has, accordingly, a set of allomorphs with two quite independent patterns of phonological variation (the four-fold vowel harmony on the one hand and the voiced/voiceless consonant variation on the other), and may therefore be represented by any one of eight different morphs.

I hope that the reader does not feel that this has been too much of a digression into Turkish. For it is important to have a grasp of the kind of system which confirms the insights of our first model, before we turn to other, often more familiar, languages whose structure calls them into question. The most important insight is that, in the structure of each word, distinct and single

FORMS correspond to distinct and single MEANINGS. For example, in the structure of *diş-çi-ler-im-in* 'of my dentists', the form *diş* corresponds to the meaning 'tooth', the form *-çi* to the meaning of the Agentive, the form *-ler* to the meaning 'more than one', the form *-im* to the meaning 'my', and the form *-in* to the meaning of the Genitive. In that sense we are dealing literally with Bloomfield's 'sames of form and meaning'.

## TYPES OF ALTERNATION

Throughout this illustration the concept of alternation has played a crucial role. It is now time to consider, more precisely, how alternations of different kinds should be described.

So far, we have made clear that, in this model, alternations hold between the allomorphs of a morpheme. In Turkish the Plural morpheme, for example, exhibits an alternation between *-ler* and *-lar*, and Dative an alternation between *-e* (in *köye*) and *-a* (in *sona*). But the reader will have noticed that the alternants of a morpheme regularly have much of their phonological make-up in common. For instance, *-ler* and *-lar* have in common the consonants *l* and *r*; in addition the vowel is in each case Open and Unrounded, the only difference being that in one form it is Front and in the other Back. Even in English CATCH the two alternants [kætʃ] and [kɔː] have in common at least the initial [k], and for the Turkish Agentive the eight allomorphs *-ci*, *-cü*, *-cı*, *-cu*, *-çi*, *-çü*, *-çı* and *-çu* share a consonant which is in general a Palatal Occlusive (Voiced [dʒ] in the first four, Voiceless [tʃ] in the last) and a vowel which is throughout Close as opposed to Open. For this reason it is helpful to speak of alternation not only between allomorphs as wholes (*-ler* alternating with *-lar*, [kætʃ] with [kɔː]), but also between the PARTS of these allomorphs which actually differ. Accordingly, within the forms which identify the Turkish Plural we will isolate a specific alternation between a Front vowel in *-ler* and a Back vowel in *-lar*. Similarly, the allomorphs of CATCH show an alternation between, specifically, the [ætʃ] and the [ɔː], and those of the Turkish Agentive morpheme show (for the moment, let us say) an eight-way alternation between Voiced consonant with Front Unrounded vowel, Voiced consonant with Front Rounded vowel, and so on.

On this basis, the SAME alternation may be said to recur in two or more different sets of allomorphs. In the case of English CATCH this is not so: there is no other morpheme which we could establish whose alternants would display an identical variation between [ætʃ] and [ɔː]. That, therefore, is a **non-recurrent** alternation – one which is instanced in one morpheme only. But in the Turkish Plural the variation is precisely the same as in the Ablative: *e* in *-ler* alternates with *a* in *-lar* and likewise *e* in *-den* alternates with *a* in *-dan*. It also takes place under conditions which can be stated identically: the Front alternants *-ler* and *-den* are found with a Front vowel in the preceding syllable, and the Back *-lar* and *-dan* whenever it is Back instead. We will therefore say that there is a **recurrent** alternation between the Open Unrounded vowels – recurring, in fact, not only in the Plural and Ablative but also in the Locative (*-de* alternating with *-da*, as we have seen), Dative (*-e* alternating with *-a*) and in many other Turkish morphemes. Similarly, our description has pointed to a recurrent alternation between the Close vowels *i*, *ü*, *ı* and *u* (as parts of the allomorphs of Accusative, Genitive and so on), and to yet another which is exemplified by the final consonants of *kitap* and *kitab* (Voiceless versus Voiced Bilabial) or *taç* and *tac* (Voiceless versus Voiced Palatal). Finally, in the case of the Turkish Agentive morpheme, we can now make explicit two distinct recurrent alternations (Voiced *c* versus Voiceless *ç*; Front Unrounded *i* versus Back Rounded *u*, and so on), each of which recurs independently throughout the language. For the vowel alternation compare again the allomorphs of Accusative or Genitive. For the alternation of the consonant we may compare the Ablative in the paradigm of Nouns such as DAMAT 'son-in-law': whereas in forms like *sondan* the allomorph of Ablative begins with a Voiced *d* (*son-dan*), here, after the Voiceless consonant of *damat*, it begins with Voiceless *t* (*damat-tan*).

In addition to classifying alternations as recurrent or non-recurrent, we may also classify them according to the different types of conditions in which they take place. In some cases, the presence of one variant or another depends entirely on the particular morphemes which form their context or environment. To return to English, the nasal alternants of the Past Participle morpheme (the *-en* of *begotten* or *swollen*) simply appear when

115

certain individual Verbal morphemes, such as SWELL or BEGET, precede them. There is nothing in the phonology of modern English (in the sense that we spoke of a phonological rationale for Turkish vowel harmony) which explains why *swollen* should have an *-en* whereas *holed*, for example, has a regular alternant with a dental. The alternation between written *-en* ([n̩] or [ən]) on the one hand and written *-ed* ([d], etc.) on the other is accordingly said to be **morphemically conditioned**. To be more specific, SWELL, BEGET and so on are lexical morphemes, and we will therefore say that the alternation in the inflectional morpheme is **lexically conditioned**. Another morphemically conditioned alternation is that of the vowel in allomorphs of SWELL itself: [swəʊl] when it is followed by Past Participle, but its counterpart [swel] elsewhere (*swells, swelled, swelling, swells*). Here the alternation may be classified more precisely as **grammatically** or **morphologically conditioned**. It is worth remarking that both grammatically and lexically conditioned alternation may, naturally, be either recurrent or non-recurrent. There is no other morpheme in English with a variation identical to that of the Past Participle. But the alternation in *tell* and *told* is identical to that of *sell* and *sold* both in the nature of the difference ([e] versus [əʊ]), and in the conditions under which the alternants appear: *tol-* and *sol-* before Past Tense and Past Participle (more widely than the *swoll-* of *swollen*), but *tell* and *sell* in the remainder of the paradigm.

In other cases an alternation is **phonologically** (or **phonemically**) conditioned. In all our Turkish examples, as we have seen, the conditions may be stated in terms of the vowel in the preceding syllable (whether Rounded or Unrounded, Front or Back), of the nature of the immediately following phoneme (whether vowel, in *kitab-ı*, or otherwise, in *kitap-lar*) and so on. It is not necessary to refer to the particular morphemes (e.g. the particular Nouns KÖY, SON, etc.) which form the environment in a grammatical or lexical sense. But one may also recognise a subsidiary distinction within the phonologically conditioned type. In the case of the Noun morphemes *kitap/kitab-, çocuk/çocuğ-,* etc., we mentioned that the pattern was not entirely regular. Among monosyllables, Absolute *çok* 'much' has a corresponding Accusative *çoğu*, and Absolute *gök* 'sky' has as one possibility the

Accusative *göğü*. But the normal pattern for monosyllables is that of *kök* 'root', Accusative *kökü*, and with the morpheme for 'sky' the Accusative may also be *gökü* instead (LEWIS, p. 10). Now we might define the **domain** of an alternation as the set of morphemes which exhibit it: so, for example, the English alternation between [ætʃ] and [ɔː] has as its domain the single morpheme CATCH, and (less trivially) the alternation now under discussion has a domain including çOK 'much' and çOCUK 'child', but excluding KÖK and others. In this case, therefore, we may go on to say that the domain is **lexically** (or, more generally, **morphemically**) **restricted**. Although the alternation itself is conditioned solely by phonological factors (position before a vowel, before a consonant, at the end of a word), we have to indicate specifically which morphemes enter into it and which do not.

For our remaining Turkish alternations the domain is un-restricted. Any non-initial morpheme with an allomorph in *e* in one set of paradigms will have an *a* in others, and vice versa. Any Close vowel in the allomorphs of such a morpheme will alternate between *i, ü, ı* and *u* under identical conditions. Any such allomorph beginning with *c, d* or *g* will alternate with another beginning with *ç, t* or *k*, and again vice versa. In such circumstances the alternation may be said to be **automatic**. The same rule holds automatically for any morpheme meeting the appropriate conditions (namely, those with allomorphs containing Close vowels, Open Unrounded vowels, and so on), in addition to applying automatically in any appropriate environment. A further point, for these examples at least, is that the variation is in some way forced by the phonological structure of words in general. 'Villages' must be *köyler* and 'ends' must be *sonlar* because, as we remarked, the alternatives *köylar* or *sonler* are not of a native Turkish shape. This is an important point, and we will return to it when we look more closely at the relation between morphology and phonology (chapter 8).

When a morpheme exhibits several different alternations we will naturally expect that some may be of one type and others of another. Among the English Past Participles, phonological factors alone determine that *swollen* is [swəʊlən] not [swəʊln̩]: in my speech, final syllabic nasals are normal after an alveolar plosive (e.g. *garden* [gɑːdn̩]) provided no other consonant precedes (e.g. *Eastern* [iːstən]), but not after the lateral [l] amongst others. The same rules in reverse determine that *begotten* is [bɪgɒtn̩] and not, in normal speech, [bɪgɒtən]. But the nasal as such is selected by the grammatical items specifically. Both types of alternation must therefore be stated in order to account for the allomorphs of Past Participle in general.

The same point can also be made for the alveolar alternants in *sailed*, *fished*, etc. But here the facts are a little more complex. Let us begin (the reason will appear directly) with the regular alternants of three other morphemes. One is the Plural morpheme in Nouns, whose usual forms were set out earlier in this chapter. The others are the Possessive morpheme in, for example, *John's* and the morpheme in Verbs traditionally called 3rd Singular Present. As we have noted already for the Plural, each of these has three forms which are phonetically [ɪz], [s] and [z]:

| | | |
|---|---|---|
| fishes [fɪʃɪz] | Chris's [krɪsɪz] | pushes [pʊʃɪz] |
| sticks [stɪks] | Pat's [pæts] | rips [rɪps] |
| seas [siːz] | John's [dʒɒnz] | cries [kraɪz] |

The alternation is also phonologically conditioned. If the preceding Noun form ends in a sibilant (as in the first row) the allomorph of each morpheme takes the form [ɪz]: examples with other sibilants are *batches* [bætʃɪz], *badges* [bædʒɪz] or *buzzes* [bʌzɪz]. If it ends with a voiceless consonant (other than a sibilant), the allomorph is [s]: other examples are *cliffs* [klɪfs], *Jack's* [dʒæks] or *deaths* [deθs]. Finally, if it ends with anything else (voiced non-sibilant or vowel) the allomorph is [z]. We may sum up by saying that all three alternants have an alveolar sibilant in common; if it is preceded by a sibilant in the Noun or Verb then it is voiced and separated by an intervening [i], but when anything else precedes it is simply voiced ([z]) or voiceless ([s]) as required.

If we now return to the Past Participle morpheme, we will find a very similar alternation among its *-ed* forms. In *waited* [weɪtɪd] the alveolar plosive is voiced ([d]) and is separated from a preceding alveolar plosive by the same vowel [ɪ]: so also in *faded* [feɪdɪd], where the preceding alveolar is [d] instead of [t]. After any other voiceless consonant it too is voiceless ([t]): for example, in *pushed* [pʊʃt] or *ripped* [rɪpt]. Likewise it too is voiced ([d]) in contexts such as those of *cried* [kraɪd], *hugged* [hʌgd], and so on. Apparently the same general pattern may be recognised in all four morphemes: Plural, Possessive and 3rd Present with a constant alveolar sibilant and Past Participle with constant alveolar plosive. The same pattern with the plosive also appears in the regular Past Tense allomorph: *I waited, I pushed, I cried.* So far, then, everything appears very neat. But what of the [t] in *I caught* and *I have caught*, in *I burned* and *I have burned* (which are both [bɜːnt] in my normal speech), in *learned* [lɜːnt] and so on? We cannot say that this is a further detail of phonological conditioning; if it was, why is *turned* phonetically [tɜːnd] (to the best of my knowledge, no English speaker says [tɜːnt]), or *cawed* phonetically [kɔːd] and not a homonym of *caught*?

The normal way of resolving this difficulty is to say that the [t] of *caught* or [bɜːnt] is an irregularity distinct from the [t] of *pushed* or *ripped*. The grammatically conditioned alternations of Past Participle will accordingly lie between a nasal [n̩] or [ən] in one group of cases, an inherently voiceless alveolar plosive [t] in another, and another alveolar plosive which is inherently neither voiced nor voiceless, but which alternates between [ɪd], [t] and [d] depending on circumstances. The advantage of this analysis is that within this third group strict phonological conditioning may again be maintained.

In handling this one morpheme, we are compelled to recognise a number of typologically different alternations among its allomorphs. But at the grammatical level it remains an identical unit throughout (Past Participle). The distinctions which we have drawn in this section will also be of value in the context of other models. But the basic notion, of the word split into units that are grammatically invariant but phonologically variable, is the heart of morpheme-based morphology.

## RELATED READING

The model expounded here is largely the creation of Harris and Hockett. For the distinction between segments and abstract units see Z. S. Harris, 'Morpheme alternants in linguistic analysis', *Lg* 18 (1942), pp. 169–80; for 'morph' and 'allomorph', C. F. Hockett, 'Problems of morphemic analysis', *Lg* 23 (1947), pp. 321–43: both reprinted, with other contemporary articles, in *RiL* (pp.

109–15, 229–42). For the distributional approach see HARRIS; but the motive is explained more clearly in his retrospective lectures, Z. S. Harris, *Language and Information* (New York, Columbia University Press, 1988). For the analysis of proportions compare LYONS, *Introduction*, pp. 182f. On the history of distributionalism see my 'Distributional syntax', in T. Bynon & F. R. Palmer (eds.), *Studies in the History of Western Linguistics* (Cambridge, Cambridge University Press, 1986), pp. 245–77; for the emergence of the American model generally see R. D. Huddleston, 'The development of a non-process model in American structural linguistics', *Lingua* 30 (1972), pp. 333–84.

Complementary and contrastive distribution are still central criteria in phonology: thus, for example, LASS, pp. 18ff.

The term 'morpheme' has a complex history and it is not always clear in what sense it is being used. In the work referred to here it is an abstract unit: in *sails*, Plural is realised or represented by [z], but the morpheme is not [z] itself. This view is developed most fully in a thirty-year-old article by C. F. Hockett, 'Linguistic elements and their relations', *Lg* 37 (1961), pp. 29–53. But in structural linguistics generally the morpheme is a minimal sign: thus for BLOOMFIELD, p. 161; also many of the European writers in, for example, *RiL II*. In this view, [z] in *sails* is a morpheme with the meaning 'more than one' (BLOOMFIELD's 'sememe', p. 162), or the semantic feature 'Plural'. Finally, in the French tradition 'morphème' tends to be reserved for grammatical as opposed to lexical units: thus, in particular, MARTINET, §1.9.

Present usage is confused. I do not find BAUER's definition (*Morphology*, p. 247) very helpful. In the history of generative grammar, Chomsky began with what was then the usual American concept: see CHOMSKY, *Structures*, p. 32 especially. But in later work, a 'formative' is represented in the lexicon by a pairing of a 'phonological distinctive feature matrix' with a 'collection of specified syntactic features': see N. Chomsky, *Aspects of the Theory of Syntax* (Cambridge, Mass., MIT Press, 1965), pp. 3 (formatives as minimal syntactic units), 84 (lexical entries). For 'formative' one might as well say 'morpheme', and that is what most followers of Chomsky now do. For a careful recent definition see WURZEL, p. 28: note that, like my 'formative' (chapters 4 and 7), Wurzel's morpheme is a formal unit that does not have to bear a consistent meaning (p. 29). For the morpheme as a minimal form see also Lyons's textbook: J. Lyons, *Language and Linguistics* (Cambridge, Cambridge University Press, 1981), p. 103. He too has shifted his account (compare LYONS, *Introduction*, pp. 183ff.).

My sources for the typology of alternations are quite old: see, in particular, R. S. Wells, 'Automatic alternation', *Lg* 25 (1949), pp. 99–116; also BLOOMFIELD, pp. 210f. (in the context of 'phonetic modification'); HARRIS, pp. 208–12, 220ff.; HOCKETT, *Course*, pp. 277ff. I have not seen recent accounts which add anything. For the morphology of the English Past Participle see PALMER, ch. 11.

See later chapters for defects of the morpheme-based model. But since it was in part a product of analytical procedures, it is worth referring to contemporary criticism, especially by Haas and Bazell: see W. Haas, 'On defining linguistic units', *TPhS* 1954, pp. 54–84 (general critique of Harris); C. E. Bazell, 'Phonemic and morphemic analysis', *Word* 8 (1952), pp. 33–8 (on false parallels between morphology and phonology).

In some recent work the term 'allomorphy' is restricted to alternations that cannot be brought under a productive rule: see, for example, R. Lieber, 'Allomorphy', *Linguistic Analysis* 10 (1982), pp. 27–52, for a definition in this sense and a discussion that is useful in the generative context.

# 7
# Morphological processes

Problems with irregular forms in English (*man*:*men*, *come*:*come*). 'Zero morphs'; the model works but its spirit is broken. An alternative model: morphological operations. Item and Arrangement vs Item and Process. *Inflectional formations.* Parallel with 'derivation'. Grammatical representation of words: lexemes vs features. Inflectional formatives; addition of formatives to roots and stems; semantic role of operations; link-up with the lexicon. Vowel-change as an operation (English *teeth*, etc.); sequences of operations (English *caught*). Inflectional classes: regular and exceptional processes. Identity operations. *Types of morphological process.* Lexical and inflectional processes. Affixation: base vs affix. Prefixation, suffixation, infixation; boundaries not always clear-cut. Reduplication, partial vs complete. Modification: vowel-change; patterns of vowel-change in Verbs in English. Direction of modifications: problems in Indo-European and in Arabic; in suppletion. Accentual and tonal modifications; 'superfixes'. Addition vs subtraction: problem of Adjectives in French.

We remarked in the last chapter that there were difficulties when the morphemic model was applied to English. What are the difficulties and how do we respond to them?

Let us return once more to two of the examples introduced in chapter 1. In

> That is no country for old men

*men* is Plural. Syntactically, a proportion such as

> man:men = sea:seas

is exact. But where *seas* and other regular Plurals have the ending -*s*, *men* has no ending. The distinction between *man* and *men* is marked differently, by a vowel change. Where then is the allomorph of the Plural morpheme? If *seas* is grammatically SEA + Plural, how can *men* be MAN + Plural? In

> And therefore I have sailed the seas and come

*come* is a Past Participle, just as *sailed* is a Past Participle. There is again a proportion:

> sail:sailed = come:come

But there is no formal difference between plain *come* and Past Participle *come*. If the latter is grammatically COME + Past Participle, where again is the allomorph of the morpheme Past Participle?

The 1940s and 1950s saw several desperate attempts to answer these and similar questions. In cases like *come*, the usual solution was to supply what was called a '**zero morph**'. Between *sailed* and *sail* the difference lies, as we said, in the ending. So, in terms of morphs, *sailed* is [seɪl] + [d]. Between *come* and *come* there is zero difference. So (the argument runs) the *come* of *have come* may be said to consist of a morph [kʌm] followed by a morph 'zero'. Just as in arithmetic we use two digits to represent the number '10' (symbolising a one in the 'tens' position plus zero in the 'units' position), so this word-form may be represented as *come* + o, symbolising *come* in the 'root' slot plus zero in the 'inflection' slot. Now in *sailed* the morph [d] is an allomorph of Past Participle. In the same way (it was argued) the 'o' of *come* + o was another allomorph of Past Participle.

Some scholars also posited a zero morph in cases like *men*. *Seas*, as we said, is SEA + Plural. That again establishes a 'root' slot and an 'inflection' slot. But now consider a Plural like *those*. Morphemically it is THAT + Plural; in terms of morphs it may be analysed into [ðəʊ] + [z], where the allomorph of THAT differs from the one found in the Singular. This analysis is like that of *caught* ([kɔː] + [t]) in the last chapter. But, as Plural [ðəʊ] is opposed to Singular [ðæt], so Plural [men] is opposed to Singular [mæn]. The only difference is that after [men] the 'inflection' slot is empty. Or, to put it another way, the inflection is zero. Just as *come* is [kʌm] + o, so *men* is [men] + o. The first morph, [men], is an allomorph of the morpheme MAN; the second, 'o', is the allomorph of Plural.

These accounts were never universally accepted, even within the North American school, whose model this was. Forty years later, one is tempted to consign them entirely to the dustbin of history. Nevertheless, the arguments are still instructive. For what we have here is a classic instance of an analysis which preserves the letter of a model perfectly. But it does so at the expense of its spirit. To restore the spirit, we need a new model.

Let us begin with *come*. What we want to say, and what we did in fact say when this example was first discussed, is that 'Past Participle' is not marked. But to say that something is not marked is one thing; to say that it is marked by zero is another. Suppose that I am walking down a road in search of someone's house. I have been told that every other house has got a front gate, whereas theirs has not. In that case it would make sense to say that it is 'marked' by the absence of a front gate. Similarly, in morphology, it makes sense to say that *sail* is marked by the absence of an ending, in opposition to *sailed*, *sailing* and *sails*. If we like, *sail* is marked by zero. But then suppose that I am looking for a house with such and such a number. I find that numbers 1 and 2 have '1' and '2' on their gate, but numbers 3 and 4 have nothing. It makes sense to say that the last two are 'not marked'. It does not make sense to say that they are marked by 'zero forms' of their numbers. Similarly, in linguistics, it does not make sense to say that *come* in *have come* is marked by a zero form of Past Participle.

Now let us return to *men*. What we want to say – and what again we did say – is that Plural is marked by the vowel [e], in opposition to [æ]. But the solution proposed does not say that. If treating [kʌm] as an allomorph of COME is to say that it marks the Verb, treating [men] as an allomorph of MAN is to say that all it does, [e] included, is mark the Noun. If the zero morph of *come* is a device for saying that a morpheme Past Participle is not marked, a zero morph in *men* must be interpreted similarly as saying that Plural is not marked. But that is the opposite of what we wanted to say. It is like pretending that number 3 is marked by a zero '3' on its gate when in fact there is a real '3' nailed to a tree alongside.

To repeat, the letter of the model is not broken. *Sailed* and *come*, *seas* and *men* are assigned to the same grammatical construction. Each has a sequence of morphemes and a sequence of morphs corresponding to them. But the whole point of representing words in that way was that the successive morphemes, in such forms as *sailed* or *seas* or in the Turkish examples of chapter 6, are marked or identified by their successive allomorphs. In neither *come* nor *men* can the presence of Past Participle or Plural be indicated by something that is not there.

These forms are exceptions and, in seeking an alternative model, we must take care that the tail does not wag the dog. But consider again a form like *seas*. Qua form, it is [siː] plus [z]; that no one will dispute. Nor will anyone dispute that, as a whole, it is syntactically Plural. But it does not follow that it is syntactically a sequence of two elements ('SEA + Plural'). That is merely one form of representation; and, if it is alright for most Plurals, the exceptions, as we have just seen, raise problems. Let us therefore say no more about the syntax of this form than we strictly must say. We have to say that, as a whole, it is Plural. We have to say that, in the terms of chapter 2, it is a form of the lexeme SEA. But that is already enough to distinguish it from every other word in the language. In the traditional formula, it is simply 'the Plural of SEA'.

Now let us consider not the form [siːz], but the relation between it and its component form [siː]. It is natural to describe this as an operation: as *sea* is to *seas*, so *arm* is to *arms*, *tree* to *trees*, *table* to *tables*, and so on. Thus, in general, $X$ (where $X$ is a variable) → $X + [z]$. The operation forms Plurals; and, by that token, the ending [z], which it adds, is a Plural marker. But operations do not have to add endings. In the same way, we can say that [men] is derived from [mæn] by an operation which replaces the vowel. This too forms a Plural; so, the resulting vowel [e] is another Plural marker. Nor do all forms have to undergo a change. The relation between *sailed* and *sail* will be mediated by an operation ($X → X + [d]$). It derives Past Participles; so, in *have sailed*, [d] will be described as a Past Participle marker. But for *come* in *have come* the relation is one of identity. In that way, Past Participle is described as having no marker.

Nor, finally, is it necessary that a word should be derived by one operation only. Consider again a form like *caught* in *have caught*. In terms of morphemes, we assumed that this consisted of [kɔː], representing CATCH, plus [t], representing Past Participle. By implication, [t] alone marked the inflectional morpheme, while [kɔː] marked only the lexical morpheme. But in reality the difference between *caught* and *catch* is made by both [ɔː] and [t]. Let us therefore think afresh in terms of operations. We might derive *caught* in two stages, first changing [kætʃ] to [kɔː], then adding [t]. Both operations contribute to the Past Participle. Therefore, in *have caught*, the forms supplied by both are defined as markers of Past Participle.

The model of chapter 6 is often referred to as the '**Item and Arrangement**' model. Its basic feature is that words are built up of arrangements of morphemes. A model based on processes has been called, perhaps less felicitously, an '**Item and Process**' model. Its advantage for English is precisely that it allows all forms, both regular and exceptional, to be described naturally and consistently.

## INFLECTIONAL FORMATIONS

How then do we formulate it? The answer is in part contained in the title of this section. In chapter 4 we dealt with what are commonly called 'derivational' formations. For example, the Agentive ACTOR (form *actor*) was derived from the Verb ACT (*act*). We are now concerned with **inflectional formations**. *Sailed*, for example, illustrates a regular formation of the Past Tense and Past Participle. *Come* in *have come* represents an irregular formation.

Let us begin with the grammatical representation of words. *Seas*, for example, has two properties: (a) it is Plural; (b) it is a form of SEA. In a notation which is widely established, properties or features of a unit are listed vertically between square brackets. To say that *seas* is the Plural of SEA is thus to say, in this notation, that it has the representation:

$$\begin{bmatrix} \text{Plural} \\ \text{SEA} \end{bmatrix}$$

Similarly, *sailed* in *I have sailed* will be represented as

$$\begin{bmatrix} \text{Past Participle} \\ \text{SAIL} \end{bmatrix}$$

while in *I sailed* it is:

$$\begin{bmatrix} \text{Past Tense} \\ \text{SAIL} \end{bmatrix}$$

Now let us turn to the operations. To form *seas* the operation will add [z]. In its formal aspect, therefore, we may represent it like this:

$$X \rightarrow X + [z]$$

$X$ being again a variable with the possible values [si:], [ɑːm] (in *arms*) and so on. As in chapter 4, the operation adds a **formative**; in the case of inflectional formations, it is an **inflectional formative**. The form to which it applies is, by our earlier definitions, either a root or a stem. A **root** was defined in chapter 4 as a form that underlies at least one paradigm or partial paradigm, and is itself morphologically simple. So, in *seas*, the operation adds [z] to the root [si:]. A **stem** was defined as a form that underlies at least one paradigm or partial paradigm, but is itself morphologically complex. For example, in *generations* the operation adds [z] to the stem [dʒenəˈreɪʃn]. In the case of Verbs, an operation

$$X \rightarrow X + [d]$$

similarly adds an inflectional formative [d] to roots like [seɪl] and stems like, for example, [ˈdʒenərəlaɪz] (*generalise*).

But the formations also have a semantic aspect. In the case of *seas*, the operation applies to Nouns and it specifically derives the Plural. We may therefore expand its representation in this form:

$$\begin{bmatrix} \text{Plural} \\ X \end{bmatrix}_N \rightarrow X + [z]$$

where the part of speech is again shown by a subscripted 'N'. The forms to which it can apply are obtained by supplying possible values for $X$. One such form is, formally and semantically:

$$\begin{bmatrix} \text{Plural} \\ \text{[si:]} \end{bmatrix}_N$$

It is then changed in the way shown, all else staying constant. The result, accordingly, is:

$$\begin{bmatrix} \text{Plural} \\ \text{[si: + z]} \end{bmatrix}_N$$

Similarly, an operation

$$\left[\begin{matrix} \left\{\begin{matrix} \text{Past Participle} \\ \text{Past Tense} \end{matrix}\right\} \\ X \end{matrix}\right]_V \rightarrow X + [d]$$

(braces indicating that it is valid either for Past Participles or Past Tenses) will apply to

$$\left[\begin{matrix} \text{Past Participle} \\ [\text{seɪl}] \end{matrix}\right]_V$$

deriving:

$$\left[\begin{matrix} \text{Past Participle} \\ [\text{seɪl} + \text{d}] \end{matrix}\right]_V$$

Finally, the values of $X$ must be supplied by a lexicon. The entry for SEA must indicate, among other things, that it has a root [siː]. So, our initial form

$$\left[\begin{matrix} \text{Plural} \\ [\text{siː}] \end{matrix}\right]_N$$

is obtained, more precisely, by substituting root for lexeme in the purely grammatical representation:

$$\left[\begin{matrix} \text{Plural} \\ \text{SEA} \end{matrix}\right]_N$$

The entry for SAIL must similarly indicate that it has a root [seɪl]. For complex lexemes such as GENERATION and GENERALISE stems will be derived by the lexical processes of chapter 4. For compound lexemes such as BLACKBIRD or OVERGENERALISE the roots or stems of the component lexemes will be combined by those of chapter 5.

These are regular formations, as we said. What then of the exceptions? Let us take for illustration the formation of *teeth*, *geese* and *feet*. Formally, the operation changes the vowel of the root ([tuːθ], [fʊt], [guːs]) to [iː]. So, one way to represent it would be like this:

$$C\ V\ C \rightarrow C\ [iː]\ C$$

$C$ being any consonant, $V$ being any vowel. Grammatically, it forms Plurals; but with the limitation that it is valid only for TOOTH, FOOT and GOOSE. Let us therefore assign these to a class, mnemonically the class '$\bar{I}$'. The process as a whole may then be shown as follows:

$$\begin{bmatrix} \text{Plural} \\ \bar{I} \\ C\ V\ C \end{bmatrix}_N \rightarrow C\ [iː]\ C$$

In words – since, in these notations, we are still saying nothing that cannot be said quite clearly in plain English – the Plural of Nouns in class $\bar{I}$ is formed by changing the vowel to [iː].

Now let us return to *caught*. We suggested that it might be derived by two operations: first [kætʃ] → [kɔː], then [kɔː] → [kɔː + t]. In that respect, CATCH would resemble other Verbs like THINK (first stage [θɪŋk] → [θɔː]), BUY or BRING. The first operation could then be as follows:

$$\begin{bmatrix} \left\{ \begin{array}{l} \text{Past Participle} \\ \text{Past Tense} \end{array} \right\} \\ \bar{ɔ} \\ C_n X \end{bmatrix}_V \rightarrow C_n\ [ɔː]$$

'$\bar{ɔ}$' symbolises the class CATCH, THINK and so on; $C_n$ = any sequence of consonants; $X$ is again anything. The form derived by this would then be extended by the second operation:

$$\begin{bmatrix} \left\{ \begin{array}{l} \text{Past Participle} \\ \text{Past Tense} \end{array} \right\} \\ T \\ X \end{bmatrix}_V \rightarrow X + [t]$$

'T' is here a larger class, including other Verbs like LEARN, whose Past Tense and Past Participle ([lɜːn + t]) will be formed by this operation only.

In these formations, $\bar{I}$, $\bar{ɔ}$ and T are **inflectional classes**. They are classes of lexemes that go together in respect of some inflection; and, in the case of exceptions or irregular formations, they must be specified. But let us now reflect on what we mean by the term '**regular**'. To say that a form has a regular inflection is to say that it has the inflection one would expect unless one knew that it was different. Suppose, for example, that there is a Noun '*glud*' which I have not heard previously. Unless I am given some indication to the contrary, I will assume that its Plural is *gluds*, with the regular inflection of *seas*. Or suppose that a child learns the lexeme MAN in the Singular. It will naturally form a Plural *mans*, unless or until it has learned *men* and can make the connection. For this reason we have not specified the inflectional class for regular formations. The dictionary will say that TOOTH belongs to class Ī, CATCH to both class Ɔ and class T, and so on. These are the exceptions, and irregular processes apply. The regular processes simply apply for every lexeme that is NOT an exception.

We can now return to one final case, which was illustrated earlier with Past Participle *come*. This is identical to the root and, if that were all, we would establish no formation for it. But it is an exception to the regular formation of *sailed*. We must therefore describe it by an operation which makes no change:

$$\begin{bmatrix} \text{Past Participle} \\ \text{o} \\ \text{X} \end{bmatrix}_{\text{v}} \rightarrow \text{X}$$

'o' being a class with at least the members COME, RUN and BECOME. In ordinary language, the Past Participle of Verbs in class o are formed identically to the root.

## TYPES OF MORPHOLOGICAL PROCESS

The operations which we have posited, in this chapter and earlier in chapter 4, may be described collectively as **morphological processes**. *Generations*, for example, is derived by two processes, one lexical and one inflectional. But the examples which we have chosen for illustration can give no impression of the rich variety of morphological processes to be found in different languages. So far in this chapter we have met with two main types: the addition of an independent formative (in such forms as *seas* or *sailed*), and an internal change involving one or more phonemes (in, for example, *teeth* and *caught*). But other languages have types of process that we do not find in English. The 'reduplications' in, for example, Greek and Latin are just one that will be familiar to some readers. A detailed typology might arguably be too tedious for this kind of book. But it will be useful to consider at least the main distinctions that are logically possible.

The first major division is between processes of addition or **affixation** (for example, the affixation of -*t* in *caught*) and all the remainder. Affixation is defined by two characteristics. Firstly, the form which results from the operation – we may call this the derived form – will consist of the **base** – the form that the operation applies to – plus an additional morpheme. So, for instance, *caught* consists of the base *caugh-* plus the inflectional morpheme -*t*. Secondly, the form which is added (the **affix**) will be constant; it will be the same whatever particular base the operation applies to. So, once more, the affixation of -*t* in *caught* or *bought* may be represented as follows:

$$X \to X + t$$

where '*X*' stands for any of the possible bases *caugh-*, *brough-*, *taugh-*, *burn-*, *fel-* (in *felt*), etc. and, regardless of their specific phonetic form, the same constant [t] is added to them all.

Processes of affixation may then be divided into **prefixation**, **suffixation** or **infixation**, depending on whether the affix is added before the base, after it, or at some determined point within it. By the same token, the affix itself may be a **prefix**, a **suffix**, or an **infix**. In English the commonest processes are those of suffixation: they are involved in most lexical derivations (*generate* → *generate* + *ion* = *generation*, *happy* → *happy* + *ness* = *happiness*, and so on) and in most inflectional formations (*sail* → *sail* + *ed*, *sea* → *sea* + *s*, etc.). Examples of prefixation are found, however, in the Negative formations of *happy* → *un* + *happy* – schematically:

$$X \to un + X$$

– or of *order* → *dis* + *order*. The English tendency to suffixation continues a characteristic of Indo-European which has substantially resisted change through the millennia. But outside Europe there are other families where prefixation predominates.

The following, for example, is a fragment of a Verbal paradigm in Navaho:[1]

|  | Imperfective | Optative |
|---|---|---|
| *1st Sg.* | di-ʃ-bááh | d-ó-ʃ-bááh |
| *3rd Sg.* | di-bááh | d-ó-bááh |

(acute accent = high tone) in which a root *-bááh* is accompanied by three prefixes. The first prefix *d(i)-* is part of the lexical morphology: *d(i)…bááh* as a whole means 'to start off for war'. In the second column *ó-* is a form of the Optative prefix: *d-ó-ʃ-bááh* 'would that I were starting off for war'. In the first row, *ʃ-* is the 1st Sg. prefix: *di-ʃ-bááh* 'I start off for war'. By contrast, Imperfective and 3rd Sg. are unmarked. Inflection by prefixes is characteristic of the Athapaskan family of North America, to which Navaho belongs.

An example of infixation is provided by a handful of Present or Imperfective forms in Latin. In *rupit* 'broke' or *ruptum* 'broken' we can establish a root [rup]; in the first form its vowel is lengthened (phonologically this had a long vowel, [ruːp]-), and in the second the first operation would be one which suffixes [t] ([rupt]-). Similarly, for example, [wiːdit] 'saw' is derived in part by lengthening the vowel in a root [wid], and *sectum* 'cut' by suffixing *-t* to *sec-*. But in *rumpit* 'breaks' a nasal consonant (written *m* before the bilabial *p*) is inserted after the vowel *u*. Similarly, in *fundit* 'pours', a consonant which at this level we can again characterise by the single feature 'nasal' is infixed within a root [fud]: compare, for example, [fuːdit] 'poured'. Such forms are exceptions – there is no nasal in, for example, the words for 'sees' or 'cuts' – but for a small class of lexemes (RUMPO 'break', FUNDO 'pour', …) the infix is a constant feature.

The boundary between infixation and prefixation or suffixation is not always as simple, however, as a neat typological definition may suggest. Firstly, the same morphological element may be introduced 'infixally' in some instances, but as an apparent 'suffix' or 'prefix' in others. Thus in Latin a nasal is also added in the Present *sinit* 'allows'; compare, for the root, the Participle

---

[1] See E. Sapir & H. Hoijer, *The Phonology and Morphology of the Navaho Language* (Berkeley/Los Angeles, University of California Press, 1967). The examples cited are on pp. 27 and 41.

*situm* 'allowed'. But, unlike *rup-* or *fud-*, the root *si-* has no final consonant; therefore, since the nasal is inserted before such a consonant where there is one (*rup* → *ru* + nasal + *p*, *fud* → *fu* + nasal + *d*), here it is simply added as if it were a suffix (*si* → *si* + nasal). To cover both possibilities, we may represent the operation as follows:

$$X \; V \; (C) \rightarrow X \; V \; \text{nasal} \; (C)$$

where the brackets around '*C*' indicate that this variable may or may not be present. As an operation, this is more complex than the straightforward suffixation of *-t* in *ruptum*, *sectum* or *situm*:

$$X \rightarrow X + t$$

But in *sinit* and *situm* their effects are similar (*si-* → *si-n-*, *si-* → *si-t-*).

Secondly, some confusion might arise from the order in which successive processes are applied. In our examples from Navaho, *d(i)-*, *ʃ-* and *ó-* precede the root *-báah*, and in that sense they are all prefixes. But *d(i)-* is lexical, whereas the others are inflectional. It might therefore be argued that the first operation which applies to each of these forms is the prefixation of *d(i)-*: this gives us the 'theme' (as it is called) *d(i)-báah*. Subsequent operations insert *-ó-* and *-ʃ-* within the theme, and in that sense these are infixes. The issue is of no substantive importance, but different descriptions might easily lead to discrepancies between the typologies proposed by one investigator or another.

In all processes of affixation, as we have said, the form which is derived consists of the base plus an added constant: in infixation the internal structure of the base is also broken into, whereas in prefixation and suffixation it is left intact. However, there are other processes of 'addition' in which the form added is directly determined (wholly or in part) by the form of the base itself. The following, for example, is a set of partial Verb forms in Ancient Greek:

| | *Future* | *Perfective Active* |
|---|---|---|
| 'strike' | pai-s- | pe-pai-k- |
| 'love' | pʰilɛ:-s- | pe-pʰilɛ:-k- |
| 'order' | keleu-s- | ke-keleu-k- |
| 'heap up' | kʰɔ:-s- | ke-kʰɔ:-k- |

which will in turn serve as the bases for complete forms such as *paísɔː* 'I will strike' and *pépaika* 'I have struck', *pʰilɛ́ːsɔː* 'I will love' and *pepʰílɛːka* 'I have loved', *keleúsɔː* 'I will order' and *kekéleuka* 'I have ordered', *kʰɔ́ːsɔː* 'I will heap up' and *kékʰɔːka* 'I have heaped up'.[2] In analysing these forms, we will find that the Futures are formed by the suffixation of *-s* and the Perfectives in part by the suffixation of *-k* (*pai-* → *pai-s-*, *pai-* → *pai-k-*, and so on). However, the Perfectives also have a regular 'prefixal' element – schematically *Ce* – in which the consonant (*C*) varies in harmony with the initial consonant of the root. If the latter is a labial then the 'prefixal' consonant is also a labial (*pepaik-*, *pepʰilɛːk-*; also, e.g., *be-bíɔː-k-a* 'I have lived'); if velar then it is also velar (*kekeleuk-*, *kekʰɔːk-*; also, e.g., *ge-gámɛː-k-a* 'I [a man] have married [so-and-so]'). If the root consonant is a voiced plosive, the prefixed consonant is also voiced (*bebiɔːk-*, *gegamɛːk-*); if a voiceless plosive (aspirated or unaspirated) it is voiceless unaspirated. The same principle extends throughout the consonant inventory: thus if the root begins with *l*, the prefixed form is likewise *le-* (e.g. *lé-ly-k-a* 'I have unfastened'), and so on. In the broadest terms the *e* of the prefix is constant, but the *C* simply 'repeats' the relevant features of the root initial.

Processes of 'repetition' are generally referred to under the heading of **reduplication**. In Ancient Greek, then, a process which may be represented in a very schematic form like this:

$$C^1X \to C^2e\,C^1X$$

(*C²* is in principle identical with *C¹*, but with qualifications for *pepʰilɛːk-* not *pʰepʰilɛːk-* and others) is a reduplicative operation forming part – though only part – of the formation of Perfects. In this case the reduplication also includes a constant element (*e*); furthermore, it is **partial** (in the sense that only part of the base is reduplicated), and it is prefixal and initial (in the sense that the reduplicative form is added before the base and it is the beginning of the base which is repeated). But reduplication without constants is very common, as in some Latin examples (see below).

---

[2] I will cite Ancient Greek in a form which indicates the phonology of the vowels, in particular, in classical Attic, and not in the standard transliteration.

It is also possible to have **complete reduplication** – schematically:

$$X \rightarrow X + X$$

Again, one can have suffix-like forms (forms following the base) which result from processes of final reduplication (repetition of the end of the base). One can also have cases of infixal reduplication, in which the structure of the base itself is again broken into, and moreover in such cases the reduplicated material might conceivably originate initially, medially or finally. Even in cases of complete reduplication one could decide from the general pattern of the language that it was prefixal in one case and suffixal in another.

However, it would be unwise to insist too far on this kind of logic-chopping detail. In Latin there are a handful of Perfects which are also formed with reduplication: for example, *cu-curr-i* 'I ran', *mo-mord-i* 'I have bitten', or *fe-fell-i* 'I deceived'. So far we have the same effect as in Ancient Greek, except that a back vowel in the root (*curr-*, *mord-*) is also reduplicated (*cu-curr-*, *mo-mord-*). But there are three other examples which might, in isolation, be assigned to different categories. The first is an effectively complete reduplication of the root of DO 'give': *d- →* *ded-* with *e* intervening (compare *dedi* 'I gave'). In fact this is the same process as in *fefelli*; however, just as the *-n* of *sin-* was 'suffixed' in the absence of a final consonant (see above), so the reduplication of one element appears 'complete' if, it so happens, it is the only element present. The other two examples concern the roots of SPONDEO 'pledge, pledge oneself' and STO 'stand', both of which begin with an *s* + plosive cluster. For the former one could strictly say that the reduplication is infixal and medial: *spond- → spo-po-nd-*, with repetition of the *-po-* (compare *spopondi* 'I pledged'). For the latter one might even say that it was suffixal: *st- → st-et-*, with repetition of *t* and again an intervening *e* (thus *steti* 'I stood'). But it seems better to treat them all as reflexes of a single operation – one which might perhaps be shown schematically as follows:

$$(s) \, C^1 \, (V^1) \, (X) \rightarrow (s) \, C^2 \, V^2 \, C^1 \, (V^1) \, (X)$$

($C^2 = C^1$, $V^2$ variously = either *e* or $V^1$). The unity of this process is not impugned by its apparently differing effects in differing types of instance.

The last major category of morphological processes are those which involve a **modification** (either total or partial) of the base itself. In English the partial modification of *man* to *men* is an obvious example; another is the more extensive change in *catch* → *caugh-* or *teach* → *taugh-*. In Latin, we have already referred to a process of vowel lengthening in, for example, *rupit* [ru:pit]. The possible subdivisions of this type are very numerous, and can profitably be distinguished by phonetic as well as purely logical criteria. In addition, sundry particular terms – such as the German 'Ablaut' (see below) and 'Umlaut' (see the end of chapter 9) – are conventionally employed for particular classes of operation in particular languages or groups. To survey them all would be a tour through a curiosity shop. We will therefore restrict ourselves to a handful of theoretically interesting or problematic instances.

The case of **vowel change** may be illustrated with a plethora of particular instances in English, only a few of which have been mentioned earlier. Thus [æ] → [e] in *men*, [ɪ] → [æ] in *sang* and [ʌ] in *sung*, [u:] → [ɒ] (as in *shoot* → *shot*), [aʊ] → [aɪ] (as in *mouse* → *mice*), conversely [aɪ] → [aʊ] (as in *find* → *found*), and so on. In grammars these are usually described, as here, in terms of individual phonemes; many of them are accordingly of very limited application. But when we study them further we will sometimes find that two or more apparently different processes involve the same phonetic features. Let us begin, for example, with the change in *get* → *got* (also, with the further addition of -*en*, in *beget* → *begotten*). In the system of short vowels in English:

|       | Front | Back |
|-------|-------|------|
| Close | ɪ     | ʊ    |
| Mid   | e     | ɒ    |
| Open  | æ     | ʌ    |

the vowel of *got* is, it will be seen, the Back equivalent of the Front vowel in *get*. We might therefore state this operation, in its most general form, as:

Front → Back

But now consider two further operations, one in, for example, *find*
→ *found* and the other in *break* → *broke*. In the system of 'closing'
long vowels and diphthongs (closing towards cardinal 1 if Front,
towards cardinal 8 if Back):

|       | Front | Back |
|-------|-------|------|
| Close | iː    | uː   |
| Mid   | eɪ    | əʊ   |
| Open  | aɪ    | aʊ   |

the diphthongs [aʊ] in *found* and [əʊ] in *broke* are similarly the
Back equivalents of [aɪ] and [eɪ]. In terms of features, these too are
the same process. We might also consider the change in *wear* →
*wore* (also *bear* → *bore*). One possibility would be to group this
with *catch* → *caugh-*, etc. as, in general, a change resulting in [ɔː].
But it might also be grouped with *get* → *got*, etc., since [ɔː]
(phonetically [ɔə] for many speakers) is, in another system of long
vowels and diphthongs, the Back counterpart of [eə]. The English
strong Verbs form a tangled network of proportional similarities,
and both groupings are probably valid.

Other generalisations can be made within the same schema of
oppositions. For example, upwards of twenty Verbs show a
change of [iː] to [e], either accompanied by the non-alternating
suffix *-t* (as *feel* → *fel-t*) or in a root which itself ends in either a *d*
or a *t* (*breed* → *bred* or *meet* → *met*). In terms of the vowel systems
this is a change from Front Close in the 'Closing' set ([iː]) to
Front Mid in the Short. However, *lose* → *los-t* and *shoot* → *shot*
show an identical change with Back instead of Front: Close [uː] in
the 'Closing' system → Mid [ɒ] in the Short. Again, therefore, it
would be possible to establish a single operation – or two
successive operations of 'shortening' and 'lowering' – which
would cover both. Of course, one must not pursue this à outrance.
At some point in these Verbal patterns even the most determined
generaliser will begin to feel that his generalisations are capturing
nothing that has any bearing on the maintenance of the processes.
But the major groupings are historically important.

In postulating vowel change or any other sort of 'change' one
has to check that the direction of the process can be justified.
Why, that is, do we derive *x* from *y* instead of *y* from *x*? In our
English examples the main reason will be obvious. In cases of

affixation, the Past Tense and Participle are regularly derived from the Present (or from a root identical with the Present – see earlier in this chapter); we therefore preserve the pattern by writing *get → got*, *break → broke* or *broken*, etc., and not *broke → break* and *breaks* or *got → get*. In the case of *catch → caugh-* or *teach → taugh-* the pattern is confirmed by the nature of the process. For if the Presents were formed from a root in [ɔ:], we would need a separate operation – [ɔ:] → [ætʃ], [ɔ:] → [i:tʃ], [ɔ:] → [ɪŋ] (in *bring*), and so on – for each instance. The process can be generalised in one direction, but not in the other.

Sometimes, however, it is not obvious that any direction can be justified. The processes in the Germanic strong Verb (which we have just illustrated from English) are in part a reflex of a regular pattern in Indo-European, by which a root will have an *e* in some forms, an *o* in others, and in others no corresponding vowel at all. A transparent inflectional example is provided by the forms for 'leave' and for 'see' (in a poetic style) in Ancient Greek:

| 1st *Sg. Present* | 1st *Sg. Perfect* | 1st *Sg. Aorist* |
|---|---|---|
| leíp-ɔ: | lé-loip-a | é-lip-on |
| dérk-o-mai | dé-dork-a | é-drak-on |

in which the stems vary between *leip-*, *loip-* and *lip-* in one case and *derk-*, *dork-* and *drk-* (> *drak-* by sound change) in the other. The same variation also played a rôle in the relationships of Nouns and Verbs: for example, Latin *fīdō* (< *feid-*) 'I put trust in', *foedus* (< *foid-*) 'treaty' and *fides* (< *fid-*) 'faith'.

In explaining this pattern in his *Introduction*, Meillet most happily compares it to another pattern in Semitic.[3] The following, for example, are the 3rd Singular Masculines of the Simple Perfective and Imperfective ('he *X*ed' versus 'he *X*es, will *X*') for three Verbs in Egyptian Colloquial Arabic:[4]

|  | *Perfective* | *Imperfective* |
|---|---|---|
| 'write' | kátab | yí-ktib |
| 'ask' | ṭálab | yú-ṭlub |
| 'understand' | fíhim | yí-fham |

[3] A. Meillet, *Introduction à l'étude comparative des langues indo-européennes*, 7th edn (Paris, Klincksieck, 1937), pp. 153f.
[4] Examples from T. F. Mitchell, *Colloquial Arabic* (London, Teach Yourself Books, 1962), pp. 36 and 72f. I have followed Mitchell's orthography but conflated the back and front variants of *a*.

from which it will be seen that the only elements in common to each pair are a skeleton of consonants (*C-C-C*) with the value *k-t-b* in the first, *t-l-b* in the second, and *f-h-m* in the third. The grammatical difference is then made partly by a prefix in the Imperfective (basically *y-* with *i* or *u* following), but otherwise by a variation in the pattern of vowels and syllabification: *CaCaC* or *CiCiC* in the Perfective versus Imperfective *-CCiC*, *CCuC* or *-CCaC*. Further patterns of vowel variation also appear in the lexical morphology or in the Singulars and Plurals of Nouns. For example, with the same skeleton *k-t-b* (as for 'write') we have the forms *kitáab* 'book', *kútub* 'books', *káatib* 'clerk', *kátaba* 'clerks', the Passive Participle *ma-ktúub* 'written', and so on.

What would be the direction of the processes in these examples? The practice of specialists would certainly imply that there is none. Indo-Europeanists will simply talk of the *e*-grade, the *o*-grade and the zero, weak or reduced grade of a given root (e.g. the root *derk-/dork-/drk-*). In referring to the phenomenon in general they will talk of 'vowel alternations' (Meillet, *Introduction*) or of 'Ablaut' (the German term adopted by Grimm for the Germanic reflexes in particular).[5] A Semitist will say that our Arabic roots are simply the consonantal skeletons *k-t-b*, *t-l-b* or *f-h-m* – not, for example, either *-ktib* ('becomes' *katab*, *kitaab*, etc.), or *katab*, or any other form with a specific vowel and syllable pattern. The triconsonantal *k-t-b* is the best base for all the variants. In this sense neither Indo-European nor Arabic would have directional 'vowel change' of the sort exemplified for English.

Directionality can also be a problem in the case of total modification (usually called **suppletion**). For English *go → went* it may seem obvious why we write it that way rather than as *went* (or *wen-*) → *go*; we have the pattern of suffixation also found in *mean-t* [ment], and the only additional detail is that in this case *go* is changed completely. But is it so obvious why we should write either? In Ancient Greek the Verb for 'bear' or 'carry' formed its Present as in *pʰér-ɔ* 'I carry', its Future as in *oís-ɔ* 'I will carry' and, for example, its Aorist as in *é:neŋk-a*. Clearly, there is suppletion, but nevertheless in neither the Future nor the Aorist is the form before the hyphens morphologically simple. The

[5] J. Grimm, *Deutsche Grammatik*, I (1819), p. 10 (p. 8 in the more accessible edition (Berlin, 1870)).

Future *ois-* (the accent need not concern us) consists of *oi-* plus the Future suffix *-s* which we have already seen in regular forms such as *paí-s-ɔ:* 'I will strike'. The Aorist begins with a long vowel which is found in other forms where the root begins with *e*: we can therefore see *ɛ:neŋk-* as derived from *eneŋk-*. This leaves what would be seen in 'Item and Arrangement' terms as an alternation between *pʰer-*, *oi-* and *-eneŋk-*; does it help to say anything more? Coming back to *went*, we might say that this is *wen-* plus the suffix *-t* which we have already established in forms such as *burnt* or *felt*. Do we then gain anything by talking of *go* being modified to *wen-*? Would it not be clearer to speak, IN THE DICTIONARY, of a **suppletive alternation** between two different roots?

Dictionary treatment will not do, of course, for our problems in Cairene Arabic or Indo-European. There are undoubtedly general processes to be stated. But do they necessarily belong to the category of modification with which we started? If the root is simply *k-t-b* then *katab*, for example, is that PLUS (as it were) a broken or two part infix *-a-a-*. According to many linguists the process would not be one of change or alteration of the operand, but rather a special instance of affixation, involving what has sometimes been called a 'discontinuous morph' (or morpheme realised 'discontinuously'). Likewise in Greek *dérk-o-mai* and *dé-dork-a* we might say that the root is strictly *drk-*, the so-called '*e* grade' and '*o* grade' being derived by infixation of *-e-* and *-o-* respectively. Indo-Europeanists do not speak in these terms, but one can imagine some typologist insisting (on strictly logical grounds) that they should.

Another important type of modification involves an accent or a tonal pattern. In some cases, this is in close association with a process of affixation. For example, in Italian *canta* 'sings' the stress is on the root (*cánta*); we will take this as its basic position. But in the Imperfect *cantava* 'was singing' it shifts to the vowel immediately preceding the Imperfect suffix *-va* (*cantá-va*). This shift always accompanies the suffix (compare, for instance, the 3rd Plural *cantá-va-no*). But in the 1st and 2nd Plurals the accent is then shifted again to the vowel immediately before the suffixes which mark these categories: *canta-vá-mo* 'we were singing', *canta-vá-te* 'you (Pl.) were singing'. These suffixes too are ones which always require the stress in that position: compare, for instance, the Presents *cantiámo* 'we sing' and *cantáte*. In such cases, the accentual modification can be seen as a direct repercussion of the process of suffixation. There are similar instances in English word-formation: for example, in *generátion* or *automátion* the stress changes from its position in the bases *génerate* and *áutomate* to the syllable before the suffix *-ion*.

In other cases, an accent or tonal pattern functions on its own. The following, for example, are a selection of Verbs and derived Nominals in Birom, a language of northern Nigeria:

|          | *Verb* | *Nominal* |
|----------|--------|-----------|
| 'surpass'| dàl    | dál       |
| 'break'  | mɔ̀pɔ̀s | mɔ́pɔ́s    |
| 'follow' | ra:    | rá:       |
| 'roast'  | halaŋ  | hálàŋ     |
| 'see'    | dí     | dí        |
| 'run'    | télé   | télé      |

In the first column, *dàl* and *mɔ̀pɔ̀s* have distinctively Low tones, *ra:* and *halaŋ* have Mid tones, and *dí* and *télé* have High tones. But whatever the tones of the Verb, the Nominals have High tones. Therefore *dàl* and *mɔ̀pɔ̀s* → *dál* and *mɔ́pɔ́s*; *ra:* and *halaŋ* → *rá:* and *háláŋ*; *dí* and *télé*, which already have High tones, are unchanged. This rule holds for all monosyllables, and for all disyllables except one where the first syllable has a higher tone than the second. In that case, the tone is changed to High, where necessary, only on the first; for example, *hotòk* 'dry out' (Mid + Low) → *hótòk*, and *dúŋa* 'show' and *gílì* 'jump' (High + Mid, High + Low) are unchanged.[6]

In this illustration the direction of the process is quite clear. But in other cases it is again less obvious that either form is the base. There is a pattern in English, for example, in which a Noun is accented on the first syllable (*cónflict*, *ínsult*, *éxport*) and a corresponding Verb on the second (*conflíct*, *insúlt*, *expórt*). It is a growing pattern, and moreover grows in both directions. One will often hear talk of, for instance, 'an industrial díspute', where the earlier form (and indeed mine) would be *dispúte*. An opposite

---

[6] L. Bouquiaux, *La Langue Birom* (*Nigeria septentrional*): *phonologie, morphologie, syntaxe* (Paris, Les Belles Lettres, 1970), pp. 193f.

example is the Verb 'to contact', earlier *cóntact* (which I think is the form that I most often use) but also *contáct*. In most grammars, the Noun is said to derive from the Verb (e.g. QUIRK *et al.*, p. 1556); and, if the relation has to be directional, that is arguably the better choice. But an alternative view is that the two stress patterns ('– for Nouns, – ' for Verbs) are added equally to roots that, in themselves, are unaccented. In this analysis, both *cónflict* and *conflíct* consist of the root *conflict* (unstressed) plus what has sometimes been called a 'superfix' – an accentual affix superimposed on it.

In all typological work the most elementary error is to forget that different linguists will inexorably describe things differently. For a final subtype of modification we may turn to the Adjectives in French, where the Masculines have often been seen as deriving from the Feminines by a process of **subtraction**. Thus Feminine *blanche* [blɑ̃:ʃ] → Masculine *blanc* [blɑ̃] by the removal of final [ʃ], *bonne* [bɔn] → [bɔ̃] by removal of [n] (with accompanying nasalisation of [ɔ]), *longue* [lɔ̃:g] → *long* [lɔ̃], and so forth. The reason for this treatment is similar to the one which we gave for English *teach* → *taught* or *bring* → *brought*. If the Masculines are derived from the Feminines, we can postulate a single operation: subtract the final consonant. But if the Feminines were to be derived from the Masculines, we would need a separate operation for each consonant: add [ʃ] to form *blanche*, [g] for *longue*, etc. This has become the standard example of subtraction or of 'minus formation', dealt with many times since Bloomfield's classic exposition in the 1930s (BLOOMFIELD, p. 217).

But in the heyday of generative phonology many scholars wanted to treat it differently. Their solution, in effect, followed the spelling. Masculine *bon*, for example, was phonologically [bɔn]. However, final consonants often fall, in this case nasalising the preceding vowel, unless they are in what are traditionally called positions of 'liaison' (before a vowel in a variety of grammatical structures). The Feminine *bonne* was then derived by the suffixation of [ə]: [bɔn + ə]. However, this [ə] is generally, as the tradition has it, 'silent'. Yet another view is that an Adjective such as BLANC is irregular. A correct account should eschew Bloomfield's generalisation and say simply that its root is [blɑ̃] and it forms its Feminine by suffixing [ʃ]. To resolve this issue would require a detailed study of French. But the crucial lesson is that the same facts may be handled in an entirely contrary way by different analysts. Hence the same process (in a real sense) stands in danger of falling under two quite contrary typological headings.

## RELATED READING

For the device of zero morphs see especially B. Bloch, 'English verb inflection' *Lg* 23 (1947), pp. 399–418, reprinted in *RiL*, pp. 243–54; compare HOCKETT, 'Models', on alternative analyses of *took* (*RiL*, p. 393f.). For contemporary criticism see E. A. Nida, 'The identification of morphemes', *Lg* 24 (1948), pp. 414–41, reprinted in *RiL*, pp. 255–71 (pp. 256, 263 especially); later and fuller critique by W. Haas, 'Zero in linguistic description', in *Studies in Linguistic Analysis* (Supplement to *TPhS*, Oxford, Blackwell, 1957), pp. 33–53. It should be stressed that zero does have a rôle in morphology: to condemn its abuse is not to condemn all use whatever. For 'Item and Process' vs 'Item and Arrangement' see again HOCKETT, 'Models'. But Hockett's concept of 'IP' was very general.

My account of inflectional formations derives in part from generative work at the end of the 1960s: see, in particular, W. U. Wurzel, *Studien zur deutschen Lautstruktur* (Berlin, Akademie-Verlag, 1970); K.-H. Wagner, *Generative Grammatical Studies in the Old English Language* (Heidelberg, Groos, 1969). See chapter 9 below for further development. For regularities and exceptions compare, for example, my *Inflectional Morphology*, pp. 191ff.; this employs the technical device of rule ordering (flowchart, p. 195). But there is much more to be said about the notion of regularity, especially in a historical context. See WURZEL, chs. 3–5 for an important and penetrating study.

For the typology of processes compare MAYERTHALER, §6.1; BAUER, *Morphology*, pp. 19ff.; WURZEL, pp. 43f.: see also earlier accounts by SAPIR, ch. 4, and E. M. Uhlenbeck, 'Limitations of morphological processes', *Lingua* 11 (1962), pp. 426–32. My main categories are basically from Uhlenbeck, except that I have treated compounding separately. In an early article, I drew the main distinction between processes that are not sensitive to the internal structure of the base ($X \rightarrow X +$ suffix, $X \rightarrow$ prefix $+ X$) and all the remainder, including infixing. See P. H. Matthews, 'The inflectional component of a Word and Paradigm Grammar', *JL* 1 (1965), pp. 139–71 (§2.2, pp. 147ff.). I won no support for this; however, it does have the advantage of dividing processes which are common from those that are rarer, and perhaps, in the case of infixation, of explaining WHY it is rarer. On the relative rareness of modification see WURZEL, pp. 166ff. For a specialist study of reduplication see A. Marantz, 'Re reduplication', *LIn* 13 (1982), pp. 435–82. Reduplication as an inflectional process should be distinguished from complete reduplication in compounding or in syntax. For a very interesting instance of the latter see R. P. Botha, *Form and Meaning in Word-formation: a Study of Afrikaans Reduplication* (Cambridge, Cambridge University Press, 1988).

# 7 Morphological processes

On vowel changes in English Verbs see, for example, PALMER, pp. 251ff. For Arabic see the summary of an influential technical treatment in J. Durand, *Generative and Non-linear Phonology* (London, Longman, 1990), pp. 257ff. For an account of French Adjectives in generative phonology see F. Dell, *Les Règles et les sons : introduction à la phonologie générative* (Paris, Hermann, 1973), pp. 178ff. The argument against subtraction is given very briefly by W. U. Dressler, 'Word formation as part of natural morphology', in DRESSLER, *Leitmotifs*, pp. 99–126 (see p. 106, with reference).

# 8
# Morphophonemics

Basic forms and morphophonemic processes (English *-ed*). Forms may be partly specified (vowel harmony in Turkish); or abstractions (*tʰrikʰ-* in Ancient Greek). Processes phonetically natural: 'euphony' and 'ease of articulation'.

*Sandhi.* Morphophonemics as a process of joining: sandhi forms and rules of sandhi. Types of sandhi: assimilation, regressive and progressive; dissimilation; epenthesis; fusion. Examples of fusion in Ancient Greek: dentals before *s*; extended discussion of contracted Adjectives.

*The scope of morphophonemics.* Morphophonemics as a transitional field: what then are its boundaries? Alternations in Italian: purely morphological vs purely phonetic. Nasal assimilation in Italian: as case of neutralisation; morphology predictable from phonology. Further examples of neutralisation. Consonants before *s* and *t*: rules phonologically motivated; but not predictable; therefore need for explicit statement. Limits to motivation. Palatalisation of velars: morphophonemic only if we posit diacritic features.

We have argued that the 'Item and Process' model is better, for a language like English, than the 'Item and Arrangement' model. But our account of it is not complete.

Take, for example, the Past Participle formations. We have dealt with the [d] of *sailed* and distinguished it from sundry irregularities. But what of [t] in *fished* or [ɪd] in *faded*? [t], [d] and [ɪd] all have an alveolar plosive, and the choice between them, as we pointed out in chapter 6, is phonologically conditioned. All three are regular. When the Verb *blitz* was created or borrowed in the 1940s, its Past Tense and Past Participle were automatically [blɪtst]. If someone were to tell me that there is a Verb '*to glud*' I would automatically derive a form ['glʌdɪd], just as, for a Verb '*to beer*', I would derive [bɪəd]. All three are variants of ONE formative, not separate formatives.

The best solution is to posit a single morphological process:

$$
\left[ \begin{array}{l} \left\{ \begin{array}{l} \text{Past Participle} \\ \text{Past Tense} \end{array} \right\} \\ \text{X} \end{array} \right]_V \rightarrow X + [d]
$$

Since FISH and FADE will not be listed as exceptions, this adds [d] to all three roots: [seɪl+d], [fɪʃ+d], [feɪd+d]. But in *fished* and *faded* the formative is modified in contact with the consonant that precedes it. In *faded* the root ends in an alveolar plosive and [ɪ] is inserted: [feɪd+d]→[feɪdɪd]. By the same rule [weɪt+d] (*waited*) →[weɪtɪd]. In *fished* this rule does not apply, since [ʃ] is not an alveolar plosive. But it is voiceless; therefore, by another rule, [d] is devoiced: [fɪʃ+d]→[fɪʃt]. Similarly, [kɪs+d] (*kissed*)→[kɪst], [kɪk+d] (*kicked*)→[kɪkt], and so on. In *sailed* the root ends neither in an alveolar plosive nor in a voiceless consonant. Therefore there is no change: [seɪld].

In this account, [d] is the **basic form** of the suffix. In terms of the 'Item and Arrangement' model, it as a **basic allomorph**. The processes by which it is modified – the insertion of [ɪ], the devoicing of [d] – are **morphophonemic processes**. This term reflects their intermediate status. They are not purely phonological, since they apply to morphological elements. But neither are they purely morphological. The forms to which they apply are defined phonologically (alveolar plosive+[d], voiceless consonant+[d]), and not by reference to classes of lexemes. They also reflect the phonological structure of the language. A form like [feɪd+d] is not possible in English: there is no double [dd] as opposed to single [d]. Nor can words end in sequences like [sd] or [kd]. Morphophonemic processes are thus transitional between morphology and phonology.

In this example, the basic form is identical to one of the actual alternants: [d] as in *sailed*. But it is not necessarily so. In a Turkish word like *köye* (Dative for 'village'), the ending (-*e*) is phonologically conditioned. With the word for 'end', as we saw in chapter 6, it would be -*a* (*son-a*). But there is no reason to argue either that -*e* is derived from basic -*a* or vice versa. The two alternants are simply opposite sides of the coin. The Turkish Accusative morpheme is represented by -*ü* in *köy-ü* ('village'), by -*u* in *son-u* ('end'), by -*ı* in *kitab-ı* ('book') and by -*i* in *diş-i* ('tooth'). By convention, this and similar morphemes are traditionally cited in the form with *i* (thus LEWIS's index). But that is a convention only. In reality no vowel is more basic than the others.

What should the basic forms be? In the light of what we have said, they are not identical to any actual alternant. Instead they are abstractions in which vowels are represented solely by the features that are constant. For the Dative we can establish a basic

$$\begin{bmatrix} \text{Open} \\ \text{Unrounded} \end{bmatrix}$$

where Open and Unrounded are the phonological features that *e* and *a* have in common. In *sona*, a morphophonemic process will add the feature Back; in *köye* Front will be added instead. Similarly, the basic form of the Accusative will be

[Close]

Close being the only vocalic feature that all allomorphs share. In *köyü* a morphophonemic process will add Front and Rounded to form *ü*, in *sonu* Back and Rounded to form *u*, and so on.

In this account, the basic forms are only partly specified; the rest is determined by the rules of harmony. But even when a basic form is fully specified it may still be modified in every context. For illustration, let us cross the Aegean and turn back twenty-four centuries. In Ancient Greek, the lexemes for 'sentry', 'goat' and 'hair' had the Nominative and Genitive Singulars:

|  | 'sentry' | 'goat' | 'hair' |
|---|---|---|---|
|  | (φύλαξ) | (αἴξ) | (θρίξ) |
| *Nominative* | pʰýlaks | aíks | tʰríks |
| *Genitive* | pʰýlakos | aigós | trikʰós |

each form consisting of a root and an ending. Accents apart, the Nominatives are marked by *-s*, the Genitives by *-os*. But whereas the root for 'sentry' is constant (*pʰýlak-s*, *pʰýlak-os*) the others alternate: *aik-* versus *aig-*, *tʰrik-* versus *trikʰ-*. Now in the word for 'goat' we might already guess, from the evidence presented, that it has a basic form *aig-*. If it were *aik-* and *k* were voiced between vowels, why is *pʰýlakos* not, by the same rule, *pʰýlagos*? If it is *aig-*, then in the Nominative *aíks* we simply have another case in which a consonant devoices in contact with one which is already voiceless. This guess is confirmed by other forms. For example, in the words for 'vulture' and 'vein':

|  | 'vulture' | 'vein' |
|---|---|---|
|  | (γύψ) | (φλέψ) |
| *Nominative* | gý:ps | pʰléps |
| *Genitive* | gy:pós | pʰlébos |

the first root is *gy:p-*, with constant *p*. For the second we can establish basic *p$^h$leb-*, with *b* similarly devoiced before *s*. In the word for 'whip' we find the same alternation as in 'goat': Nominative *másti:k-s* (μάστιξ), Genitive *másti:g-os*. We also find it before other endings: for example, Dative Plural *aik-sí*, Accusative Singular *aíg-a*.

What of the Noun for 'hair'? As we can see, there are two alternations: *t$^h$* versus *t* at the beginning of the root, *k* versus *k$^h$* at the end. If we take the second alone we can guess that the basic form has *k$^h$*. We will also find that the same rule covers both this and the case of 'goat' or 'vein'. In Ancient Greek there were three series of plosives (Labial, Dental, Velar) and within each series there were three types (Aspirated, Voiced, and Voiceless Unaspirated). The complete table is thus:

| Labial | Dental | Velar |
|--------|--------|-------|
| p$^h$ | t$^h$ | k$^h$ |
| b | d | g |
| p | t | k |

(in spelling φ, β, π; θ, δ, τ; χ, γ, κ). Before vowels, all three types contrasted. But before *s* they did not. In that position a consonant had to be Voiceless and it had to be released directly by the sibilant. Hence *aíg+s*, with basic *g*, → *aíks*. Likewise, in the word for 'hair', basic *-k$^h$+s* → *-ks*.

The remaining alternation is separate but it too is phonologically conditioned. When the root ends in Unaspirated *k*, it begins with Aspirated *t$^h$r* (phonetically [tr̥]). Thus Nominative *t$^h$rík-s* and, in the Dative Plural, *t$^h$riksí*. When it ends in Aspirated *k$^h$* it begins with Unaspirated *tr* or [tr]: Genitive *trik$^h$-ós* or Accusative Singular *trík$^h$-a*. In the development of Greek from Indo-European, this is explained by a sound-change ('Grassmann's law') whose synchronic effect is that a consonant which is otherwise Aspirated loses its aspiration if, after a following vowel, there is another Aspirated consonant. Although the alternation is not automatic, there are many other instances of it. We may therefore posit a basic form *t$^h$rik$^h$-*. It is evidently an abstraction. In the Nominative and Dative Plural the second aspirate is, in effect, deaspirated: *t$^h$rik$^h$+s* → *t$^h$ríks*, *t$^h$rik$^h$+sí* → *t$^h$riksí*. Therefore the first remains. In the Genitive or Accusative Singular the second remains. Therefore the first is deaspirated: $t^h rik^h + \acute{o}s \rightarrow$ $trik^h \acute{o}s$, $t^h rik^h + a \rightarrow trik^h a$. In no actual alternant is the abstract form unaltered.

In older grammars, processes like this were commonly referred to under the heading of 'euphony' (thus, for Greek, GOODWIN, pp. 13ff.). Another frequent explanation is in terms of ease of articulation. For example, the principle of vowel harmony in Turkish is 'due to the natural human tendency towards economy of muscular effort' (LEWIS, p. 15). Now such accounts are clearly relative to the phonologies of particular languages. Sequences of vowels that must harmonise for native words in Turkish are pronounceable without inordinate muscular effort in, for example, French or German. A sequence of aspirates which might be 'non-euphonious' in Ancient Greek is quite normal in my own pronunciation of an English word like *tricky*. Nevertheless these explanations point to something important. If we do not expect a morphophonemic process to reflect an absolute phonetic law, we do expect it to make phonetic sense. It is phonetically understandable that consonants should be devoiced before [s] (Greek *aík-s*, English *cat-s*). It is understandable that features such as rounding should be consistent, where possible, across syllables. Thus in a Turkish word like *köyü*, every phoneme, consonants included, is rounded phonetically.

This is also important heuristically. In practice, we will often suspect that a process exists precisely because the change from one alternant to another is phonetically plausible. The phonetic principle may be either auditory ('euphony') or articulatory ('ease of articulation'). By contrast, a process is not morphophonemic if it is phonetically arbitrary.


## SANDHI

Morphophonemic processes can sometimes operate in the absence of a specific context. In Latin the root for 'milk' was *lact-* (Genitive Singular *lact-is*). But in the Nominative and Accusative Singular there is no ending and the form is simplified to *lac*. The explanation was given by a native speaker, Julius Caesar, in the first century BC. In Latin, no word can end in two plosives (in

ancient terminology, two 'mutes').[1] Therefore, in our terms, *lact*
→ *lac*.

Usually, however, they are processes affecting forms in contact.
Thus, in our illustration from Greek, *aig-*, *pʰhleb-* and *tʰrikʰ-* are
modified in contact with the *-s* of the Nominative Singular or the
*-si* of the Dative Plural. We can accordingly see them as processes
that join forms together. In the Nominative of the word for
'goat', a basic form in *-g* is joined to *-s* to form a [k] which is
released directly by the sibilant. The term '**sandhi**' is a Sanskrit
word for 'joining' which has been borrowed from the grammarians of ancient India to describe this kind of modification.
Thus, in Greek, *aik-* is a **sandhi form** of *aig-*; a form which has
been modified according to a **rule of sandhi**.

In these examples, the process of joining is traditionally called
**assimilation**. In Greek *aíks* ('goat') or *pʰléps* ('vein'), basic *g*
and *b* are adapted or assimilated, in respect of voicing, to the
inherently voiceless *s*. More precisely, it is a case of **regressive
assimilation** – the voicelessness of *s* having an effect backwards,
as it were, on the preceding element. In English *fish* + [d] → [fɪʃt]
we have a case of **progressive assimilation**. The voicelessness
of the [ʃ] extends forwards to unvoice the following [d]. Turkish
vowel harmony also has an effect of progressive assimilation (see
LEWIS, p. 16), the vowels in each morpheme adapting to the
vowels preceding.

Assimilation is a process by which elements are made more
alike. Its opposite, **dissimilation**, is one in which they are made
more different. This is far less usual as a phenomenon of contact.
It would be phonetically odd if, for example, a back [q] were to be
fronted to [c] before back vowels, while a front [c] became [q]
before front vowels. But dissimilation at a distance has been
illustrated in the Greek word for 'hair'. In the Genitive *trikʰós*
(← *tʰrikʰ* + *ós*), a repetition of two aspirated consonants is avoided.
The first plosive, basically *tʰ*, is accordingly differentiated or
dissimilated, in respect of aspiration, from the second. A third
type of process is illustrated in English *faded* or *fishes*. Whereas in
*fished* and *cats* the final consonant is assimilated – another example
of progressive assimilation – in these forms it is joined to the root

---

[1] H. Funaioli (ed.), *Grammaticae romanae fragmenta* (Leipzig, Teubner, 1907), p. 152,
fr. 14.

with, as it were, a buffer element ([feid-ɪ-d], [fɪʃ-ɪ-z]. In the tradition, this is generally called **epenthesis** (a Greek term meaning 'insertion').

These are the only types in our material so far. But joining (if we may pursue the metaphor) can be carried to varying degrees. Sometimes units are joined or stuck together like bricks, so that each still occupies its separate place. Thus in Greek *aîks*, despite the joining of the consonants, we can still segment between a [k] phoneme and an [s] phoneme. In other cases they are slotted together or dovetailed: the analogy here is with a phoneme, perhaps, that may yet be analysed into features that belong to different morphemes. But they can also be welded or woven into a continuous piece. Turkish *çocuğum* 'my child' is grammatically the 'child' morpheme (basic *çocuk*) plus the 1st Singular morpheme (-*um*). But in its actual form [tʃɔdʒuːm] there is no way of saying where one morph ends and the other begins. In the process of joining:

çocuk + um → [tʃɔdʒuːm]

the velar consonant is 'swallowed up' (see again LEWIS, p. 5) and the boundary obliterated.

Sandhi phenomena of this more drastic type can best be considered under the special heading of **fusion**. In the realisation of written Turkish *ğ*, the preceding and following phonemes **fuse** into a single long vowel in which the quality of the former (again, by the overall progressive pattern) will prevail. Thus, to give a more striking example, the written *alacağiz* 'we will take' is simply [aladʒaːz] (compare LEWIS, p. 5), with the Open Unrounded quality over the whole final syllable. In Turkish, fusion is relatively rare. Phonetically, let alone in writing, the word-forms have a structure in which the patterning of morphemes is largely transparent.[2] But in many other languages, Ancient Greek among them, it is very widespread. For a simple example, let us return to the same pattern of Noun inflection (that of the traditional 3rd Declension), but with roots ending in Dentals instead of Labials or Velars. The following are the

---

[2] I MEAN 'phonetically'. In practical analysis a student will often be sure of the morphemes BEFORE knowing how many phonemes (or even syllables) to put in a phonemic transcription.

corresponding forms of lexemes meaning 'bird', 'hope' and 'hired worker':

|  | 'bird' (ὄρνις) | 'hope' (ἐλπίς) | 'hired worker' (θής) |
|---|---|---|---|
| *Nominative* | órni:s | elpís | tʰéːs |
| *Genitive* | órni:tʰos | elpídos | tʰɛːtós |

On the evidence of the Genitives (suffix -*os*), we may establish the roots *ornitʰ*-, *elpid*- and *tʰɛːt*-; these are confirmed by the Accusative Singulars and other forms in which a vowel follows. But whereas the velars and labials merely lose their voiced or aspirated character before the -*s* of the Nominative (*aig-s → aîks* or *tʰríkʰ-s → tʰríks*), the dentals lose their identity entirely. Any Dental plosive (whether Aspirated *tʰ*, Voiced *d* or Voiceless Unaspirated *t*) is simply run together with the following fricative: *órni:tʰ-s → órni:-s*, *elpíd-s → elpís*, *tʰéːt-s → tʰéːs*.

In these examples we could maintain a division between segments if we liked. The form *elpís*, for instance, might be said to consist of an alternant *elpí*- of the root followed, once more, by an unaltered suffix -*s*. In *elpíd-os*, the root has another alternant *elpíd*-. We would then establish the form with *d* as basic and posit a rule by which a dental is deleted in the appropriate environments. Hence *elpíd-s → elpí-s* (likewise *órni:tʰ-s → órni:-s*, *tʰéːt-s → tʰéː-s*), where the hyphen in the sandhi form shows that the integrity of the morphs *elpí*- etc. has been technically preserved. However, the notion of *tʰ*, *d* or *t* being 'deleted' is phonetically unilluminating. What is truly involved is a process in which an occlusive (a consonant with closure) and a fricative (without closure) are no longer distinguished as separate articulations. In *tʰríks* the fricative hypothetically 'swallows up' the aspiration of the velar. The result is a velar occlusive with a sibilant release. In *órni:s* etc. (so far as we can judge from the spelling) the fricative 'swallows up' not only the release of the occlusion but the occlusion itself. The result is an indivisible sibilant in which the articulation of what would otherwise be a plosive and what would otherwise be an [s] are run together. The reason why this happens with dentals but not with velars or labials is that the *s* itself has a dental place of articulation.

Despite the fusion, the grammatical structure of these words is still fairly transparent. But elsewhere (in particular where vowels and accents are involved) it can be considerably obscured. In the following, for example, we contrast (a) the paradigm of a Masculine Noun meaning 'gold', (b) the corresponding Masculine forms of a regular Adjective meaning 'clever', and (c) the same forms (specifically in the Attic or Athenian dialect) for the Adjective meaning 'golden':[3]

|  | (a)<br>'gold'<br>(χρυσός) | (b)<br>'clever'<br>(σοφός) | (c)<br>'golden'<br>(χρυσοῦς) |
|---|---|---|---|
| *Nom. Sg.* | kʰryːsós | sopʰós | kʰryːsûːs |
| *Acc. Sg.* | kʰryːsón | sopʰón | kʰryːsûːn |
| *Gen. Sg.* | kʰryːsûː | sopʰûː | kʰryːsûː |
| *Dat. Sg.* | kʰryːsɔ̂ːi | sopʰɔ̂ːi | kʰryːsɔ̂ːi |
| *Nom. Pl.* |  | sopʰoí | kʰryːsôi |
| *Acc. Pl.* |  | sopʰúːs | kʰryːsûːs |
| *Gen. Pl.* |  | sopʰɔ̂ːn | kʰryːsɔ̂ːn |
| *Dat. Pl.* |  | sopʰôis | kʰryːsôis |

(All sequences of vowels, please note, are diphthongs; of the accents, which are marked at the beginning of a long vowel or long diphthong, the acute represents a high tone and the circumflex a high plus low or falling tone on the whole syllable.) In these paradigms we observe, first of all, that the endings are identical in columns (a) and (b): Nom. Sg. -*os*, Gen. Sg. -*uː*, and so on. This observation would be confirmed by many other Masculine Nouns and Adjectives. We would therefore expect, at least, that these should also be valid as basic forms in column (c). So *kʰryːsûːs*, for instance, should have a form before sandhi which in some way ends in -*os*. It also seems clear that the Noun 'gold' and the Adjective 'golden' are systematically related. This too is confirmed by other lexemes: e.g. Nom. Sg. *árgyros* 'silver' (Noun), but *argyrûːs* 'made of silver, silvery'. We would hope, therefore, to establish some further basic form which makes the difference between columns (a) and (c). For example the Nom. Sg. *kʰryːsûːs* must, as it were, be *kʰryːs-X-os* with something else (*X*) before the ending. But what precisely?

---

[3] For the phonology of these and earlier forms see W. S. Allen, *Vox graeca*, 3rd edn (Cambridge, Cambridge University Press, 1987). Note, in particular, that I assume written *ου* = [uː] and that forms with an iota subscript represent long diphthongs.

Readers who have learnt Greek can supply an answer, of course. But even they will appreciate that it is by no means transparent in the forms themselves. If we look at the apparent endings for 'golden' and 'clever' we find that in two cases there is a difference of vowel accompanied by an accentual difference: Nom. Sg. *-ós* versus *-û:s*, Acc. Sg. *-ón* versus *-û:n*. In two others we find the accentual difference on its own: Nom. Pl. *-oí* versus *-ôi*, Acc Pl. *-ú:s* versus *-û:s*. Elsewhere (i.e. in half the paradigm) the endings are the same for both. Faced with this data in the field (if we can imagine for a moment that we are working with a fourth-century informant) we might well guess that the consistent accentuation of column (c) is the most important feature. Let $X$ as a hypothesis be simply a high plus low accent: thus *kʰry:s-^-* plus the endings, as it were. In the Genitives and Datives these endings (as exemplified by *sopʰû:* etc.) would have such an accent anyway: hence no difference is made. In the Nom. and Acc. Pl. the high plus low tone overrides the high tone: thus *kʰry:s-^-oí* → *kʰry:sôi*, *kʰry:s-^-ú:s* → *kʰry:sû:s*. For the Nom. and Acc. Sg. we would then go on to establish basic *kʰry:s-^-ós* and *kʰry:s-^-ón*. Here the processes are more complicated, but as a first step the high plus low accent will again override the high: so far as that is concerned we would therefore expect *kʰry:sós* and *kʰry:sôn*. However, in Greek phonology the high plus low can only be carried by a long vowel or diphthong; as a second step it will therefore seem reasonable to suppose that the vowels are lengthened in order that they may carry it here. As a third and final factor we will then find that the language has no long *o:* [o:], but only the short *o*, the long *ɔ:* [ɔ:] of *sopʰɔ́:n* etc., and the long *u:* [u:] which in fact appears in the word-forms now under consideration (*kʰry:sû:s*, *kʰry:sû:n*). Is the *u:* anything more, we will surmise, than a secondary effect of the vowel lengthening – an adjustment which is merely necessitated by the non-existence of an '*o:*' as distinct from *u:*?

This hypothesis is very reasonable, and (whether right or wrong) may serve to illustrate the tonal and accentual phenomena that are possible. It is phonetically very plausible that one tone should override another, and that a vowel should be lengthened to receive a complex (high plus low) unit. The proposed changes of *o* to *u:* (*kʰry:s-^-ós* → *kʰry:sû:s*) are also plausible – given, in particular, that the maintenance of the half close quality is phonologically excluded. We could happily proceed with our analysis of the language on this basis. But in fact any classicist will argue that we have grasped the wrong end of the stick. The true basic forms, he would say, should be established with $X$ (the 'unknown' Adjectival suffix) $= e$: thus $k^hry{:}s\text{-}e\text{-}os$, $k^hry{:}s\text{-}e\text{-}on$, $k^hry{:}s\text{-}e\text{-}u{:}$, etc. His most crucial evidence – crucial for the quality of the vowel especially – is that trisyllabic forms such as these are attested by the spelling of other dialects: $k^hrý{:}seos$ (χρύσεος), Genitive $k^hry{:}séu{:}$ (χρυσέου), and so on. The falling accent, which seems at first to be the basic feature of column (c), is in fact a special secondary effect which accompanies fusions in this class of Adjective in the Attic dialect.

Nor is this the end of what may be discovered in these examples. If we now bring in the Feminine Adjectives:

|            | (b)          | (c)         |
|------------|--------------|-------------|
|            | 'clever'     | 'golden'    |
| *Nom. Sg.* | sop$^h$έ:    | k$^h$ry:sê: |
| *Acc. Sg.* | sop$^h$έ:n   | k$^h$ry:sê:n |
| *Gen. Sg.* | sop$^h$ê̂:s   | k$^h$ry:sê̂:s |
| *Dat. Sg.* | sop$^h$ê̂:i   | k$^h$ry:sê̂:i |
| *Nom. Pl.* | sop$^h$aí    | k$^h$ry:sâi |
| *Acc. Pl.* | sop$^h$á:s   | k$^h$ry:sâ:s |
| *Gen. Pl.* | sop$^h$ɔ̂:n   | k$^h$ry:sɔ̂:n |
| *Dat. Pl.* | sop$^h$âis   | k$^h$ry:sâis |

we see that, where the Masculines have a back vowel ($o$, $ɔ$: or $u$:), the Feminines have a front $ε$: in the Singular and an open $a$ in all but one of the Plurals. Thus, for example, $sop^h\text{-}ó\text{-}n$ versus $sop^h\text{-}ε{:}\text{-}n$ in the Accusative Singular, $sop^h\text{-}o\text{-}í$ versus $sop^h\text{-}a\text{-}í$ in the Nominative Plural. The difference evidently marks the Gender. In a form like $sop^hû{:}$ (Gen. Sg. Masc.), the ending $-u{:}$ is a fusion of the Gender suffix and the Case/Number suffix. In the corresponding form for 'golden' ($k^hry{:}s\text{-}û{:}$), both are fused with $-e-$.

For 'clever', we might establish basic forms as follows. In the Accusative Plural, the Feminine has a final $s$ with the preceding Gender suffix lengthened: basic $-a{:}s$, as it were. The Masculine would accordingly have basic $-o{:}s \rightarrow o{:}s$ except, as we remarked earlier, that there is no distinct '$o$:' in the language. Instead we have the long $u$:, which is phonologically nearest:

| | |
|---|---|
| *Acc. Pl. Masc.* | $sop^h + o + $:s $\rightarrow sop^h$u:s |
| *Acc. Pl. Fem.* | $sop^h + a + $:s $\rightarrow sop^h$a:s |

The same $u$: is found, as we have seen, in the Genitive Singular Masculine ($sop^h\hat{u}$:); although other basic forms might be suggested (-$o$-: or -$o$-$u$: in particular), the following is one possibility:

| | |
|---|---|
| *Gen. Sg. Masc.* | $sop^h + o + o \rightarrow sop^h$u: |

In the Feminine, $sop^h$-$\hat{\varepsilon}$:-$s$, the -$s$ is a different basic formative.

In the Nominative Singular the Masculine is transparent ($sop^h$-$\acute{o}$-$s$); the Feminine also, except that in this case there is no Case/Number suffix ($sop^h$-$\varepsilon$:). The only remaining problems are the Genitive Plural and Dative Singular. In the latter the Feminine at first appears straightforward: basic $sop^h + \varepsilon$: +$i$. But why is the Masculine ending -$ɔ$:$i$ instead -$oi$? That is what we would expect, in particular, from the Dative Plural ($sop$-$\hat{o}$-$is$). So far as the length is concerned, the best answer is to say that the Feminine is basically in -$\varepsilon$: + :$i$, where -:$i$ would have a lengthening effect (compare the Accusative Plural) except that the preceding $\varepsilon$: is long already. As for the quality, we note again that there is no long $o$:. Neither is there a long $u$:$i$; the only long back vowel which is possible in a diphthong is, in fact, $ɔ$:. We may therefore posit:

| | |
|---|---|
| *Dat. Sg. Masc.* | $sop^h + o + $:i $\rightarrow sop^h$ɔ:i |
| *Dat. Sg. Fem.* | $sop^h + \varepsilon$: + :i $\rightarrow sop^h$ɛ:i |

Finally, in the Genitive Plural the basic forms are modified as follows:

| | |
|---|---|
| *Gen. Pl. Masc.* | $sop^h + o + ɔ$:n $\rightarrow sop^h$ɔ:n |
| *Gen. Pl. Fem.* | $sop^h + a + ɔ$:n $\rightarrow sop^h$ɔ:n |

with the distinction between the Gender suffixes obliterated.

This is not the place to discuss the Ancient Greek vowel sandhi in further detail. The reader will sense that we have glossed over certain problems with the accent. Other complications would confront us as we turned to other classes of lexemes, among them the many Verbs whose forms show similar fusions (traditionally 'contractions'). But enough has been said to illustrate its far-reaching effect on the basic structures of the word-form. In the forms for 'golden' the endings may be regularly analysed into three basic suffixes. Thus in summary:

|  | *Masculine* |  | *Feminine* |  |
|---|---|---|---|---|
| Nom. Sg. | '-e-o-s | → -û:s | '-e-ɛ: | → -ɛ̂: |
| Acc. Sg. | '-e-o-n | → -û:n | '-e-ɛ:-n | → -ɛ̂:n |
| Gen. Sg. | '-e-o-o | → -û: | '-e-ɛ:-s | → -ɛ̂:s |
| Dat. Sg. | '-e-o-:i | → -ɔ̂:i | '-e-ɛ:-:i | → -ɛ̂:i |
| Nom. Pl. | '-e-o-i | → -ôi | '-e-a-i | → -âi |
| Acc. Pl. | '-e-o-:s | → -û:s | '-e-a-:s | → -â:s |
| Gen. Pl. | '-e-o-ɔ:n | → -:n | '-e-a-ɔ:n | → -ɔ̂:n |
| Dat. Pl. | '-e-o-is | → -ôis | '-e-a-is | → -âis |

– assuming, as it were, a basic $k^h ry$:s- with accent (´) following. The modifications so set out would be described in terms of three general sandhi processes: first, the fusions of the last two elements (these or similar processes hold for all Greek dialects); secondly, the further fusions or contractions for the endings as wholes; thirdly, the special reorganisation of the accent. The result is that in some forms both the lexical formative (-*e*-) and the Gender marker (-*o*-, -*ɛ:*-, -*a*-) lose their basic identity. The former loses it throughout. When fusions are as drastic as this, working out the structure of the word can be a fascinating puzzle.

## THE SCOPE OF MORPHOPHONEMICS

I remarked in the introduction to this chapter that morphophonemic processes are transitional between morphology and phonology. But transitional fields are often the hardest to delimit. Is there a simple way to determine what belongs to morphophonemics and what belongs to morphology or phonology proper? The answer, alas, is No. There is, precisely, a transition. But along the road a number of mile posts may be set up, and it is at one or another of these that different theorists have tended to draw their boundaries.

Let us take Italian as the language of illustration. At one extreme, Italian has many alternations which – as everyone will agree – are purely morphological. For a regular Verb like FERIRE 'wound', the Past Participle is formed with the vowel of the Infinitive (*fer-i-[re]*) and a suffix -*t*-: *fer-i-t-* (Masc. Sg. *ferito*). Other regular examples are *sal-i-to* 'gone up', *and-a-to* 'gone'

(Infinitive *and-a-re* 'to go'), and so on. One might expect, therefore, that APPARIRE 'appear' or MORIRE 'die' would have similar Participles of the form *apparito, morito*. But they do not. In the case of MORIRE the suffix -*t*- is added to the bare root: *mor-t-* (*morto*). For APPARIRE the suffix is also different: Masculine Singular *appar-s-o*. There is no phonological reason why any of this should be so. These are simply morphological exceptions to the regular pattern.

At the other extreme, it would be easy to set up 'alternations' which are purely phonetic in character. In the forms *cade* '[he] falls' and *cadde* 'fell', the difference in consonant length (shown by the single and double *d*'s in the spelling) is matched by a complementary difference in vowel length. The *a* in *cade* is noticeably long ([ka:de]), but the one is *cadde* is short ([kadde]); that is undoubtedly how we would transcribe them if we were not already familiar with the language. Morphologically, both forms contain a root of the shape $CVC$, followed in one case by a bare vowel (*cad-e*) and in the other by a reduplication of the final consonant (*cad-d-e*, with the same vowel following). For the root itself we might therefore be led to establish an alternation between a variant in [a:] ([ka:d]) and another in [a] ([kad]), the conditions being, apparently, the presence of a vowel (e.g. *e*) or a consonant (e.g. *d*) as the element following. But in fact we will do no such thing. According to the accepted phonological analysis, consonant length is distinctive (the *d* of *cade* being phonemically opposed to the *dd* of *cadde*), but vowel length is merely an accident of the type of syllable in which the vowel appears. In non-final stressed open syllables ('open' = ending in the vowel itself), the phonetic variants or allophones are at their longest: this is the case in *cade* (with the syllabic structure ['ka:]+[de]). In closed syllables (syllables ending in a consonant) the allophones are shorter: thus *cadde* is ['kad]+[de]. This can be discovered and stated without any reference to the grammar. In analysing the morphology we may therefore take it as read and assume that *a* is identical throughout.

Examples like these mark the ends of the transition. But between them there are many phenomena which are a problem for both phonology and morphology. Let us take, for example, the phonology of nasals before consonants. At the beginning of a syllable, Italian has three nasal phonemes: written *m* [m] as in *matto* 'mad', *n* [n] as in *nostro* 'our', and *gn* [ɲ] as in *gnocchi* 'dumplings'. But at the end of a syllable the only nasal is one that is homorganic (identical as to its place of articulation) with whatever consonant follows. Before a bilabial we find only the bilabial [m] (written as *m* in *impossibile* 'impossible' or *ambedue* 'both'). Before a labiodental there is only the labiodental [ɱ] (written as *n* in *infelice* 'unhappy' or *inverno* 'winter'). Before a dental there is only the dental [n] (compare *insolito* 'unusual' or *andare* 'to go'), before an alveolo-palatal only the matching [ɲ] (e.g. *ingiusto* 'unjust' or *lancia* 'launch'), and before a velar only the velar [ŋ] (written as *n* in *incolto* 'uncultivated' or *lungo* 'long'). This is a feature of syllable structure (or of medial clusters across syllable boundaries), which may be stated quite independently of grammar.

At the same time it has morphological repercussions. The first of each pair of examples (*impossibile, infelice, insolito, ingiusto, incolto*) is an Adjective formed with a Negative prefix written *im-* or *in-*: compare *possibile* 'possible', *felice* 'happy', *solito* 'usual', *giusto* 'just' and *colto* 'cultivated'. Even in the spelling this has two forms, and in phonetics it has all five variants [im], [iɱ], [in], [iɲ] and [iŋ]. Since the dental variant [in] is also found before vowels (compare *inelegante* 'inelegant', *elegante* 'elegant') that must be the basic form; the others will be due to assimilation in one form or another. A second, slightly different repercussion can be found in the Past Participles of ASSUMERE 'take up, assume' and SPEGNERE 'put out, extinguish'. Before a vowel their roots have different nasal consonants: bilabial [m] in *assum-* (e.g. Infinitive *assum-e-re*), palatal [ɲ] in *spegn-* (*spegn-e-re*). But in the Participles both have a dental [n] (*assun-t-o, spen-t-o*). Here too we must speak of assimilation: just as basic *in-* is assimilated as *im-* in *impossibile* so basic *assum-* is assimilated as *assun-* in *assunto*. Likewise in *spento* basic *spegn-* is assimilated as *spen-*.

In phonology, this is a case of **neutralisation**: although the three nasal phonemes are distinct before vowels, the oppositions between them are suppressed or **neutralised** whenever another consonant follows. The nasal which appears in that position may be phonetically like one or another of them. For example, the [m] of *impossibile* is phonetically like that of *matto*. But phonologically it is identical to none. In *matto*, [m] has the phonological features Nasal and Labial; [n] in *nostro* is Nasal and Dental; [ɲ] in *gnocchi* is Nasal and Palatal. But the homorganic nasal is simply Nasal. Its only phonological feature, as distinct from its varying phonetic realisation, is the one that all three phonemes have in common.

This account is not accepted by all phonologists, and for that reason assimilations like that in *impossibile* have often been called morphophonemic. But if we do accept it, no further rule is needed. The prefix, as we said, is basically *in-* (*in-elegante*). By similar reasoning, the root of SPEGNERE is *spe*[ɲ]- and of ASSUMERE *assum-*. But in the position of neutralisation [n], [m] and [ɲ] do not contrast; all three must reduce to the single feature Nasal. It follows that *in-* before *possibile* and so on can only be *i*+Nasal; *spegn-* and *assum-* before *-t-o* can only be *spe*+Nasal and *assu*+Nasal. The rest belongs to the level of phonetic realisation. In *in-solito*, *spen-to* and *assun-to* the nasal element is realised as [n]; it merely happens that in the first example there is also a basic Dental. In *im-possibile*, *in-giusto* and *in-colto* it is realised as [m], [ɲ] and [ŋ]. This follows from exactly the same rules that apply in cases where there is no morphological boundary.

Examples of neutralisation form a large part of the sandhi in many languages. In Ancient Greek we remarked that consonants like *kʰ*, *g* and *k* did not contrast before, for instance, *s*. Hence *tʰríʹ*[k]*s* 'hair' and *aíʹ*[k]*s* 'goat'. In Italian, the pattern of SPEGNERE 'extinguish' may at once be extended to the corresponding forms of SCEGLIERE 'choose'. Phonologically, just as the Palatal *gn* contrasts before vowels with the Dental *n*, so a Palatal Lateral (written *gl* or *gli*) contrasts with a Dental Lateral *l*. It is these Palatals which appear in the basic roots: *spegn-e-re* (with long [ɲɲ], as we said), and *scegli-e-re* (likewise with long [ʎʎ]). But before *t* both oppositions are equally neutralised: phonologically, the units are the features Nasal (as before) and simply Lateral (the only feature common to Palatal Lateral and Dental Lateral). It is this neutralised unit that is realised in the Participle *scelto* 'chosen'. Although the *l* is phonetically dental (and there is thus an alternation between *scel-* and the *scegli-* of *scegliere*), no further rule is needed to account for it. Neutralisation is also common in vowel systems. In the form of Italian widely taught to foreigners, Half-close [e] and [o] are phonologically opposed to Half-open [ɛ] and [ɔ]. The first two appear, for example, in the roots of *vendo* ' I sell' and *pone* '[he] puts' and the others (though spelled the same) in *sento* 'I feel' and *volge* '[he] turns'.[4] But the oppositions hold only in stressed syllables. It follows that *vendiámo* 'we sell' (with the stress marked by the acute accent) must have an *e* identical to that of *sentiámo* 'we feel', and *ponéva* 'was putting' an *o* identical to that of *volgéva* 'was turning'. It follows literally, just as, in *cadde* 'fell', it followed that *a* was phonetically short, without reference to the morphological context.

In these cases we can argue that an apparent morphological alternation is explained entirely by the rules of phonology. But when we have passed this mile post there are other alternations that are less straightforward. Let us pick up again the forms of the Past Participle. In *morto* or *apparso* there is merely an irregular formation; the roots *mor-* and *appar-* are in their normal form. In *spento* or *scelto* the morphophonemic problem has already been dealt with. But consider, for example, *volto* 'turned' and *chiuso* 'closed'. For the Verb 'to turn' the root is basically *volg-* (Infinitive *volg-e-re*) and for 'to close' it is *chiud-* (*chiud-e-re*). So, in the Participles, we can posit basic *volg+t*, *chiud+s*. In addition, neither *lgt* nor *ds* is allowed phonologically. We may therefore posit rules of sandhi by which:

$$volg + t + o \ \rightarrow volto \qquad \text{'turned'}$$
$$chiud + s + o \rightarrow chiuso \qquad \text{'closed'}$$

These processes are **phonologically motivated**. Sequences of phonemes that would not be in accordance with the rules of phonology are changed into ones that are. But they do not follow automatically from the rules of phonology alone. We have to state explicit **morphophonemic rules**.

To understand why, we must look at a wider range of alternations. For roots which end in simple *c* or *g*, there is a general process by which, for example:

$$fac + t + o \quad \rightarrow fatto \qquad \text{'made'}$$
$$ereg + t + o \quad \rightarrow eretto \qquad \text{'erected'}$$

Schematically, *c* or *g* + *t* → *tt*. When -*s* follows, we can posit a

---

[4] I will follow the markings in the *The Cambridge Italian Dictionary*, ed. Barbara Reynolds, vol I (Cambridge, Cambridge University Press, 1962).

similar process by which *c* or *g* + *s* reduce to *ss*. This is shown, for example, by the irregular Preterites:

$$\text{dic} + \text{s} + \text{i} \quad \rightarrow \text{dissi} \qquad \text{'I said'}$$
$$\text{ereg} + \text{s} + \text{i} \quad \rightarrow \text{eressi} \qquad \text{'I erected'}$$

The same processes apply if the consonant of the root is itself double:

$$\text{legg} + \text{s} + \text{i} \quad \rightarrow \text{lessi} \qquad \text{'I read'}$$
$$\text{legg} + \text{t} + \text{o} \quad \rightarrow \text{letto} \qquad \text{'read'}$$

All else being equal, this would give us *voltto* for 'turned'. However, the distinction between double and single consonants is valid only between vowels and, after *l*, *t* is phonetically single. similarly:

$$\text{volg} + \text{s} + \text{i} \quad \rightarrow \text{volsi} \qquad \text{'I turned'}$$

and, with a nasal preceding:

$$\text{vinc} + \text{t} + \text{o} \quad \rightarrow \text{vinto} \qquad \text{'won'}$$
$$\text{vinc} + \text{s} + \text{i} \quad \rightarrow \text{vinsi} \qquad \text{'I won'}$$

In all these cases, the sandhi is phonologically motivated. There are again no clusters *ct* or *gt*, *cs* or *gs*, and so on.

But now let us turn to roots in dentals. In the examples which follow, *t* or *tt* plus *s* again reduce to double *ss*:

$$\text{scot} + \text{s} + \text{o} \quad \rightarrow \text{scosso} \qquad \text{'shaken'}$$
$$\text{annett} + \text{s} + \text{o} \rightarrow \text{annesso} \qquad \text{'annexed'}$$

But in *chiuso* 'closed' we have posited a reduction of *d* + *s* to single *s*. Similarly, for example:

$$\text{rid} + \text{s} + \text{o} \quad \rightarrow \text{riso} \qquad \text{'laughed'}$$

Why are these not *chiusso* and *risso*? Why, for that matter, are *scosso*, *dissi* and *eressi* not *scoso*, *disi*, *eresi*? Neither process follows directly from the distribution of phonemes. All that tells us is that, for *d* + *s*, *g* + *s* and so on, there must be some form of sandhi. What it is must then be made explicit.

On the evidence presented so far, there are two rules. One is the general rule that holds for *dissi*, *fatto*, and so on. In fact it holds more widely:

$$\text{mov} + \text{s} + \text{o} \quad \rightarrow \text{mosso} \qquad \text{'moved'}$$
$$\text{scriv} + \text{t} + \text{o} \quad \rightarrow \text{scritto} \qquad \text{'written'}$$

– and, as we have seen, it also holds for $(t)t$ plus $s$. The other, which would hold for $d$ plus $s$, is an exception. But when we look at other roots in $d$, we find fresh complications. Let us begin with *preso* 'taken'. The root is *prend-* (Infinitive *prend-e-re*) and, from what we have said so far, we would expect the Participle to be *prenso*. There is nothing wrong with the cluster $ns$: compare already *vinsi* 'I won' ($\leftarrow vinc\text{-}s\text{-}i$). Why the further reduction to *preso*?

There is no answer – except that the reduction of $n+s$ may also be posited for two other Verbs:

$$\text{pon}+\text{s}+\text{i} \;\rightarrow \text{posi} \qquad \text{'I put'}$$
$$\text{riman}+\text{s}+\text{i} \;\rightarrow \text{rimasi} \qquad \text{'I remained'}$$

(compare *pon-e* 'puts' and Infinitive *riman-e-re*). It is therefore tempting to say that *preso* is derived by two exceptional processes. First, $d+s$ reduces to $s$. That, as we have seen, is phonologically motivated. Then $n+s \rightarrow s$. This is NOT phonologically motivated. Furthermore, we must make clear that it does not apply to forms like *vinsi*. There are ways of doing that; but it is evident that another mile post has been passed.

We must also consider the phonetic quality of the $s$. In the variety of Italian that is normally taught, [s] and [z] are in contrast between vowels. *Chiuso*, *riso* and *preso* all have [s],[5] but other similar Participles have [z]:

$$\text{uccid}+\text{s}+\text{o} \;\rightarrow \text{ucci[z]o} \qquad \text{'killed'}$$
$$\text{persuad}+\text{s}+\text{o} \rightarrow \text{persua[z]o} \qquad \text{'persuaded'}$$

There is no phonological reason why this should be so. The reduction of $d+s$ is phonologically motivated and, in general, it applies to nearly a dozen Verbs. But not only is it exceptional when compared with that of $t+s$ or $g+s$; in this variety, it also varies from lexeme to lexeme.

Some scholars have maintained that processes like this are phonological. Others will say that the forms are irregular, and would be better listed. But there are degrees of irregularity; and, even when they must be lexically restricted, general processes are still attractive.

For illustration – and it will be the last, I promise – let us return to roots with written -*c* or -*g*: for example, *dic-* 'say' or

---

[5] I again follow the markings in the *Cambridge Italian Dictionary*.

*volg-* 'turn'. We have seen that the consonant is assimilated before *t* or *s*; but at the beginning of a syllable it also alternates between a Palatal phoneme before Front vowels (*dice* ['ditʃe] '[he] says', *volgi* ['vɔldʒi] 'you turn') and the corresponding Velar before Back or Open (*dico* ['diko] 'I say', Subjunctive *volga* ['vɔlga]). The same alternation can be found with double consonants (*leggo* ['lɛggo] 'I read' but *legge* ['lɛddʒe] '[he] reads'); nor is it confined to the Verbs (compare *ami*[k]*o* 'friend' but Plural *ami*[tʃ]*i* 'friends'; *astrolo*[g]*o* 'astrologist' but *astrolo*[dʒ]*i* 'astrologists'). The cluster [sk] alternates, under the same conditions, with the phonetically double [ʃʃ]: thus *fin-i-sc-o* [fi'nisko] 'I finish', but *fin-i-sc-e* [fi'niʃʃe] '[he] finishes'. Obviously, a tempting solution is to treat this as a phenomenon of palatalisation. By the first and most important rule, basic Velar Occlusives would be modified to Palatals before a 'palatal' vowel': thus *di*[k]*-e* → *di*[tʃ]*e*, *vol*[g]*-i* → *vol*[dʒ]*i*, and also *fin-i-s*[k]*-e* → *finis*[tʃ]*e*. By a subsidiary rule, the [stʃ] of the last form (which is phonologically excluded) would be further adjusted to [ʃʃ]. The basic morphological formations (1st Singular with suffixed *-o*, Noun Plural in *-i*, and so on) would remain quite regular.

Unfortunately, the process is BOTH phonologically unmotivated (like *pon* + *s* + *i* → *posi*) AND lexically restricted. In Italian, Velars readily appear before Front vowels (*chilo* 'Kilo', *ghiro* 'dormouse'). There are also other roots which do not alternate. For example, the Verb PAGARE 'pay' has 1st Singular ['pago] 'I pay' and likewise 2nd Singular ['pagi] 'you pay'; although these are spelled *pago* and *paghi*, the '*gh*' is merely a spelling convention for [g] before *i* and *e*. The Noun LUOGO 'place' has Singular *luogo* and Plural *luoghi* ['lwɔgi], CIECO 'blind' the Singulars *cieco* and *cieca* and the Plurals *cie*[k]*i* (*ciechi*) and *cie*[k]*e* (*cieche*), BOSCO 'wood' Singular *bosco* and Plural *bos*[k]*i* (*boschi*), and so on. On the strength of this, we might argue that the alternation is purely morphological.

But there are two considerations which might be brought against this. Firstly, the alternation is not only recurrent (in the sense defined in chapter 6) but it recurs in several morphological contexts. We would need a separate formation of Noun Plurals, also of the 2nd Singular of Verbs (*-i* with palatalisation versus *-i* without), also of the 1st Plurals (compare *volgiamo* 'we turn', also with [dӡ]), and so on. Although the process itself is identical, we would have to posit a separate rule for each formation. Secondly, the change is phonetically natural. The fronting of velars is widespread before Front vowels (e.g. in English and still more in Turkish), and this readily leads to affrication. It is by just such a process (subsequently overlaid by analogy and other developments) that the alternation in Italian has historically arisen. We are clearly approaching our final mile post. But, by this reasoning, palatalisation is one process and is still morphophonemic.

If we take this line, we must distinguish 'palatalising' from 'non-palatalising' consonants. The root of CIECO, for example, has a normal [k] which remains [k] in whatever context. But AMICO has a special [k] which is distinguished from it by a **diacritic feature** 'Palatalising'. For convenience we may write this with a capital $K$ (*amiK-*). Similarly, the Verb 'to say' has the root *diK-* and, in *finisce*, *-sc-* is basically *-sK-*. For LUOGO or PAGARE we establish a normal [g]; but in the roots of ASTROLOGO or VOLGERE 'to turn' there is again a special 'Palatalising' [g]. This too we can write with a capital *astroloG-*, *volG-*). Before back or open vowels, $K$ and $G$ are phonetically the same as normal [k] and normal [g]. But when a front vowel follows, $amiK+i \rightarrow$ *ami*[tʃ]*i*, $volG+i \rightarrow vol$[dӡ]*i*, and so on. In this way, we can state one general rule. We then show, in the dictionary, which form of root each lexeme has.

This is a technique that works. But it is plainly open to abuse: whenever we are left with a recurrent alternation, we may be tempted to say that form $x \rightarrow$ form $y$ because of some diacritic feature 'y-ish'. It is also no more than a technique: there is still no reason why some [k]s and [g]s should be palatalisable and others not. In this example, the process is phonetically plausible (and it may be relevant that it is the reflex of a genuine sound change). But it has a status unlike any of the assimilations with which we began.

## RELATED READING

DRESSLER, *Morphonology*, is the best recent treatment of this topic: it would be even better if it had an index or an analytic table of contents. The term 'morpho(pho)nology' is equivalent to 'morphophonemics'; both date from the

1930s, and both have been used with senses variously wider than the one adopted here. For a survey of their history see J. Kilbury, *The Development of Morphophonemic Theory* (Amsterdam, Benjamins, 1976).

For the concept of basic forms see BLOOMFIELD, p. 164; but Bloomfield's 'phonetic modification' also includes morphological processes. To understand Bloomfield, it is also essential to read his later article, 'Menomini morphophonemics' (1939), reprinted in C. F. Hockett (ed.), *A Leonard Bloomfield Anthology* (Bloomington, Indiana University Press, 1970), pp. 351–62. LASS, ch. 4, includes an interesting restatement of Bloomfield's method (pp. 59ff. on 'process morphophonemics'). For 'base forms' in a morphemic model compare HOCKETT, *Course*, pp. 281ff.; or H. A. Gleason, *An Introduction to Descriptive Linguistics* (2nd edn, New York, Holt Rinehart and Winston, 1965), pp. 82ff. Ancient Greek $t^hrik^h$- is an example of what Hockett calls a 'theoretical base form'. In generative phonology Bloomfield's basic form became part of an underlying 'phonological' representation: thus CHOMSKY & HALLE, §5.1 (with the example of *telegraph*, §5.2). See below for the collapse of morphophonemics into phonology; the fundamentals were otherwise unchanged.

Notions of 'euphony' and 'ease of articulation' are even more important in historical phonology. It is distressing that one cannot recommend a comprehensive study.

For sandhi in Sanskrit and in general see W. S. Allen, *Sandhi* (The Hague, Mouton, 1962); for a traditional Sanskritist's account, A. MacDonnell, *A Sanskrit Grammar for Students* (3rd edn, London, Oxford University Press, 1927), ch. 2 ('Rules of sandhi or euphonic combinations of letters'). On assimilation, dissimilation and other kinds of process see LASS, ch. 8. The analysis of Ancient Greek employs what Lounsbury once called the 'method of internal reconstruction': see F. G. Lounsbury, *Oneida Verb Morphology* (New Haven, Yale University Press, 1953), Introduction ('The method of descriptive morphology', reprinted *RiL*, pp. 379–85). But note that Lounsbury uses 'fusion' in a wider sense (following SAPIR, pp. 129ff.).

For the last section compare my earlier article on Latin, 'Some reflections on Latin morphophonology', *TPhS* 1972, pp. 59–78. For a study of an interesting aspect of Italian dialects, see M. Maiden, *Interactive Morphonology : Metaphony in Italian* (London, Routledge, 1991). For neutralisation see LASS, ch. 3; its origin, as of so much that is worthwhile in phonology, is in the work of Trubetzkoy (see TRUBETZKOY, ch. 5). For its application to the present problem see *Inflectional Morphology*, p. 237 (with references to Martinet and Bazell). At the end of the 1950s, Halle used a case of neutralisation in Russian to argue against the current American concept of the phoneme: see M. Halle, *The Sound Pattern of Russian* (The Hague, Mouton, 1959), pp. 22ff.; also, for this and other arguments, N. Chomsky, *Current Issues in Linguistic Theory* (The Hague, Mouton, 1964), §§4.2–5. It was then assumed that NO concept of the phoneme was valid; therefore morphophonemic processes, which had been thought to deal with alternations among phonemes, were no different from phonological processes. This became the classic view in generative phonology: see CHOMSKY & HALLE, part 1; for its eventual break-up see LASS, §9.6 (and references, p. 235).

On phonological (= phonotactic) motivation see A. H. Sommerstein, 'On phonotactically motivated rules', *JL* 10 (1974), pp. 71–94: this discusses, among other things, my treatment in *Inflectional Morphology*. See also Maiden's critique (*Interactive Morphonology*, ch. 2). For diacritic features see CHOMSKY & HALLE, p. 138 and elsewhere. But they are a version of a very old device: see Bloomfield, 'Menomini morphophonemics', §5 for morphophonemes that are distinct from actual phonemes; for similar units in Italian (K, G as distinct from /k/, /g/) see R. A. Hall, *Descriptive Italian Grammar* (Ithaca, N.Y., Cornell University Press, 1948). DRESSLER, *Morphonology*, has a whole chapter (pp. 168ff.) on Italian palatalisation. But I have suggested elsewhere that, in the case of Verbs, the alternations now reflect an opposite process of velarisation: see P. H. Matthews, 'Present stem alternations in Italian', in H. Geckeler, B. Schlieben-Lange, J. Trabant and H. Weydt (eds.), *Logos Semantikos : Studia Linguistica in Honorem Eugenio Coseriu* (Berlin, De Gruyter, 1981), 4, pp. 57–65 (and compare BYBEE, pp. 68ff., on Spanish).

# 9
# Properties and their exponents

Types of language: agglutinating; fusional but basically agglutinating; flectional but non-fusional; flectional and fusional.

*Flection.* Some illustrations from Ancient Greek: Number and Case in Nouns; patterns of marking in the regular Verb (*elelýkete* 'you had unfastened'). Extension of the process model; exponence. Derivation in stages: inflectional stems and terminations; rules for *elelýkete*. Exponence and the marking of categories.

*Types of exponence.* Simple exponence. Cumulation: vs fused markers; vs overlapping. Extended exponence: main and subsidiary exponents; distinction not always feasible; comparison with treatment in the 'Item and Arrangement' model. Extended exponence and overlapping; extended exponents parallel to the positions of simple exponents (Plurals of Nouns in Luxembourgish).

Let us drag ourselves back from the edges of phonology and see where our search for models has got to. In summary, we have distinguished a model in which words are sequences of morphemes:

SEA + Plural

from one in which they have a list of properties:

$$\begin{bmatrix} \text{Plural} \\ \text{SEA} \end{bmatrix}$$

In the first model, we must say which allomorphs the morphemes have. Thus SEA is represented by [si:] and Plural by the basic allomorph [z]. In the second, we must show how the form is derived from a root. Thus SEA has the root [si:] and its Plural is formed by suffixing [z]. In either case, the form may be modified by morphophonemic processes.

It is also possible to see the glimmerings of a typology. At one extreme, the 'Item and Arrangement' model might work to perfection. Each morpheme has one basic allomorph; each basic allomorph is different from every other; in every word-form the sequence of allomorphs is transparent. Of the languages which have a rich morphology, those conventionally called '**agglutinating**' meet these conditions most nearly.

In another case, the 'Item and Arrangement' model might work perfectly except for the morphophonemics. Each morpheme would have one basic allomorph; again each basic allomorph would be different from any other; but, in actual word-forms, the sequence of allomorphs is obliterated by fusion. Let us return, for a moment, to Turkish *çocuğum* 'my child'. By a rule of sandhi, written *çocuğ-* fuses with *-um*: [tʃɔdʒuːm]. Hence the sequence of morphemes (ÇOCUK + 1st Singular) is no longer transparent. But if we ignore the fusion it is [tʃɔdʒuk + um], just as *köyüm* 'my village' is *köy + üm* and so on. In Turkish 'soft' *ğ* is an exception. But we can imagine a language whose morphology is like that of Turkish except that fusion is general. It would be at once **fusional** but **basically agglutinating**.

For the next type we can return, for a moment again, to English. In *sailed* or *missed*, Past Participle is marked by basic [d]. But in *taken* it is marked by basic [n]; in morphemic terms, one morpheme has two basic allomorphs. In *sailed* or *missed*, [d] also marks Past Tense; the allomorphs of two morphemes are the same. In *sold* or *stolen*, Past Participle is marked by both a suffix and a change of vowel. In terms of morphemes, SELL and STEAL have the further allomorphs [səʊl] and [stəʊl]. In *come* Past Participle is not marked, and in *sung* or *won* it is marked by a change of vowel alone. Apparently there is no allomorph. For the exceptions at least, we have argued that the 'Item and Arrangement' model works rather badly. But the reason lies solely in the basic processes, not in the morphophonemics. Where there IS a suffix it is in general not fused: *sailed* is transparently [seɪl + d], *taken* [teɪk + ən], and so on. Let us imagine that English was consistently like this. Its basic structure would be of the type conventionally called '**flectional**'. But it would have little sandhi and, in particular, no fusion. In that sense it would be flectional but **non-fusional**.

Finally, we can foresee a type which is basically flectional AND fusional. We have seen that Ancient Greek will often satisfy the second criterion: $k^h rys' + e + o + n \rightarrow k^h rys\hat{u}{:}n$ and so on. We are now about to see how thoroughly it satisfies the first.

## FLECTION

What, more exactly, is the character of a flectional language? We have implied that it is a language for which the 'Item and Arrangement' model works badly. But that can be for more than one reason.

One reason, as we have seen, is that it has morphological processes other than prefixation and suffixation. We had an example from Greek in chapter 7. In the Present, the Verb 'to leave' had what Indo-Europeanists call the *e*-grade (1st Singular *leíp-ɔ:*). But in the Perfect it had the *o*-grade (1st Singular *lé-loip-a*) and in the Aorist the zero grade (*é-lip-on*). This is an alternation among basic forms; only by the most elaborate fiddle could it be disguised as morphophonemic. The morphemic model would handle it no better than it handled English *man* and *men* or *sing* and *sung*.

In the case of English this was our main argument for the 'Item and Process' model. But English has relatively little morphology. Each word-form has at most one inflection, and only one category is marked. But in a language with a rich morphology word-forms may have many inflections and many categories may be marked. The more it is agglutinative the more the relationship between them will be one to one. This is a striking feature of Turkish, as we saw in chapter 6. The more it is flectional, the more the relation will be anything but one to one.

For a simple example, let us look again at forms like *p^hýlakos* 'of a sentry'. Two categories are marked, the Case (Genitive) and the Number (Singular). There is no doubt that they are grammatically separate. In a Possessive construction, the Noun identifying the possessor will be Genitive regardless of its Number: 'the sentry's cloak' (*p^hýlakos*), 'the sentries' cloaks' (Genitive Plural *p^hylákɔ:n*). In, for example, a Relative construction the Relative Pronoun will agree in Number with an antecedent in whatever Case: 'the sentry who (Sg.) I saw', 'of the sentries who (Pl.) died', and so on. But both Case and Number are marked by a single ending. If we set *p^hýlakos* in its paradigm:

|  | *Singular* | *Plural* |
|---|---|---|
| *Nominative* | pʰýlaks | pʰýlakes |
| *Accusative* | pʰýlaka | pʰýlakas |
| *Genitive* | pʰýlakos | pʰyláko:n |
| *Dative* | pʰýlaki | pʰýlaksi |

we see that there are eight endings:

| -s | -es |
|---|---|
| -a | -as |
| -os | -ɔ:n |
| -i | -si |

none of which can be divided further.

This pattern runs right through the system. The lexeme pʰYLAKS 'sentry' has one set of endings; soPʰos 'clever', which we also analysed in chapter 8, has another. But there too Case and Number are marked simultaneously, as for every other Noun and Adjective in Greek. It is a pattern also found in other Indo-European languages; and, since these are archetypally flectional, it has become a standard illustration of the type. But it is only the simplest illustration of a principle that is much more radical.

For a more complex illustration, let us take the Verb form *elelýkete* 'you had unfastened'[1] and look in detail at the categories it marks. Firstly, it is a 2nd Plural ('you') and as such is directly opposed to 2nd Singular and 2nd Dual, 1st Plural and 3rd Plural. These distinctions are marked by the suffix *-te*: compare, for instance, 1st Plural *elelýkemen* 'we had unfastened' and 3rd Plural *elelýkesan*. The 2nd Plural has the same suffix throughout the Active paradigm (*lý:ete* 'you are unfastening', *elý:ete* 'you were unfastening', and so on). But note that this holds only for the Actives. Note too that Person (2nd) and Number (Plural) are not marked separately. It is conceivable that separate markers might be posited in some Duals. But in the Singular and Plural at least they are always marked simultaneously.

---

[1] Given as the normal form by GOODWIN, p. 101. But there is an alternative *elelýke:te* with a different vowel before the ending ('not classic' according to GOODWIN, §684.2). In all the forms to be cited the accent is predictable by general rules applying regularly to Verb forms (GOODWIN, pp. 29f.); we can therefore ignore it for the purposes of our present analysis.

Secondly, the form belongs to the Perfective Aspect ('had unfastened') as opposed to the Imperfective and Aorist. But whereas Number and Person were marked together by one formative, in this case a single category is identified in concert in three separate places. One marker is the reduplicative prefix *le-* which we described in chapter 7. Contrast *elý:ete* 'you were unfastening', which is the corresponding Imperfective, and Aorist *elý:sate*. This is a regular formative for Verbs whose roots begin with a consonant, and is found in all their Perfective forms. Another marker is the vowel of the root itself: short *ly-* as opposed to long *ly:-*. Finally, Perfective is marked by the *-k-*. This is a suffix that appears in every form that is both Perfective and Active, and is regular for Verbs with this type of vocalic root. Note, though, that it is another formative which is restricted to the Actives.

Next, the word is Past Tense as opposed to Present and Future. Leaving Future aside, the distinction between Past Perfective *elelýkete* and Present Perfective *lelýkate* 'you have unfastened' is made in two ways. First, the Past Tense has a prefix *e-* (traditionally called the 'augment'). This has a fairly consistent rôle; however, it also marks the Aorist (for example, in the corresponding 2nd Plural *elý:sate*). Secondly, the Present Perfective has an *-a-* before the final *-te* while the Past Perfective has *-e-*. This is not so widespread. In other parts of the paradigm Present and Past may be distinguished by the augment alone (Imperfective *lý:ete* 'you are unfastening' versus *elý:ete* 'you were unfastening') or by the augment with a different final suffix (*lý:ɔ:* 'I am unfastening', *ély:on* 'I was unfastening'). In addition, *-a-* and *-e-* recur in other contexts: compare again the Aorist *elý:sate* and add Imperfective Future *lý:sete* 'you will be unfastening'. But the distinction is systematic at this point. Compare, for example, the 1st Plurals *lelýkamen* 'we have unfastened' and *elelýkemen* 'we had unfastened', or 2nd Singular *lélykas* and (with a long vowel as an added complication) *elelýkɛ:s*.

Next, the word belongs to the Indicative Mood as opposed to the Subjunctive, Optative or Imperative. In these other Moods there is no distinction between Past and Present, the forms being correspondingly without an augment. However, the distinctions between the Present Perfective Indicative, Perfective Subjunctive and Perfective Optative are most consistently marked by the same pre-final vowel: if we take the 2nd Plurals alone the forms are *lelýkate* as above, *lelýkɛːte* (the vowel in the Subjunctives being regularly ɛː in some Person/Number forms and ɔː in others), and *lelýkoite* (*oi* being found in every Optative).

Finally, it is Active in Voice as opposed to Middle or Passive. As may be clear already, this is another distinction which is marked in more than one place. The following are the Plurals for the Past Perfective:

|          | *Active*    | *Middle/Passive* |
|----------|-------------|------------------|
| 1*st Pl.* | elelýkemen  | elelýmetʰa       |
| 2*nd Pl.* | elelýkete   | elélystʰe        |
| 3*rd Pl.* | elelýkesan  | elélynto         |

– from which it may be seen that the whole ending of the word-form differs from the first column to the second. The Middle/Passive has no -*k*- (as we have already remarked) and no following vowel. Furthermore, there is a different set of final suffixes. As 2nd Plural -*te* is general in the Active, so the contrasting -*stʰe* is general in the Middle and Passive. The Duals show a similar pattern; also the Singulars, except that in them and in the 3rd Plural the Middle/Passive endings also vary with the Tense. Thus 3rd Singular *elélyto* (Past Perfective) versus *lélytai* (Present Perfective) or, in the Imperfective, *elýːeto* versus *lýːetai*.

To sum up, the form *elelýkete* may be analysed into a sequence of formal elements:

$$e - le - ly - k - e - te$$

(the accent falling predictably on the antepenultimate syllable), where each formative is isolated by its recurrences elsewhere in the paradigm. As a semantic unit the word is marked for Aspect (Perfective), Tense (Past), Mood (Indicative), Person and Number (2nd Plural) and Voice (Active). But categories and formatives are in nothing like a one-to-one relation. That the word is Perfective is in part identified by the reduplication *le*-, but also by the suffix -*k*-. At the same time, -*k*- is one of the formatives that help to identify the word as Active; another is -*te* which, however, also marks it as 2nd Plural. The following table shows each formal element in sequence and, above it, each of the semantic elements which it marks or helps to mark:

|  | (Root) | Perfective | Indicative | Active |
|---|---|---|---|---|
| Past | Perfective | Perfective | Active | Past Active 2nd Plural |
| e | le | ly | k | e | te |

As can be seen, the markers of a given category need not even be next to one another. Perfective and Past are both identified at once by prefixes before the root and by suffixes following it.

None of this involves any crucial irregularity. The paradigm of the Verb 'to loose' or 'to unfasten' is in fact the first that generations of schoolchildren used to commit to memory. But it would clearly be very hard to analyse this word into a sequence of morphemes. Does the morpheme Past come before Perfective or after it, and how does the position of either of these relate to that of the lexical morpheme LY-? Perhaps we will say that Past is the first morpheme in the word, since the augment *e-* is its most consistent marker. But in forms like *lý:-ɔ:* 'I am unfastening' versus *é-ly:-on* 'I was unfastening', or *lé-ly-tai* 'has been unfastened' versus *e-lé-ly-to* 'had been unfastened', the morphemes at the end of the word (1st Singular, 3rd Singular) would have allomorphs that are morphologically conditioned by one that is never adjacent to them. How do we explain such conditioning at a distance? Finally, which is the right sequence for the Person and Number: 2nd + Plural, as it were, or Plural + 2nd? There seems no way of deciding. Some theorists would avoid the issue, saying that 2nd Plural is syntactically a single morpheme. That is less awkward, perhaps, than saying that Genitive Singular is a single morpheme in words like *pʰýlakos*. But Person and Number will have to be distinguished at some level. Is there any other reason for saying that they are different from Aspect, Tense, and so on?

These and other questions arise only if we start by thinking in terms of the 'Item and Arrangement' model. It creates gratuitous problems of analysis and gratuitous problems of explanation. Nor did anyone dream of treating flectional languages in that way until the theory of the morpheme as an abstract unit was invented in the 1940s. The marking of these categories is non-linear and is at once many to one and one to many. The 'Item and Arrangement' model is strictly linear and implies that one-to-one relations are the ideal. Not surprisingly, it works badly and many theorists will now agree that it is a mistake to apply it.

For a better treatment, let us begin with the simpler example of *pʰylak-os* 'of a sentry'. In the traditional formula, it is 'the Genitive Singular of pʰYLAKS'. In the notation which we introduced in chapter 7 it is thus

$$\begin{bmatrix} \text{Genitive} \\ \text{Singular} \\ \text{p}^{\text{h}}\text{YLAKS} \end{bmatrix}$$

The lexeme has the root *pʰylak*; that is again a matter for a dictionary. It also belongs to a large but irregular class whose endings are an exception to the regular pattern. Traditionally they form the 3rd Declension and we will assign them to an inflectional class 'III'. On this basis, the rule for the Genitive Singular is as follows:

$$\begin{bmatrix} \text{Genitive} \\ \text{Singular} \\ \text{III} \\ \text{X} \end{bmatrix} \rightarrow \text{X} + \text{os}$$

In words, the Genitive Singular of the 3rd Declension is formed by suffixing *-os*. This rule follows the model in chapter 7, except that it refers to two categories (Case and Number) instead of one. By the rule which we gave for English *seas*:

$$\begin{bmatrix} \text{Plural} \\ \text{X} \end{bmatrix} \rightarrow \text{X} + [\text{z}]$$

the suffix [z] is related to the single property Plural. By the rule for *pʰylakos*, *-os* is related simultaneously to both Genitive and Singular.

Let us describe this relationship as that of **exponence**. Thus, in *seas*, [z] is the **exponent** of Plural and, by the similar rule for *sailed*, [d] is defined as the exponent of Past Tense or Past Participle. In *pʰylakos*, the Case and Number together have the exponent *-os*. So, in setting out the rules for *elelýkete*, our task is to ensure that each successive formative (*e-*, *le-*, and so on) is assigned as an exponent to just the categories that it marks. In that way, we will derive it and the other word-forms which are related to it by the simplest or most general processes, and the function or functions of each formal element will be described exactly.

Since there are several formatives, it is obvious that there will be several processes. It is also clear that their order must be partly fixed. Starting from the root, the suffixes are added in the order *-k-e-te* not, for example, *-te-e-k*. The root must likewise be reduplicated (*le-*) before the augment (*e-*) is prefixed. Finally, although the marking of categories is not linear, not every category is marked in every position. Person and Number are marked only by the final suffix. Aspect is marked only by formatives adjacent to the root (*le-ly-k-*), and Tense only by formatives before and after these. We can therefore distinguish three layers:

$$_3[\,_2[e\,_1[\text{le ly k}]_1\,e]_2\,\text{te}]_3$$

and, correspondingly, three stages in their derivation. If we assume a root *ly:*, the first stage will derive *le-ly-k-* by three operations: shortening the vowel, reduplication and the suffixing of *-k-*. In the second stage, the augment is prefixed and a further *-e-* is suffixed: *e-le-ly-k-e-*. The third and last stage adds *-te*.

In the tradition *-te*, which ends the derivation, is a **termination**, and the form to which it is added, *elelyke-*, is a **stem**. In the definition of chapter 4, this is again a form that underlies at least one paradigm or partial paradigm: more specifically, however, it is an **inflectional stem** as opposed to a lexical stem. Within the stem *elelyke-* there is a smaller stem *lelyk-*. Let us simply call the smaller 'Stem 1' and the larger 'Stem 2'. So, the structure of the whole form is

$$[e\,[\text{lelyk}]_{\text{Stem 1}}\,e]_{\text{Stem 2}}\,[\text{te}]_{\text{Termination}}$$

and our rules must deal with three inflectional formations, between which the successive operations have been parcelled out. The formation of Stem 1 involves, as we have seen, three operations; that of Stem 2 two; the addition of the Termination one.

For the rest, we can once more follow the 'Item and Process' model. The word is grammatically the '2nd Plural Active Past Perfective Indicative of LYO'. We assume that LYO has a root $ly:$-; so, in the columnar notation, our starting form is

$$\begin{bmatrix} \text{2nd} \\ \text{Plural} \\ \text{Active} \\ \text{Past} \\ \text{Perfective} \\ \text{Indicative} \\ \text{ly:} \end{bmatrix}_\text{V}$$

(subscript 'V' again = Verb). Stem 1 is derived according to three rules. Two refer to the single property Perfective and might be formulated (provisionally perhaps) as follows. First,

$$\begin{bmatrix} \text{Perfective} \\ \text{X V:} \end{bmatrix} \rightarrow \text{X V}$$

($ly:$- $\rightarrow$ $ly$-). This can again be put as easily in words: 'If the form is Perfective, a long vowel at the end of the root is shortened.' Then:

$$\begin{bmatrix} \text{Perfective} \\ \text{C X} \end{bmatrix} \rightarrow \text{C e} + \text{C X}$$

($ly$- $\rightarrow$ $le$-$ly$-). 'In the Perfective', that is, 'the root is reduplicated.' The third rule refers to both Perfective and Active, and says that if a word has both these properties -$k$- will be suffixed:

$$\begin{bmatrix} \text{Active} \\ \text{Perfective} \\ \text{X} \end{bmatrix} \rightarrow \text{X} + \text{k}$$

($le$-$ly$- $\rightarrow$ $le$-$ly$-$k$-). Note that we are assuming that these rules are regular; *lé-loip-a* 'I have left' is clearly one form that at this point is exceptional. In summary, the three rules will define the relation of exponence as follows:

|  |  | *Perfective* |
| *Perfective* | *Perfective* | *Active* |
| [le | ly | k]$_\text{Stem 1}$ |

(categories again listed above each formal element).

For the formation of Stem 2 there are two rules. First,

$$
\begin{bmatrix} \begin{Bmatrix} \text{Aorist} \\ \text{Past} \end{Bmatrix} \\ \text{X} \end{bmatrix} \rightarrow e + X
$$

So, if the form is either Past or Aorist, *e*- is prefixed. For the Aorist we cited earlier the form *e-lý:-s-a-te*. Then, if we can assume very tentatively that this is the general rule,

$$
\begin{bmatrix} \text{Active} \\ \text{Past} \\ \text{Indicative} \\ \text{X} \end{bmatrix} \rightarrow X + e
$$

So, unless a word falls under some other more specific rule, *-e-* is suffixed if it is Active AND Past AND Indicative. By these rules, *le-ly-k-* → *e-le-ly-k-* → *e-le-ly-k-e-* and the relation of exponence, for Stem 2, is defined thus:

*Active*

*Past*

*Past*               *Indicative*

[e      [Stem 1]    e]$_{\text{Stem 2}}$

Finally, the Termination is added by a rule which suffixes *-te* if the form has all three properties 2nd, Plural and Active:

$$
\begin{bmatrix} \text{2nd} \\ \text{Plural} \\ \text{Active} \\ \text{X} \end{bmatrix} \rightarrow X + te
$$

(*e-le-ly-k-e-* → *e-le-ly-k-e-te*). The relation of exponence is correspondingly:

*2nd*

*Plural*

*Active*

[te]$_{\text{Termination}}$

The last few pages have been rather spotty with notation, spottier than I would like a book of this kind to be. But it is instructive to take at least one complicated example and see how the marking of categories can be handled. In the model which we have followed, each rule refers equally to each of the properties that is relevant to the distribution of each formative. So, if *x* marks *y*, *x* is defined as an exponent of *y*. At the same time, certain categories are characteristically marked in certain positions. These positions are defined by the establishing of stems; where necessary, stems within stems.

## TYPES OF EXPONENCE

As we have seen, exponence may be one to one, or one to many, and so on. At least one case has a widely accepted name, and it will be useful to have names for others.

For the one-to-one type, no term is in use. But it could appropriately be called **simple exponence**. In English *sailed*, for example, [d] is the **simple exponent** of Past Tense or Past Participle. A simple exponent, like any other, need not be an affix. For example, in *sung* the modified vowel [ʌ] is the simple exponent of Past Participle.

In Greek *pʰýlakos* 'of a sentry' the relation, as we saw, is one to many. This type is usually referred to by the term '**cumulation**'. We will therefore say that, by our rule, -*os* is the **cumulative exponent** of both Genitive and Singular. For an example in a modern Indo-European language we can take the paradigm in Russian of the Masculine Inanimate Noun STOL 'table':

|  | *Singular* | *Plural* |
|---|---|---|
| *Nominative* | stol | stalý |
| *Genitive* | stalá | stalóv |
| *Dative* | stalú | stalám |
| *Accusative* | stol | stalý |
| *Instrumental* | stalóm | stalám'i |
| *Prepositional* | stal'é | staláx |

The pattern is again that of a root (*stol*) with or without an ending; and, although it may seem that in certain forms the root is also modified, this is purely morphophonemic. When there is an ending it is stressed (′) and in unstressed syllables the opposition between the vowels *o* and *a* is neutralised. In the Prepositional Singular, *l* is also palatalised (*l′*) before *e*. The only basic processes are those that introduce the endings and here there is again cumulative exponence throughout.

Cumulative exponence is common, and some scholars see it as THE characteristic of flectional languages. However, it is important to distinguish it from two other cases that are superficially similar. The first is the **fused marking** that can sometimes result from processes of sandhi. The Ancient Greek word for 'golden' had a Genitive Singular Masculine, *kʰrysûː*, whose ending *-ûː* represents a fusion of three formatives. One is a lexical formative (*-e-*); the second (*-o-*) is the exponent of Masculine; the third (perhaps *-o*) is that of Genitive and Singular. It is only in this last instance that there is cumulation. By the basic rule Masculine will have the simple exponent *-o-*, while *-e-* will be part of the lexical stem. Only through sandhi does *-uː* represent all of them.

The second case is that of **overlapping**. In Ancient Greek, the Termination of the Verb is a regular exponent of Person and Number. It is also a consistent exponent of Voice: compare again *elelýke-te* 'you had unfastened' with the corresponding Middle/Passive *elély-stʰe*. It can be, in addition, an exponent of Tense (*elély-to* 'had been unfastened' versus *lély-tai* 'has been unfastened' or *lýː-ɔː* 'I am unfastening' versus *élyː-on* 'I was unfastening'). But both Voice and Tense can have exponents in other positions. For example, in *elelýkete* (*e-le-ly-k-e-te*) *-k-* is an exponent of Active Voice and the augment (*e-*) of Past Tense. In that sense, their exponents merely overlap those of Person and Number. Those of Person and Number coincide completely, and here alone there is cumulative exponence.

The opposite of cumulation is the case in which exponence is many to one. In English *sold*, for instance, Past Tense or Past Participle has as its exponent both the vowel ([əʊ] versus [e]) and the suffix. Let us speak in this case of **extended exponence**. Similarly, in Ancient Greek, Perfective has **extended exponents** in *e-le-lýː-k-e-te* (*le-*, *y* not *yː*, *-k-*); likewise Past (*e-*, *-e-*); likewise Active (*-k-*, *-e-*, *-te*). In this whole word only Indicative has a simple exponent (*-e-*), and in that position there is still overlapping.

In most instances of extended exponence it is possible to identify one formative as the **main exponent**. In English, regular Past Tenses and Past Participles have a suffix and it is, moreover, identical with that of *sold*. We can therefore say that, in *sold*, [d] is the main exponent and [əʊ] a subsidiary exponent. But it may not always be so. In the example from Greek we might say that the main exponent of Perfective is *le-*; of the different markers, reduplication is the most consistent across Verbs and across the paradigm. For Past the main exponent is, more obviously, the augment (*e-*). But it is less clear that there is a main exponent of Active. Of its exponents in *e-le-lý-k-e-te*, *-te* is the best candidate. However, that is also the only – therefore vacuously the main – exponent of Person and Number. The preceding *-e-* is in the position in which we find the main exponents of Mood. Finally, *-k-* is an exponent of Active only in the Perfective. In reality, the contrast is carried by the whole word ending.

In the 'Item and Arrangement' model, extended exponence will be rendered in part as 'grammatically conditioned allomorphy' (final section of chapter 6). In *sold*, for example, SELL would have an allomorph [səʊl] whose form is determined by the following inflectional morpheme. Similarly, in *e-le-lý-k-e-te*, we would be forced to say that, if *e-* is the allomorph of Past, this morpheme also determines, by remote grammatical conditioning, the form of *-e-* as an allomorph of, say, Indicative. In *é-ly:-on* 'I was unfastening' versus *lý:-ɔ:* 'I am unfastening' it is at least one morpheme that grammatically determines the allomorph of 1st Singular, and so on. If flectional languages are those for which the 'Item and Arrangement' model works badly, this is a characteristic of them which is at least as striking as its opposite, cumulation.

Where several categories are marked, extended exponence leads naturally to overlapping. In Greek, the extended exponents of Voice overlap the cumulative exponents of Person and Number, and so on. But English *sold* forms part of a different pattern. In some forms, like *come* in *have come*, the category is not marked. In others it has a simple exponent, sometimes in one position (*sung*) and sometimes in another (*sailed*). In others, like *sold*, it has extended exponents in both positions. For a much more regular illustration of the same kind let us look at the Plural formations in, for example, Luxembourgish. Of the Nouns which follow:[2]

|  | Singular | Plural |
|---|---|---|
| 'leg' | Been | Been |
| 'fish' | Fësch | Fësch |
| 'brother' | Brudder | Bridder |
| 'mouse' | Maus | Mais |
| 'animal' | Déier | Déieren |
| 'table' | Dësch | Dëscher |
| 'book' | Buch | Bicher |
| 'house' | Haus | Haiser |

the first two have a Plural identical with the Singular. In the next two, Plural is marked by a change of vowel: [ʊ] in *Brudder* → [ɪ] in *Bridder*, [æːʊ] in *Maus* → [aɪ] in *Mais*. These are reflexes in Luxembourgish of the Germanic sound-changes that are conventionally called 'Umlaut': compare, for instance, German *Bruder* 'brother', Plural *Brüder*. In the next two examples the Plural has a suffix: *-en* in *Déier-en*, *-er* in *Dësch-er*. Finally, in the last two it is marked by both *-er* and a change of vowel. We might add to these four other examples, in which there is a change of consonant:

|  | Singular | Plural |
|---|---|---|
| 'dog' | Hond | Honn |
| 'ground' | Grond | Grënn |
| 'child' | Kand | Kanner |
| 'mouth' | Mond | Mënner |

In *Honn*, Plural is marked by *-nn* alone. In *Grënn*, it is marked by *-nn* and by Umlaut: in this case [o] in *Grond* → [ø]. In *Kanner*, it is marked by *-nn-* and by *-er*: note that medial *-nd-* is also possible in Luxembourgish. Finally, in *Mënner* it is marked by Umlaut and by *-nn-* and by *-er*.

Only one category is marked. Of the system of Cases that survives in German, the only reflex is an occasional fossil. But it

---

[2] The spellings follow those of the *Luxemburger Wörterbuch* (Luxembourg, Buchdruckerei P. Linden, 1950–77). The phonetic forms vary, in some cases, between speakers.

is clear that in our typology the Luxembourgish Noun is rudimentarily flectional, not rudimentarily agglutinative.


## RELATED READING

The argument in this chapter is part of the justification for what HOCKETT, 'Models', called a 'Word and Paradigm' morphology. See, in particular, ROBINS, 'WP'; also my *Inflectional Morphology*. But there is no simple opposition between Hockett's 'IP' and 'WP'; there is also more to be said about paradigms (see chapter 10).

For a systematic treatment of 'inflecting' languages, and the difficulties caused for the morphemic model, see *Inflectional Morphology*, ch. 6 (with examples from Latin); see my survey article, 'Recent developments in morphology', in J. Lyons (ed.), *New Horizons in Linguistics* (Harmondsworth, Penguin, 1970), pp. 97–114, for an illustration from Italian (pp. 107ff.). For a direct comparison with a morpheme-based description see E. F. Stairs & B. E. Hollenbach, 'Huave verb morphology', *IJAL* 35 (1969), pp. 38–53, and my reanalysis, 'Huave verb morphology: some comments from a non-tagmemic viewpoint', *IJAL* 38 (1972), pp. 96–118. Huave is a Mexican language spoken on the south side of the Tehuantepec Isthmus. These studies are quite old: for the later development of 'Word and Paradigm' models see, in particular, ANDERSON, 'Where's morphology?' (§4, 'The formal description of inflection'). A book by Anderson, *A-morphous Morphology* (Cambridge, Cambridge University Press) is at the time of writing still forthcoming.

For the form and notation of rules compare ANDERSON, 'Where's morphology?' which in turn refers to ARONOFF (see reading for chapter 4) on word-formation. In my earlier writings, I developed a different system, in which rules referred explicitly to stems: see *Inflectional Morphology*, ch. 9; also, for an extended illustration, 'The main features of Modern Greek verb inflection', *Foundations of Language* 3 (1967), pp. 262–84. For a generous exposition (and an alternative notation) see BAUER, *Morphology*, ch. 10. But note that my system also allowed for 'parasitic' formations (*Inflectional Morphology*, pp. 86, 173f.), in which the stem for one part of a paradigm is derived from that of another. See chapter 10 (on morphological transformations) for the reasons why one might want to do this.

For exponence compare *Inflectional Morphology*, pp. 185f. In the strict sense I am talking about a relation defined by rules: 'is an exponent of' has thus a similar status to (in a morphemic system) 'is an allomorph of'. In some work in the United States one finds what is in effect a compromise between a word-based and a morpheme-based approach, in which features are initially located in specific formatives, but then 'percolate' upwards to word level. See most recently R. Lieber, 'On percolation', *Yearbook of Morphology* 2 (1989), pp. 95–138 (specifically for morphosyntactic features and with examples from flectional systems). This is fine: but why should the features be assigned to formatives in the first place? For the original purpose of feature percolation, which was rather different, see textbook account by BAUER, *Morphology*, pp. 135ff.

For types of exponence I can refer only to my own work. But cumulation has long been recognised: for the difference between it and other cases of what are commonly called 'portmanteaus' compare *Inflectional Morphology*, §6.2.

## 10
# Paradigms

In the last three chapters we have seen how word-forms can be built up from their roots. Take, for example, Ancient Greek $sop^h\acute{ɔ}:n$ (σοφῶν). This is the Genitive Plural (all Genders) of the Adjective sop$^h$os 'clever', and can be built up as follows. First, the lexeme (sop$^h$os) has a root $sop^{h'}$-, the acute accent indicating, as before, that a basic high tone follows. To this is added a Gender suffix: for example, Feminine Plural -$a$-. Accordingly, $sop^{h'}$- → $sop^h + \acute{a}$, with the floating accent now assigned to a vowel. By another rule, the form must take the Genitive Plural suffix (-$ɔ:n$): $sop^h + \acute{a} → sop^h + \acute{a} + ɔ:n$. Finally, $a + ɔ:$ are fused to $ɔ:$ and, arising from the fusion, there is a falling tone: $sop^h + \acute{a} + ɔ:n$ (high $\acute{a}$ plus low $ɔ:$) → $sop^h\acute{ɔ}:n$. In this way, we construct each word-form by an ordered series of operations, some morphological (add -$a$-, add -$ɔ:n$), some morphophonemic.

In developing this model, we have followed a method which is typical of twentieth-century structural linguistics. We begin by trying to divide words into morphemes – Bloomfield's 'minimal sames of form and meaning'. Sometimes we could do it easily (English $sail + ed$) and at that point we were content. Sometimes we were obliged to speak of processes instead of morphemes (English *man* → *men*); but still the process had one meaning and the form to which it applied another. Sometimes we were forced to posit underlying forms that were modified by fusion (Turkish *çocuğ* + *um* → *çoc*[u:m] 'my child'). But still the basic forms conformed to the model, even if the actual form did not. In this way, we explained each large form as a combination of smaller forms. Each small form recurred in other large forms that are partly similar in meaning (English *sail-* in *sailing* or in *sails*; Turkish *-um* 'my' in, for example, *köyüm* 'my village'), and each rule of combination (add *-ed* [d] to form the Past Tense, fuse vowels across *ğ*) was made to apply as widely as possible.

But there is an alternative method, whose sources lie in the work of the ancient grammarians of Greek and Latin. This is simply to relate words as wholes. Take, for example, the opposition between *sop$^h$ɔ:n* (Genitive Plural) and the Accusative Singular Masculine *sop$^h$ón*. In terms of formatives, the latter is transparently *sop$^h$ + ó + n*, with *-o-* the Masculine and *-n* an Accusative Singular suffix. The former, as we have seen, is *sop$^h$* (root) plus a Gender suffix (Masculine/Neuter *-o-* or Feminine Plural *-a-*) which fuses with the Genitive Plural suffix. But if the forms are compared as wholes, the difference is simply that one ends in *-ɔ:n* and the other in *-ón*. Or, to reduce it to the minimal difference, one has *ɔ:* (falling tone and long vowel) where the other has *ó* (high tone and short vowel). For ANT$^h$ROPOS 'man', the corresponding forms are *ant$^h$rɔ́:pɔ:n* (Genitive Plural *-ɔ:n* and accent on the second syllable) and *ánt$^h$rɔ:pon* (*-on* or *-o-n* and accent on the first syllable). The accent of the first can be explained morphophonemically: Genitive Plural *ánt$^h$rɔ:p + ɔ:n*, with a long vowel in the final syllable, → *ant$^h$rɔ́:pɔ:n*. The different endings again derive from different processes of suffixation. But if we compare the forms as wholes these explanations are neither here nor there. They are distinguished equally by BOTH the endings AND the accent. Let us, finally, compare *sop$^h$ɔ́:n* (Genitive Plural Feminine) with its homonym *sop$^h$ɔ́:n* (Genitive Plural Masculine). We have posited different underlying forms: *sop$^h$ + á + ɔ:n* (Feminine Plural *-a-*) versus *sop$^h$ + ó + ɔ:n* (Masculine/Neuter *-o-*). If we follow the method of earlier chapters that is clearly right. But if we compare the forms as wholes, there is simply no difference at all.

Which method is best? With a language like English there is often little to choose between them. For example, we can say that *sailed* derives from a root *sail-* by the suffixation of *-ed*. Alternatively, we can say that *sailed* differs from other forms of SAIL in having *-ed* at the end of it. The analyses are effectively the same. But for languages like Ancient Greek different methods bring out different things. If we distinguish Feminine *soph + á + ɔ:n* from Masculine *soph + ó + ɔ:n*, it is because we are trying to generalise the rules of suffixation. We can then say that all Masculines and Neuters add *-o-*, while all Feminine Plurals add *-a-*. But there is a penalty, since, in these particular forms, we are obliged to posit a distinction which does not actually exist. The method followed in earlier chapters – the structuralist method, as we may call it – has in that sense led us to obscure the facts. If, instead, we simply say that *sophɔ:n* is homonymous with *sophɔ:n*, we say what is indeed the case, and we say it in a direct rather than a roundabout fashion. But, from the structuralist viewpoint, we have not explained WHY they are homonymous – WHY, at this point in the paradigm, Genders which are otherwise distinguished are not distinguished. To renounce our earlier methods is, in that sense, to renounce a deeper analysis.

Which end of the stick should we grasp? The modern method has already been explored, and its attractions do not need to be laboured further. But there are at least three reasons why the opposite approach should not be neglected.

Firstly, it conforms very closely to the method by which languages of this kind are traditionally taught. Pupils begin by memorising **paradigms**. These are sets of WORDS AS WHOLES, arranged according to grammatical categories. They learn that different members of a paradigm are distinguished by their endings – just as *sophón* and *sophɔ:n*, for example, are distinguished by *-ón* versus *-ɔ:n*. They can then transfer these endings to other lexemes, whose paradigms they have not memorised. They will learn that different members can be identical – as *sophɔ:n* and *sophɔ:n* – sometimes in a particular class of lexemes, sometimes for all. But they are not taught rules for separate formatives – for Masculine/Neuter *-o-* or Feminine *-ɛ:-/-a-*. Nor are they taught rules of sandhi. This is not only traditional, it is also effective. It seems unlikely that, if a structuralist method or a method derived from structuralism were employed instead, pupils learning Ancient Greek or Latin – or, for that matter, Russian, Modern Greek or Italian – would be served nearly so well.

Secondly, it is not clear that, when native speakers learn a flectional language, they do not themselves learn words as wholes. Children acquiring Ancient Greek will have learned the grammar of a phrase like $sop^h\grave{o}{:}n$ $ant^hr\acute{o}{:}p\mathfrak{o}{:}n$ 'of clever men'; they will have learned to identify its members, to distinguish their form and meaning from those of other units, and master the rules which governed their use. In doing so, they will undoubtedly have divided the phrase into words. But it is not clear what they would have gained by further analysis. At most, they needed to learn that both forms ended in $-\mathfrak{o}{:}n$. As children or as adults, they needed to recognise such words when they heard them – for example, to distinguish this phrase from the Accusative Singular $sop^h\acute{o}n$ $\acute{a}nt^hr\mathfrak{o}{:}pon$. Again, it does not seem improbable that they recognised words as wholes; nor that, in recognising both $sop^h\grave{o}{:}n$ as distinct from $sop^h\acute{o}n$ and $ant^hr\grave{o}{:}p\mathfrak{o}{:}n$ as distinct from $\acute{a}nt^hr\mathfrak{o}{:}pon$, the suffixes and accentuation served as equal cues.

A sceptic will demand hard evidence and, even for a living language, it is hard to get. But, finally, both Latin and Ancient Greek had native grammarians; and it is significant that, as native speakers writing for and teaching other native speakers, they too dealt with words as wholes. Let us therefore try to elucidate the model that they used. We can then compare the ancient and modern methods in more equal terms.

## AN ANCIENT MODEL

The history of ancient grammar does not concern us; mercifully, since it is still debated. But from an early period scholars recognised four basic units. Two were merely units of form: the 'letter' (Latin *litera*) which, like the modern phoneme, was the smallest unit of sound; and the syllable, which consisted of one or more sounds grouped together. Two were units of form that also had meanings. The word (Latin *dictio*) was the smallest meaningful unit, and the sentence or 'utterance' (Latin *oratio*) was in turn made up of one or more words. Note already that there was no unit like the modern morpheme. Words were forms, and could be divided into letters and syllables. But they were not divided into smaller meaningful units.

The problem of the word was, above all, a problem of classification. At the highest level, each word was assigned to a part of speech: Noun, Pronoun, Verb, and so on. The term which we translate by 'part of speech' (Latin *pars orationis*) meant, more precisely, 'part of the utterance' or 'element of the sentence'. At this level, therefore, the Latin sentence *Nihil enim semper floret* 'For nothing flowers for ever' would be analysed into a Noun *nihil* 'nothing', a Conjunction *enim* 'for', an Adverb *semper* 'always, for ever' and a Verb *floret* 'flowers'. To analyse a sentence was precisely to assign each word to its *pars* or 'part' – in what is originally a schoolroom term, to 'parse' it.

Each part of speech was then subclassified according to what in Latin were called its *accidentia* or 'accidents'. Take, for example, the Verb *floret* 'flowers, is flowering'. According to Donatus (fourth century AD), the 'accidents' of the Verb are as follows. First, a Verb is of a certain type or 'quality' (Latin *qualitas*). This included its Mood: *floret* is in this respect Indicative. But it also included other properties. A Verb like *florescit* 'is coming into flower' is Inchoative (descriptive of a process that is beginning); that too was part of its 'quality'. By contrast, *floret* is not Inchoative.

Next, a Verb belongs to a certain Conjugation. For 'conjugation' we can effectively read 'inflectional class': in our terms, the lexeme FLOREO ('to flower') belongs to an inflectional class that is traditionally called the 2nd Conjugation. In ancient terms, all classification is of forms and *floret* itself, like *floreo* 'I flower, I am flowering' and other forms of this lexeme, itself belongs to the Conjugation.

Next, it is classified with respect to Voice – or, in Latin, *genus* ('kind'). *Floret* is a form with Active endings, but no Passive – no form *floretur* 'is being flowered' – corresponds to it. In ancient accounts, it is therefore neither Active nor Passive, but 'Neuter' (literally, 'neither').

The remaining accidents were those of Number (Singular),

Tense (Present) and Person (3rd), plus what was called a formation or 'shape' (Latin *figura*). The distinction here was between simple forms and forms compounded with, in particular, Prepositions. The formation of *floret* is accordingly Simple, as opposed, for example, to Compound *defloret* 'sheds blossom' (*de-* 'down from, away from').

In summary, the classification of *floret*, taking the accidents in the order in which Donatus lists them, would have been as follows:

QUALITY: Indicative, not Inchoative, etc.

CONJUGATION: 2nd

VOICE: Neuter

NUMBER: Singular

FORMATION: Simple

TENSE: Present

PERSON: 3rd

The accidents are thus quite heterogeneous. 'Second Conjugation' refers to an inflectional class, and 'Simple' to the fact that the form has not, in general, undergone one kind of lexical process. 'Inchoative' as an accident of *florescit* 'is coming into flower', refers to a specific process of word-formation. But the other categories are of the kind that we have described as morphosyntactic. For a lexeme like FLOREO ('to flower'), the paradigm does not distinguish Passive from Active; in modern terms, we would describe the lexeme itself as Neuter. But, within the morphosyntactic category of Person, *floret* is specifically 3rd Person; within the morphosyntactic category of Number it is specifically Singular, and so on.

What was common to all the forms of what we call 'FLOREO'? The answer – and it is important to note the change of typeface – is that they are all inflections of *floreo*. The term 'inflection' is from a Latin Verb whose basic meaning was 'to bend'. But in this context we can best translate it as 'to modify'. Forms like *floret* 'flowers, is flowering' or 3rd Plural *florent* '(they) flower, are flowering' were modifications or 'bendings' of *floreo* 'I flower, am flowering'. So, for example, was the Future *florebo* 'I will flower'; and, just as *floret* and *florent* are modifications of *floreo*, so *florebo* in turn can be modified to 3rd Singular *florebit* '[it] will flower' or

3rd Plural *florebunt* '[they] will flower'. In each paradigm (as we recognise it) there is a basic, unmodified or **leading form**. It is the one which still supplies the conventional representation of the lexeme (in capital letters 'FLOREO'). But for the ancient grammarians it was, once more, a form. Its special status is that all the other forms are modifications, or 'inflections', of it.

Similarly for Nouns. The paradigm of FLOS 'flower' is a set of interrelated forms all of which were seen as modifications of the Nominative Singular *flos*. In ancient terms, the Nominative was the 'upright' – that is, the 'unbended' – Case. The other forms were bendings of it and were therefore 'oblique' or slanted. So *floris* (Genitive Singular) was an oblique form modifying *flos*. *Florum* (Genitive Plural) was similarly an oblique form modifying *flores* (Nominative Plural). Plural *flores* was, in turn, another modification of *flos*.

A grammarian then had, ideally, two tasks. One was to specify the parts of speech and their accidents. This was the backbone of grammar, and in classroom manuals of the late Empire, like those of Donatus, it dominates the morphological chapters. The other was to indicate the different patterns of modification. Take, for example, *flos* → *floris*. Formally, *-s* is replaced by *-ris*; on the plane of meaning, Nominative changes to Genitive. The same happens in the word for 'mouth' (*os* → *oris*), and something largely similar in, for instance, the word for 'guardian' (*custos* → *custodis*) or the word for 'dowry' (*dos* → *dotis*). That is one pattern, with variants, that some Nouns follow. Now take the words for 'master' and 'slave'. For the same semantic modification (Nominative → Genitive), the formal change is different: *dominus* 'master' → *domini*, *servus* 'slave' → *servi*. Here there is another pattern. A modern grammarian would speak of different Genitive Singular suffixes, or different allomorphs of a Genitive Singular morpheme. For the ancient grammarian, these were different formal changes by which oblique Cases were derived from the 'upright' Case.

The most familiar way of bringing out such patterns is by the use of what we may call **exemplary paradigms**. The Greek term, *parádeigma*, meant precisely that, a 'pattern' or an 'example'. Suppose, for instance, that one already knows the paradigm of the word for 'master'. (It was set out, in fact, towards the end of chapter 2.) Suppose too that one knows that the word for 'slave' (Nominative Singular *servus*) is of the same inflectional class. One can then take the inflections of *dominus* 'master' as a pattern or model for those of *servus*. As *dominus* → *domini* to form the Genitive Singular, so *servus* → *servi*. As Nominative *dominus* gives Vocative Singular *domine*, so *servus* gives *serve*; and so on.

This method is well known to anyone who has learned Latin or other flectional languages in the traditional way. Nevertheless it is worth pausing to consider what it involves. In effect, we are predicting the inflections of *servus* by **analogy** with those of *dominus*. As Genitive Singular *domini* is to Nominative Singular *dominus*, so *x* (unknown) must be to Nominative Singular *servus*. What then is *x*? Answer: it must be *servi*. In notation, *dominus*:*domini* = *servus*:*servi*. The pattern holds for many other Nouns of what is traditionally called the 2nd Declension. Take, for instance, *locus* 'place' or *rogus* 'funeral pyre'. By the same process of analogy, we deduce the proportions *dominus*:*domini* = *locus*:*loci* = *rogus*:*rogi*. In the passing fashions of language teaching, processes of analogy have often been made explicit in the form of blank-filling exercises. It is an ancient technique made mechanical. So, in this case, we start with what might be shown as a partly filled-in table.

|  | Nom. Sg. | Gen. Sg. |
|---|---|---|
| 'master' | dominus | domini |
| 'slave' | servus | ——? |
| 'place' | locus | ——? |
| 'pyre' | rogus | ——? |

Exercise: supply the gaps. Answers: *servi, loci, rogi*.

Analogy is an important concept in linguistic theory. It plays a major role in morphological change, as we have noted earlier. It also forms a large part of the process by which children learn their native language. One of the most banal and often repeated observations of children's speech concerns the extension of regular inflectional patterns (English *-ed*, *-s*, and so on) as analogical replacements of irregular forms. Thus a child will use forms like *He oughted to do it*, or *She bringed it* for *She brought it*. Irregular patterns may also be extended at the expense of regular: *dove* for *dived*, by analogy with forms like *drove*, is an illustration that we gave earlier. It is hardly surprising that traditional language teaching has made good use of the same instinct.

The use of paradigms belongs particularly to the period after the end of the Western Empire, when Latin had to be taught increasingly as a foreign language. But throughout the tradition analogies were also covered by explicit rules. Let us return, for example, to *flos → floris*. The Nominative is one of a set that end in *-os*, and it is Masculine. In a long and scholarly grammar composed around 500 AD, Priscian takes these as the condition for a rule. 'Masculines ending in *-os*', he writes, 'form the Genitive by the removal of the *s* and the addition of *ris.*' In our notation, *-s → -ris*: other examples, *ros → roris* ('dew') or *mos → moris* ('custom'). Nouns in *-os* which are not Masculine follow a different rule by which *-s → -tis*; the word for 'dowry', which we mentioned earlier, is Feminine and therefore *dos → dotis*. Now rules can have exceptions, and *custos* 'guardian', because it is from the Verb *custodio* 'I guard', is one (*custos → custodis*). But in book 6 of his grammar, from which this illustration is taken, Priscian goes through every class of Noun, defined by Declension, ending and Gender, and gives general rules for the Genitive wherever possible.[1]

Rules of this form may be seen as **morphological transformations**, in which a formal operation is paired with a semantic operation. In notation, the rule for *floris* could be shown like this:

$$
\begin{bmatrix} \text{Masculine} \\ \text{in -os} \\ \text{Nominative} \\ \text{Singular} \\ \text{X}+\text{s} \end{bmatrix}_{\text{N}} \rightarrow \begin{bmatrix} \text{Genitive} \\ \\ \text{X}+\text{ris} \end{bmatrix}
$$

On the formal or phonetic plane, *s* changes to *ris*; on the semantic, Nominative changes to Genitive. In his next book, Priscian gives rules for other Noun inflections, among them the Nominative Plural. The word for 'flower' belongs to the class traditionally called the 3rd Declension, and the rule that applies there can be shown, in the same notation, thus:

---

[1] *Grammatici latini*, ed. H. Keil, vol. II (Leipzig, Teubner, 1855), pp. 194–282. Nouns in *-os*, pp. 253f.

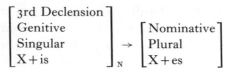

$$\begin{bmatrix} \text{3rd Declension} \\ \text{Genitive} \\ \text{Singular} \\ \text{X + is} \end{bmatrix}_{\text{N}} \rightarrow \begin{bmatrix} \text{Nominative} \\ \text{Plural} \\ \text{X + es} \end{bmatrix}$$

So, given Genitive Singular *floris* – by the first rule – this derives in turn Nominative Plural *flores*.[2] When all the relevant rules have been applied, we can say that the paradigm has been assigned at once a **semantic structure** and a **derivational structure**. Its semantic structure is given by the intersecting morphosyntactic categories. It has a Nominative Singular, our starting point, and, by these two rules, a Nominative Plural; a Genitive Singular and, by another rule or sequence of rules, a Genitive Plural; and so on. Its derivational structure is given by the order in which the operations have applied. Starting from the Nominative Singular, we have derived first the Genitive Singular and then, from that, the Nominative Singular; also, in Priscian's account, the Accusative Singular, and so on.

Now a modern reader might expect at this point that the derivational structure should always follow the semantic structure. Take, for instance, the Verb *floreo*. We might expect that other forms of the Present Indicative should be derived systematically from the 1st Singular: so, 2nd Singular *flores* (*-eo* → *-es*), 3rd Singular *floret* (*-es* → *-et*), and so on. We might then expect that the 1st Singular of the Present Indicative should be the source for the other Tenses: *floreo* → Imperfect Indicative *florebam* (*-o* → *-bam*), and so on. Each semantic operation would involve a minimum of categories, and formal operations would, as far as possible, distinguish what we now call formatives.

But that is not what we find, either in the ancient grammars or in the classroom tradition derived from them. In modern teaching, rules are given only sporadically; however, one that I learned could be written like this:

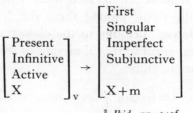

$$\begin{bmatrix} \text{Present} \\ \text{Infinitive} \\ \text{Active} \\ \text{X} \end{bmatrix}_{\text{V}} \rightarrow \begin{bmatrix} \text{First} \\ \text{Singular} \\ \text{Imperfect} \\ \text{Subjunctive} \\ \text{X + m} \end{bmatrix}$$

[2] *Ibid.*, pp. 349f.

The categories are as the tradition describes them: the Mood changes (Infinitive → Subjunctive), as does the Tense (Present → Imperfect), and the derived form, being Finite, also has a Person and Number. Thus, on the semantic plane, the transformation cuts across the paradigm. But it is justified because the rule is formally both simple and absolute. For any Verb, however irregular it may be in other respects, the Present Infinitive always predicts the Imperfect Subjunctive. For the Verb 'to flower', *florere → florerem*; for the irregular Verb 'to be', *esse → essem*, and so forth without exception.

Another illustration can be taken from the work of Theodosius of Alexandria (fourth/fifth century AD) on the Verb in Greek. Theodosius takes as his model *týptɔː* or τύπτω 'I hit', and his 'Introductory Rules' (εἰσαγωγικοὶ κανόνες) are, in effect, an annotated paradigm. The semantic structure is therefore given by the order in which the forms are listed and discussed: first those of the Present Indicative (*týptɔː* 'I hit', *týpteːs* 'you hit', *týpteː* 'hits', and so on); then the Imperfect Indicative; then the other Tenses in an order that was already conventional. The annotations give the rules. For example, under 2nd Singular *týpteːs* (τύπτεις) Theodosius says that all 1st Persons that end in *-ɔː* (as *týptɔː* 'I hit') form the corresponding 2nd Singular by changing *-ɔː* to *-eːs*. Under the next form (*týpteː*) he says that all 2nd Singulars that end in *-s* (as *týpteːs*) form the 3rd Singular by deleting it.

So far the semantic and the derivational structures are in harmony: 1st Singular → 2nd Singular → 3rd Singular. But now let us look at the other forms of the Present Indicative. For the 1st Plural, *týptomen*, one solution would be to start again from the 1st Singular (change *-ɔː* in *týptɔː* to *-o* and add *-men*). But Theodosius in fact derives it from the Genitive Singular Masculine of the corresponding Participle. This has the form *týptontos*; and, if we remove *-tos*, we are left with *týpton*. That is then taken as the source for two forms. One is the 1st Singular of the Imperfect Indicative, *étypton* 'I was hitting'; this is formed by the addition, at the beginning, of what is traditionally called the 'augment'. The other is *týptomen*: replace *-n* by *-men*. Now the Genitive Singular of the Participle is from the Nominative Singular (*týptɔːn*) and that in turn is from the unmodified 1st Singular (*týptɔː*). So, instead of the direct derivation which a modern reader might expect (1st Singular *týptɔ:* → 1st Plural *týptomen*), Theodosius gives us something much more roundabout. In summary, *týptɔ:* (1st Singular) → *týptɔ:n* (Nominative Singular of the Participle) → *týptontos* (Genitive Singular) → *týpton* (intermediate) → *týptomen* (1st Plural).

The remaining forms of the Present Indicative are the 2nd Plural (*týptete*), the 3rd Plural (*týptu:si*), and two homonymous Duals (both *týpteton*). In Theodosius' account the 2nd Plural is got directly from the 1st Plural: *týptomen* → *týptete*. It is then the natural source for the Duals: *týptete* → *týpteton*. But the 3rd Plural is homonymous with the Dative Plural of the Participle, also *týptu:si*. Theodosius points out that this holds for the Future as well as the Present: *týpsu:si* '[they] will hit' similarly equals *týpsu:si* 'to [people] going to hit'. It also holds for a class of Verbs whose unmodified 1st Singular ends not in -*ɔ:* but in -*mi*: example *títʰɛ:mi* 'I place', 3rd Plural and Dative Plural of the Participle *titʰê:si*. Therefore the natural derivation is Dative Plural *týptu:si* → 3rd Plural *týptu:si*, the former once more from *týptɔ:n* (Nominative Singular).[3]

From the viewpoint of our earlier chapters, an ancient treatment like this may appear perverse. What has the -*si* of the 3rd Plural got to do with the -*si* of the Dative Plural? What has the -*n*- of Genitive Singular *týptontos*, which divides by formatives into *týpt* + *o* + *nt* + *os*, got to do with the -*n* of the Imperfect? What indeed has the -*t*- of the 2nd Plural (*týpt* + *e* + *te*) got to do with the fortuitously recurring -*t*- of the Duals (*týpt* + *e* + *ton*)? Answers, from a modern standpoint: nothing whatever. But it is plain that Theodosius is trying to make his rules as simple and as general as possible. If we have already derived *týptete*, with an -*et*-, it is simpler to get *týpteton* from that than from some other form without an -*et*-. If 3rd Plural *týptu:si* is homonymous with Dative Plural *týptu:si*, the formal change is nil. If the former was derived from *týptɔ:* or from *týptomen*, it would be more complicated. Moreover, we would have to give a different rule for the Verbs in -*mi*.

The difference, once more, is that the modern structuralist thinks in terms of morphemes where an ancient grammarian, like

[3] *Grammatici graeci*, ed. A. Hilgard, vol. 4.1 (Leipzig, Teubner, 1894), pp. 43ff.

Theodosius, basically thought of words as wholes. The notion of the word as having functioning parts – the syllable *-men* in *týptomen*, the augment *é-* in *étypton* – was at most secondary.

## A MODERN ADAPTATION

If the ancient approach was different, can we learn anything from it? There are two possibilities. We may be able to borrow insights from the classical tradition which can be integrated with the approach developed in earlier chapters. Alternatively, we may find that their attractions are different and irreconcilable.

The most general insight is that one inflection tends to predict another. Let us return, for instance, to the Noun in Latin. The Genitive Singular of a Noun like DOMINUS 'lord, master' ends in long -[iː] (*dominī*); that of FLOS 'flower' in -[is] (*flōris*). Correspondingly, the Dative Singular of DOMINUS has a long -[oː]; that of FLOS an -[iː] (*flōrī*). This holds absolutely: for all Nouns, Genitive Singular -[iː] predicts Dative Singular -[oː] and Genitive Singular -[is] predicts Dative Singular -[iː]. Similar implications hold for other Cases. For example, Nouns like DOMINUS have a -[rum] in the Genitive Plural (*dominōrum*) and -[iːs] in the Dative/Ablative Plural. But Nouns like FLOS have a Genitive Plural either in *-um* (*flōrum*) or in *-ium*, and their Dative/Ablative Plural in -[bus] (*flōribus*). Everywhere there is an alternation: Genitive Singular -[iː] alternates with -[is], Genitive Plural -[rum] with -[um] or -[ium], and so on. But the alternations are interdependent. There are no Nouns, for instance, with a Genitive Singular in -[is] and a Dative/Ablative Plural in -[iːs]. There are only a few, like DIES 'day', which have a Genitive Plural in -[rum] (*dierum*) but their Dative/Ablative Plural in -[bus] (*diebus*). All those with a Dative/Ablative Plural in -[iːs] have a Genitive Plural in -[rum].

This insight can be incorporated into any model. Traditionally, it is the basis for the method of exemplary paradigms. If the alternations were independent, these would have to be numerous. One class of Nouns would have a Genitive Singular like DOMINUS, but all its other endings like FLOS; another would have the endings of FLOS in every form except the Dative/Ablative Plural, and so on for every possible combination. But since they are interdependent,

the number can be very small. In the tradition there are five. One
pattern is that of the 2nd Declension, including DOMINUS. The
pattern of FLOS is followed in general by all Nouns of the 3rd
Declension – 'in general' because there are some matters of detail
(like the alternation between -[um] and -[ium] in the Genitive
Plural) that subdivide them. The small class of DIES, for example,
forms the 5th Declension. It is more attractive to learn paradigms
as wholes than each alternation separately.

But suppose we persist with the model of earlier chapters. Then
for each Case we must give alternative rules. For one class of
Nouns, we must say that the Genitive Singular is formed by
suffixing -[i:]; for another class, by suffixing -[is]. We must also
say which class each Noun belongs to: DOMINUS to the [i:]-
suffixing class, FLOS to the [is]-suffixing. Likewise for other Cases.
By the rules for the Genitive Plural, for example, there is a class
that suffixes -[rum], another that suffixes -[um], another that
suffixes -[ium]. But since the alternations are interdependent,
different sets of classes will tend to correspond. Therefore we can
establish a more general classification (1st Declension, 2nd
Declension, and so on) which covers all of them.

However it is expressed, this insight is important and has
played a larger rôle in traditional teaching than in most
structuralist treatments. But can we also justify the method of
morphological transformations? That could be worse news for
the modern approach. For a rule relating complex forms as
wholes will cut across the rules that relate them individually to
their parts.

Let us turn for a moment to Spanish. The following table
shows the Present Indicative and Subjunctive of the Verb
COMPRAR 'to buy':

|  | *Indicative* | *Subjunctive* |
|---|---|---|
| 'I' | compro | compre |
| 'thou' (Familiar) | compras | compres |
| 'he', etc. | compra | compre |
| 'we' | compramos | compremos |
| 'you' (Familiar) | compráis | compréis |
| 'they', etc. | compran | compren |

– *compro* (we will assume) being morphophonemically
← *compra + o*. It will be seen that the Subjunctive is identified by

a change of *a* to *e* in the second syllable. But then look at the forms for COMER 'eat':

|  | Indicative | Subjunctive |
|---|---|---|
| 'I' | como | coma |
| 'thou' (Familiar) | comes | comas |
| 'he', etc. | come | coma |
| 'we' | comemos | comamos |
| 'you' (Familiar) | coméis | comáis |
| 'they', etc. | comen | coman |

(*como* similarly from *come* + *o*). Here the pattern is the reverse: it is now the Indicative that has *e* and the Subjunctive that has *a*. Similarly for VIVIR 'live'. For this Verb the Subjunctive again has an *a* (*viva*, *vivamos*, and so on), while the Indicative has a basic or underlying *i*: *vivo* (← *vivi* + *o*) 'I live', *vives* ← *vivi* + *s* 'thou livest', *vive* ← *vivi* 'lives', *vivimos* (*vivi* + *mos*) 'we live', *vivís* ← *viví* + *is* 'you live', *viven* ← *vivi* + *n* 'they live'. These are the regular patterns, and are found not only in Spanish, but in Italian, Portuguese and Southern Romance generally.

How should the rules be stated? If we are looking for formatives, the obvious solution is to say that *-e* and *-a* are alternating Subjunctive markers. They might be seen as added to the vowels of the Indicative: *compre* morphophonemically ← *compra* + *e*, *coma* and *viva* ← *come* + *a* and *vivi* + *a*. But is the Subjunctive truly marked by either vowel? If *e* marks it in a form like *compre* the same vowel marks the Indicative in forms like *come*. If *a* marks the Subjunctive in *coma* or *viva* it is an Indicative marker in *compra*. In reality, it is not the vowels as such that are important. A form in *e* is Subjunctive only if it belongs, as a whole, to the paradigm of a Verb like COMPRAR. A form in *a* is Subjunctive only if it belongs as a whole to the paradigm of a Verb like COMER or VIVIR.

The system in effect works by a process of vowel reversal. That of the Indicative is a general stem or conjugation vowel: it recurs in the Infinitive (e.g. *comprar* 'to buy'), in the Future (*compraré* 'I will buy') and elsewhere. If it is the open vowel (*a*), the stem of the Subjunctive has the front vowel *e*: *compra-*, for example, → *compre-*. If it is itself a front vowel (*e* or *i*), the stem of

the Subjunctive has the open vowel: *come-* and *vivi- → coma-* and
*viva-*. Now this is not quite what the ancient grammarians would
have said. For one thing, they had no notion of front and open
vowels. More important, we are deriving stems from stems
(*compra-* from *compre-*, *come-* from *coma-*, *vivi-* from *viva-*),
where they would have derived a particular form of the
Subjunctive (say, 1st Singular *compre*, *coma*, *viva*) from a
particular form of the Indicative. But the rule is a morphological
transformation. It does not derive a larger stem from a smaller
stem. Instead it relates CONTRASTING stems, just as ancient
scholars such as Theodosius would have related contrasting
words.

For our other illustrations we can return to Latin. Consider
next the opposition between the Future Participle (Active) and
the Past Participle (Passive). For a Verb like AMO 'to love', the
latter is based on a stem *amāt-* (Nominative Singular Masculine
*amāt-u-s*). The former is based correspondingly on *amātūr-*
(Nominative Singular Masculine *amātūr-u-s*). But what is the
relation between them? In terms of formatives, the Future Active
*amātūr-* seems to derive from *amāt-* by the addition of *-ūr-*. Or,
as an ancient grammarian would have put it, *amātūrus* comes from
*amātus* by the change of *-s* to *-rus*. But there is no sense in which
the meaning of the Future Active Participle includes that of the
Past Passive Participle. Formally, *amāt-ūr-* includes *amāt-*. But in
meaning all they have in common is that both are Participles.

A reader who does not know Latin may suspect at this point
that the formal correspondence is fortuitous. *Amātus* (one is
tempted to argue) is *amā-t-u-s*, with a suffix *-t-*, and *amātūrus* is
*amā-tūr-u-s*, with a separate suffix *-tūr-*. But let us look at some
more Verbs. Ones like SECO 'cut' are generally like AMO except that,
in the Past Participle, there is no vowel before the *-t-*: *sec-t-u-s*,
not *secātus*; likewise in the Future Participle (*sec-t-ūr-u-s*). Verbs
like MONEO 'advise' have Past Participles in *-it-* (*mon-it-u-s*);
likewise their Future Participles (*mon-it-ūr-u-s*). Others, such
as RADO 'shave', have Past Participles in *-s-* (*rāsus ← rād+sus*);
likewise their Future Participles (*rāsūrus*). There are a few
exceptions; but, in general, if the stem of the Past Participle is *x*,
no matter how irregular it may be, that of the Future Participle is
*x* with *-ūr-* added.

We could, in principle, list parallel rules. For class so and so, we would say that both the Past and Future Participles are formed like those of AMO; for class such and such, that both the Past and Future Participles are formed like those of SECO, and so on. But the duplication is evident. To avoid it, we may again replace one set of rules by a transformation. It could be stated over words as wholes: *amātus → amātūrus, sectus → sectūrus, rāsus → rāsūrus*. In that way we would be closest to the ancient treatment. Or, like the vowel reversal in Spanish, it too could be stated over stems: *amā-t- → amā-t-ūr-, sec-t- → sec-t-ūr-*, basic *rād + s → rād + s + ūr-*. In either case, we are deriving one form from another across the paradigm.

Here too it appears that we can learn from ancient insights. But can we reconcile the ancient model with the model of stems and formatives? Is there a method by which we can give rules of both kinds – both transformations and the rules of earlier chapters – without duplication or conflict?

There is a way, though it may seem sophisticated. Suppose that we have given a set of rules for the Latin Past Participle. For Verbs like AMO, its stem is formed by adding *-t-* to the stem vowel; for those like SECO, it is formed by adding *-t-* without a vowel; for the class of RADO, by adding *-s-*; and so on. These rules are given in our earlier ('Item and Process') format. But we can then add what is technically a **metarule**. This is a statement at a higher level, which is a rule about rules rather than directly about forms. In this case, it will refer to the set of rules for the Past Participle and derive from them a corresponding set for the Future Participle. So (exceptions apart) it will say that, where the rule for the Past Participle prescribes *x*, the rule for the Future Participle prescribes *x* plus the suffixation of *-ūr-*. Consider again a Verb like AMO. By the rule explicitly given, the stem of its Past Participle is *amā-t-*. By the derived rule, its Future Participle has the stem *amā-t-ūr-*. But this second rule is not explicitly given. It follows from the metarule. So do the corresponding rules for *sec-t-ūr-, rās-ūr-*, and so on.

The metarule says what a transformation would say, except that it is stated over rules instead of forms. The rules themselves, whether stated or implicit in the metarule, describe the familiar process by which larger forms are built from smaller. But there is no conflict, since they are on one level and the metarule on another.

Let us illustrate this further with the treatment of syncretism. A famous instance in Latin is that Nominatives and Accusatives are always identical in the Neuter. For the Masculine or Feminine, they are mostly different: Nominative *dominu-s* but Accusative *dominu-m*; Nominative *flōs* but Accusative *flōrem*. But for the Neuter BELLUM 'war', whose other inflections are like those of DOMINUS, the Nominative and Accusative Singular are both *bellum*, and the Nominative and Accusative Plural are both *bella*. This holds for all Neuter Nouns and for the Neuter forms of all Adjectives and Participles. It holds for both Singular and Plural (*bellum*, *bella*). It holds regardless of Declension. The 2nd Declension *bellum* has a suffixed *-m* (compare *dominu-m*). The 3rd Declension *caput* 'head' has no suffix. But it too is homonymously Nominative and Accusative.

This is traditionally presented as a rule of identity between forms. But we can reformulate it as a metarule: not 'for every Neuter the FORMS OF the Nominative and Accusative are identical', but 'for every Neuter, the RULES FOR the Nominative and Accusative are identical'. We can then give rules for either Case and those for the other follow automatically. For BELLUM, the Accusative Singular can be derived in the same way as for Masculines like DOMINUS 'lord, master' or for Feminines like PUELLA 'girl'. All have suffixed *-m*: *bellu-m, dominu-m, puella-m*. The last two have different forms in the Nominative: *dominu-s*, with suffixed *-s*; *puella*, with no suffix. We must therefore give two further rules for those. But we do not need one for the Neuter Nominative *bellum*. From the rule for the Accusative it follows, by the metarule, that the Nominative also suffixes *-m*.

For Nouns like CAPUT 'head' the metarule might work in the reverse direction. The root is *capit-* (Genitive Singular *capit-is*) and, like FLOS 'flower', the lexeme is 3rd Declension. If it were Masculine or Feminine, we would expect an Accusative Singular in *-em*: *capitem*, like *flōrem*. But, since we do not find it, let us give no rule for that Case. Instead we will give one for the Nominative: no suffix, but, irregularly, *-i-* (in *capit*) → *-u-*. We have seen that the Nominative *puella* 'girl' has no suffix either, and there are others in the 3rd Declension that are similar. Then, just as, for

BELLUM, an implicit rule for the Nominative was derived from the one that was stated explicitly for the Accusative, so, for CAPUT, the rule for the Accusative follows from this one for the Nominative.

For the Plurals (*bell-a*; likewise *capit-a*) the metarule might work in either direction. But again we deal with only one Case at the lower level. The metarule then supplies an identical process for the other Case.

What would an ancient grammarian say if he could return to earth and read these paragraphs? He might perhaps admire the ingenuity with which grammarians of the later twentieth century have learned to play around with rules. But ingenuity is the cheapest virtue that a scholar can have. Seriously, he might feel that we have lost sight of a vital insight. At the lower level – that of rules as opposed to metarules – we are still describing the word as an assembly of recurrent parts. We have merely added higher-level rules which, indirectly, can connect the exponents of opposing properties. But in the ancient account the word is an unanalysed whole, and parts of words, like *-rus* at the end of the Future Participle *amātūrus* or *-e* in the Spanish Subjunctive *compre*, are referred to only in passing when one word is derived, as a whole, from another. In Spanish, *compra* 'buys' can be turned into the Subjunctive by replacing *-a* with *-e*. That is the only status that either *-a* or *-e* has. The moment we start talking in terms of stems and formatives – the moment we split *amātūrus* into $am + \bar{a} + t + \bar{u}r + u + s$, or relate the *-m* of *bellum*, as such, to either Nominative or Accusative – the spirit of the ancient model is lost.

We may not agree with this; or, if we do, we may feel that the newer model is more truthful. But for a language such as Greek or Latin, it would be wise to view the argument with respect. If words are analysed into formatives, they often display what we have called extended exponence: Greek *elelýkete*, which we analysed in chapter 9, is merely an extreme instance. They show extensive fusions and other effects of sandhi, so that the boundaries of formatives are far from clear. Is *dominum*, for example, rightly *dominu-m* (compare Nominative *dominu-s*) or is it *domin-um* (compare Genitive *domin-ī*)? When formatives are isolated, they are often ambiguous. Latin *-ī* (to take another extreme case) marks the Dative Singular in *flōrī*. But in *dominī* it marks the Genitive Singular or – we may add – the Nominative Plural. In Verb forms like *amāvī* 'I loved, have loved', it marks the 1st Singular of the Perfect; in others, like *amārī* 'to be loved', the Passive of an Infinitive. Within a paradigm, words as wholes are often homonymous. They may be distinguished by a single property, like Nominative and Accusative *bellum*. Or they may have widely different meanings: thus the syncretism in Greek between *týptu:si* as 3rd Plural of an Indicative or as Dative Plural of a Participle.

Many linguists tend to boggle at such systems. They seem complicated, while agglutinating systems seem so simple. They may even seem perverse. Why should a language have rules which obscure the identity and function of its minimal elements?

An apologist for ancient grammar would answer that these elements are fictions. They are created by the modern method; and, if we foist them on a flectional system, we are bound to describe it as an agglutinating system that has somehow gone wrong. In the ancient model the primary insight is not that words can be split into roots and formatives, but that they can be located in paradigms. They are not wholes composed of simple parts, but are themselves the parts within a complex whole. In that way, we discover different kinds of relation, and, perhaps, a different kind of simplicity.

## RELATED READING

On the development and character of ancient grammar see my chapter 'La linguistica greco-latina', in G. C. Lepschy (ed.), *Storia della linguistica*, vol. I (Bologna, Il Mulino, 1990), pp. 187–310. An English edition is planned. See also, for the early stages, D. J. Taylor, 'Rethinking the history of language science in classical antiquity', in D. J. Taylor (ed.), *The History of Linguistics in the Classical Period* (Amsterdam, Benjamins, 1987), pp. 1–16; at a more difficult level, J. Pinborg, 'Classical antiquity: Greece', in SEBEOK, pp. 96–126. If I do not refer to shorter textbook accounts, it is because they are now badly dated. For a survey of the parts of speech and accidents in individual grammarians see I. Michael, *English Grammatical Categories and the Tradition to 1800* (Cambridge, Cambridge University Press, 1970), Part 1; for the adaptation of Latin grammars to foreign-language teaching, V. A. Law, *The Insular Latin Grammarians* (Woodbridge, Boydell Press, 1982). For an edition and exhaustive study of Donatus see L. Holtz, *Donat et la tradition de l'enseignement grammatical* (Paris, CNRS, 1981).

The term 'morphological transformation' is mine. There is no parallel with transformations in Chomskyan syntax (chapter 5). But there IS a parallel with what I think syntactic transformations should be: compare my *Syntax* (Cambridge, Cambridge University Press, 1981), ch. 12. For criticisms of the method, which I am afraid I once thought wholly damning, see *Inflectional Morphology*, pp. 27ff. (exposition pp. 10ff.). On analogy see again ch. 5 of PAUL and other references in Reading for chapter 4.

On the predictability of forms in paradigms see, in particular, CARSTAIRS (on the 'paradigm economy principle') and WURZEL (§5.1 on 'implicative structures'). For Carstairs's principle see also A. Carstairs, 'Paradigm economy', *JL* 19 (1983), pp. 115–25; this provoked an illuminating critique by Nyman: see M. Nyman, 'Is the Paradigm Economy Principle relevant?', *JL* 23 (1987), pp. 251–67, and rejoinders by both in *JL* 24 (1988), pp. 489–513. The controversy illustrates well the differences between a basically Chomskyan and what is widely called a 'natural' theory of universals. See chapter 12 for references for 'natural morphology'.

Both Wurzel and Carstairs segment forms, though their divisions are often of the *soph-ón/soph-ɔ:n* type. See, for example, WURZEL, p. 159 for Latin *dogma-tis* (rather than *dogmat-is*). For a treatment which is much more in the ancient mould see BYBEE, ch. 3 (with examples from Spanish, pp. 60f. and elsewhere). Bybee also gives reasons for the choice of leading form and the direction of derivations, where Wurzel, whose lexical entries include the traditional leading forms, does not (WURZEL, §2.3). For the Latin Future and Past Participles compare *Inflectional Morphology*, pp. 83ff., where it is taken as a prime example of what I called a 'parasitic' derivation. For the formal device of metarules compare, for example, the treatment of derived constructions in 'generalised phrase structure grammar': for an early and relatively informal explanation see G. Gazdar, 'Phrase structure grammar', in P. Jacobson & G. K. Pullum (eds.), *The Nature of Syntactic Representation* (Dordrecht, Reidel, 1982), pp. 131–86 (metarules §7); introductory account by G. C. Horrocks, *Generative Grammar* (London, Longman, 1987), pp. 177ff.

On ambiguity at the level of formatives see ROBINS, 'WP', pp. 127–32; following Robins, my *Inflectional Morphology*, §6.4.1. As Robins shows, this is not a problem for inflectional systems only: for a recent discussion in the context of word-formation see R. Beard in ALINEI, pp. 50ff. (on 'morphological asymmetry').

# Inflectional morphology and syntax

Is there a universal distinction? The problem of isolating languages;
problem of defining the word.
*What are words?* Words as the smallest unit of syntax; but syntax in turn
defined by words. The word as a unit of phonology: accent, restrictions
at word boundaries. Grammatical characteristics: words as minimal free
forms; cohesiveness; fixed ordering of inflections; formations in general
non-recursive. Coincidence of features that are logically independent.
*Problems and discrepancies.* What qualifications are needed? Case in Latin
and Turkish. The word in French: spelling vs phonology; forms in $C(\partial)$:
are they words or non-words? Clitics: in Latin; in English; and in
French? Auxiliary Tenses: simple forms vs periphrastic.

'Peut-on poser une définition universellement valable des
domaines respectifs de la morphologie et de la syntaxe?' ('Can
one define the fields of morphology and syntax in a way which will
be valid universally?') The question is the last of three proposed
for discussion at the Sixth International Congress of Linguists,
and the answers given by the participants are printed, with a
survey and further interventions, in the proceedings.[1] The
congress took place in Paris at a time when travel was more
difficult than now, and most people there were European. But
according to one of the few participants from North America the
answer was quite simply 'No'. It is time to ask if we can offer any
improvement on this answer, and whether, in general, the
distinction is as straightforward as we have tended to assume.

One problem is that the division between two parts of grammar
is not valid for isolating languages. In Classical Chinese, the
sentence was for the most part a succession of monosyllables.
Each was a grammatical unit, and few could be divided into
smaller units of the same kind. In particular, there was no unit
that could be described as an inflection. Nor were there many

---

[1] M. Lejeune (ed.), *Actes du VI<sup>e</sup> Congrès International des Linguistes* (Paris, Klincksieck,
1949), pp. 19–30, 261–302, 473–96.

lexical processes – a few involving a change of tone or change of consonant, some relatively loose compounds. The first reaction of European scholars was that the language 'had no grammar'. But that was nonsense. As in English, there are rules that determine how the basic units will be ordered. A more correct view is that the language only has a syntax. The division of grammar into two parts – one inflectional, the other syntactic – has no place.

This objection is perhaps not very damaging. If we say that an isolating language has no inflections we must know what an inflection is, and if we say that it only has a syntax we must know what syntax is. Our definitions may be universal, even though, in this case, they are partly inapplicable. But there is a more serious difficulty. In the traditional definition, syntax deals with successive relations between words. Thus, in Classical Chinese, the term 'word' must be applied to each basic monosyllable. Morphology, by contrast, deals with words as such. This assumes that our notion of the word is clear. It also assumes that relations between words as wholes are of a different kind or order from relations involving parts of words. But have we indeed a precise criterion for dividing one word from another? And can the second assumption always be sustained?

Let us take our first illustration from English. In *He won't come*, *he* is a word and *come* is a word. These are not statements that anyone is likely to challenge. But what about *won't*? It is written without a space; therefore one's first reaction might be to say that it too is a word. But we could also write *He will not come*, where *will* and *not* are two words. Are *not* and *n't* the same grammatical element? If so, is *won't* also two words? The problem with this is that *n't* is phonetically just [nt], and *wo-* or [wəʊ], assuming that it is the same grammatical element as *will*, is also altered. This might suggest that two words have indeed been fused into one. But *n't*, if it is the same grammatical element as *not*, retains its rôle within the sentence; therefore a part of a word would enter into the same relations as a whole word. The alternative is to say that *not* and *n't* are not the same grammatical element. But is *n't* then an inflection? Is *won't* a morphologically Negative form of WILL, [kɑːnt] or [kɑ̃ːt] the corresponding form of CAN, and so on?

It is not surprising that such problems should arise. As languages change, what were once grammatical words can gradually reduce to affixes; and perhaps, in this case, we have caught a series of changes in the middle. But problems they are; and, for this and other reasons, the issue raised by the organisers of the Sixth International Congress may never be wholly settled.

## WHAT ARE WORDS?

There have been many definitions of the word, and if any had been successful I would have given it long ago, instead of dodging the issue until now. One answer is to say that it is simply the smallest unit of syntax. That is effectively what the ancient grammarians said, and it is still a tempting line to take. But if we take it we will only turn our larger problem back to front. If words are to be defined by reference to syntax, what in turn is syntax, and why are syntactic relations not contracted by parts of words as well as whole words?

Take, for instance, the phrase *three beaches*. There is a rule by which its members have this order: it requires that Numerals, which are one kind of word, precede Nouns, which are another kind of word. There is also a rule by which one cannot say *three beach*, with *beach* in the Singular. But how should this second rule be stated? Traditionally it too affects words: if a Noun is modified by a Numeral, it must itself be Plural. But an alternative is to say that it concerns not *beaches* as a whole, but simply *-es*. If a morpheme of the class Noun is modified by a Numeral, it must be followed by the Plural morpheme. If we do not accept this, there is still a rule by which, within *beaches*, *-es* comes after *beach*. Are all these rules syntactic? If so, our definition of the word collapses. If not, why not? What is it that makes a rule relating *three* and *beaches* syntactic, but would make a rule relating *three* and *-es*, or *beach* and *-es*, not syntactic?

One answer is to say that there is indeed no difference between morphology and syntax. In the 'Item and Arrangement' model of chapter 6, the phrase is a sequence of three morphemes: THREE + BEACH + Plural. Sequence is the only relation, and therefore it makes sense to say that all rules are of the same order. It also makes sense to relate THREE directly to Plural, and not to a larger unit BEACH + Plural. Why then does the tradition view the matter differently? The reason must be that the word itself has some kind of special status. Because of that, relations within the word, even when they transparently involve a sequence, are not described in the same way as relations between words. Because of that, we do not talk of relations, like the one between THREE and Plural, which cut across the boundaries between words.

What is this special status? It must be said at once that it cannot be encapsulated in a definition, still less one that will be valid for all languages. It lies instead in a range of characteristics that words in general tend to have and other units tend not to have.

One important point is that the word tends to be a unit of phonology as well as grammar. In Latin, for example, it was the unit within which accents were determined: a word like *dóminus* 'master' was accented thus because the second to last syllable is short, while a word like *amábat* 'was loving' was stressed differently because this syllable is long ([a'ma:bat]). Of the other languages which we have cited, the same is also true of Egyptian Arabic: *kitáab* 'book' is accented finally because the final syllable is long but *kátab* 'he wrote' and *káatib* 'clerk' initially because it is short, *kátaba* 'clerks' is accented initially because all three syllables are short, *maktába* 'library' medially because the third is short but the first long, and so forth.[2] In many other languages the accent is not determined by phonology alone. But even then it is often restricted to a certain part of any polysyllabic word. In Modern Greek, for example, a word of four or more syllables may be accented on the last syllable (ἀδιαφορῶ *aðjaforó* 'I don't care'), on the second to last or penultimate (ἀδιαφορία *aðjaforía* 'indifference') or on the third from last or antepenultimate (ἀδιάφορος *aðjáforos* 'indifferent'), but not on any other syllable preceding.[3] Accent apart, there are other phonological features or restrictions which are peculiar to word-boundaries. In Italian, for example, the final syllable regularly ends in a vowel, although initial and medial syllables may readily end in a consonant. The native exceptions to this rule are a small number of monosyllables (*per* 'through', for instance), none belonging to large grammatical

[2] T. F. Mitchell, *Colloquial Arabic* (London, Teach Yourself Books), pp. 26f.
[3] See MIRAMBEL, pp. 25f.

classes. In all such cases, phonological patterns are described with specific reference to word boundaries.

The grammatical characteristics of words are themselves significantly diverse. One feature, which is again particularly striking in a language such as Latin, is that nothing smaller than a word can normally form a sentence on its own. In a play by Plautus, one of the characters questions another: 'Tell me in good faith (*dic bona fide*), you didn't get at (*surrupuisti*) that gold?' The other replies *bona* '[in] good [faith]'. A little later: 'And if you know who took it, you'll tell me?' Answer: *faciam* 'I'll do so'. To the next question the answer is simply *ita* 'just so' (*Aulularia*, IV. x). But one does not find stems on their own (unless, of course, they happen to form words as well); in answer to the first question our character in Plautus could not have said simply *bon-* (the stem of the word meaning 'good'). Nor does one find isolated inflectional formatives. The second question ends with the word *indicabis* 'you'll tell', of which the *-bis* is the Future 2nd Person Singular inflection; but in answer one could not simply pick this up and say *-bo* (1st Singular 'will do', as it were). In a classic formulation that dates back to Bloomfield, forms such as *bon-*, *-bo* or *-bis* are **bound forms** (or sequences of one or more **bound morphemes**): forms which can only appear as part of a larger form or larger sequence of morphemes. However, *bona*, *bona fide*, *dic bona fide*, *mihi indicabis* 'you will tell me', and so on, are all **free forms**: capable, that is, of appearing on their own. Of these last, all but *bona* can be divided into two or more smaller free forms: *bona fide* into *bona* and *fide*, *mihi indicabis* into *mihi* and *indicabis*. They are what Bloomfield called 'phrases'. But *bona*, *fide*, *indicabis*, etc., cannot themselves be so divided; and it is such **minimal free forms** that Bloomfield defined as 'words'.

As a definition this has often been criticised. Latin *et* 'and' would normally be called a word, and so would English *my* or *the*. But are these words that could appear on their own? *My* seems especially unlikely; apart from exclamation (*My!*), when would one use it instead of *mine*? In the case of *et*, no isolated syntactic usage is attested in the dictionaries. Perhaps we might have heard it (as it were, in the context 'Did you mean *et* or *aut*?'), but then parts of words can also appear alone in that kind of use. The following is an attested example: (A) 'Did you say révise or dévise?' – (B) 'Re'. The difficulty with *the* is one which Bloomfield himself recognised; he argued, however, that since an article is in other respects syntactically similar to *this* or *that*, and these can certainly occur freely in conversation, therefore it could be accorded word-status too. But then could not the Comparative *-er* be a word, since functionally (though not positionally) it is equivalent to *more*? For such reasons, the 'minimal free form' is regarded with misgiving by many linguists. Nevertheless, as a characteristic of words as a class (and as one criterion by which they are recognised), it is beyond dispute.

By the same token, speakers are able to split up utterances into words (e.g. to help the analyst or the learner). This cannot always be explained by writing conventions: many years ago, Sapir reported similar experiences with an unwritten language (SAPIR, p. 34) and I, at least, cannot recall a later report to the contrary. Indeed, who developed the orthography to start with, and why do children learn to space words readily? Another related point is that fragments of inflected words do not appear alone in sentence constructions. A Roman could not, for example, coordinate two different endings of Verbs – say, *indicabit vel -avit* ('will indicate or has [indicated]'), with both Future and Perfect inflections linked by a Conjunction (*vel*) to a single stem. With lexical affixes we do find exceptions. For example, an Italian has been heard to ask 'È proprio -accio?' ('Is it really bad?'), using a pejorative suffix (*-acci-*) on its own with a Masculine ending.[4] Exceptions like this are an obstacle to any strict definition. But that they are exceptions to what is otherwise a general property of elements within the word cannot be doubted.

This leads naturally to a second main characteristic (that of **cohesiveness**) which could in principle be independent. Just as a part of a word does not as a rule appear on its own (unless, of course, it is itself another word), so the parts cannot as a rule be separated by other forms (unless, of course, the whole is then a new word). In Latin, the words in a phrase may often appear with quite extraneous items intervening. For example, in the following line from Horace's *Epistles*:

Forte meum si quis te percontabitur aevum

---

[4] Observation reported to me by Professor G. C. Lepschy.

('If perhaps someone asks you my age'; 1, xx, 26), the members
of the Object phrase *meum...aevum* 'my age' are separated by the
Conjunction introducing the whole clause (*si* 'if') and also by the
Subject, Verb and the other Object (*quis* 'someone', *percontabitur*
'will ask', *te* 'you'). By contrast, the word is absolutely cohesive.
One could say nothing like *percont- aevum -abitur*, *me- si quis -um
aevum*, and so on. In English, there are marginal exceptions with
expletives. The following, for example, is from an Australian song
of the First World War:[5]

> Get a——move on, have some——sense,
> Learn the——art of self de-——-fence.

where the interrupted word *defence* might itself be regarded as the
second member of a compound. A less marginal exception might
be provided by the relatively loose cohesion, in German and
related languages, of Prepositions normally said to be compounded with Verbs. As we saw in chapter 5, they are together in
some constructions ([*Ich muss*] *ausgehen* '[I must] go out'), but in
others they are obligatorily separate. Compare *Ich geh heute abend
aus* (literally 'I go this evening out').

A third major feature is the **fixed ordering** of constituent
elements. In Latin, the order of words in the sentence is strikingly
free: in the same example, *te meum aevum percontabitur* would do
as well (metre apart) as the variant actually cited. In English,
word order often carries a difference of meaning, *John loves Mary*
being not the same as *Mary loves John*. But in both languages the
order of stems and inflections is at once fixed and non-contrastive.
In *per-cont-a-bi-t-ur* the formative elements appear only in that
sequence; there is no alternative order, such as *per-cont-ur-a-bi-
t*, which can serve either as a rhythmic variant or as another
member of the paradigm. In the Perfect *cu-curr-is-ti* 'you have
run' the stem *cu-curr-* is formed by prefixal reduplication (chapter
7) whereas in *sur-rup-u-is-ti* 'you have got at' its counterpart *sur-
rup-u-* is formed by suffixing *-u-*; but that a 'Perfect morpheme'
should come before the root in one case (*cu-*), while coming after

---

[5] The lines are to be sung to the refrain of 'Onward Christian Soldiers', with the blanks
supplied according to taste; see 'Headway in Australia's quest for new anthem', *The
Times*, 3 July 1973.

it in another (-*u*-), is a fixed feature of these forms and has no syntactic or semantic import. It is this characteristic which makes it natural to regard the grammatical properties of the word as unordered, to say that *sailed* is merely the 'Past Tense of SAIL' (see chapter 7), and *cucurristi* the traditional '2nd Singular Perfect Indicative Active of CURRO' rather than 'PERFECT morpheme followed by root morpheme CURR-' and so on.

Again there are exceptions. In the case of compounds they are obvious: English *outlet* is different from *let-out*, *cart-horse* from *horse-cart*, and so on. It is in the nature of compounds, as we saw in chapter 5, that they involve relations partly paralleling those of syntax. Other exceptions can be found in word-formation. In English, for example, -*al*, -*ise* and -*ation* have one order in a word like *nation-al-is(e)-ation* and another in a word like *sens(e)-ation-al-ise*. But it is much harder to find exceptions which involve inflectional formatives. Even in an agglutinative language such as Turkish, for which the Item and Arrangement model of chapter 6 is most appropriate, their order is at least very largely fixed.

Our fourth and final characteristic is related to the third. In any language, some syntactic constructions are **recursive**: one may build a sentence by the repetition – once, twice or, in principle, indefinitely – of the same or essentially the same process. In Latin, for example, one may take a phrase which includes a Relative clause (*milites quos saucios vidisti* 'the soldiers who you saw wounded'), make this the Object of a Verb (*adiuvabat milites quos saucios vidisti* 'was giving aid to the soldiers who...'), then put this in a larger Relative-clause construction (*feminam* 'the woman' *quae* 'who' *adiuvabat milites*, etc.), and then, since *feminam* is Accusative, have the whole form from *feminam* to *vidisti* as the Object of another Verb. But the formation of words in Latin is wholly **non-recursive**. One cannot, as it were, derive a Future stem for the Verb ADIUVO 'help' (*adiuvabi-*), then derive an Imperfect stem from that (*adiuvabi-ba-*), then a Future again from that (*adiuvabiba-bi-*), and then, with the Person/Number ending (*adiuvabibab(i)-unt*), have a form which would mean something like 'will be in a position where [they] were about to give help to'. If one wants to say that one has to use several words instead.

Here too we must recognise some qualifications. In Turkish,

for example, the stem of the Intransitive Verb form *öldü* '[he, etc.] died' may be extended with a Causative suffix to yield *öl-dür-dü* 'killed' (i.e. 'caused to die'), and this in turn might be extended with a further Causative suffix (different merely because *-dür* is excluded by the phonological context) to yield *öl-dür-t-tü* 'got [someone] to kill'.[6] To that extent recursion is possible. In Portuguese, there are circumstances in which speakers might use a double diminutive: ironically, of a baby, ['It is so'] *pequenininho* – or, in a variant recorded from Brazil,[7] *pequeninozinho*. Here *pequeno* 'small' is the form of the simple Adjective, *pequenino* is its diminutive, and these forms ('teeny-weeny-weeny') are in turn diminutives of that. In English, it is occasionally possible to double a prefix: for example, [*in his*] *pre-pre-school* [*days*].[8] With suffixes, which are more numerous, a formation can be repeated at a distance. From *sense*, as we have seen, one can form *sensation*, and from that *sensational* and then *sensationalise*. But there seems no reason, in principle, why one should not add *-ation* again to form *sensationalisation*. It may be something of a jingle, but it is hard to say that it is excluded. If we play around with the same suffixes we find derivations of the type *organ-* (also in *organic*) → *organ-ise* → *organis(e)-ation* → *organisation-al* (note, with a third possible ordering). Would it not be possible to add *-ise* again to form *organisationalise*? No doubt most readers will not like it, but can one swear that one has never heard it? It is significant that these examples are drawn from lexical morphology. In both Portuguese and English, inflectional formations are as strictly non-recursive as in Latin.

The four grammatical features which we have reviewed are logically independent. It is easy to conceive of a language in which *ab* and *c* were two minimal sentence units (the first characteristic), but *ab*, when construed with *c*, could yield the non-cohesive order *a-* + *c* + *-b*. This would be something like a regular example of the pattern *self de——— -fence*. Nor does cohesiveness rule out either a contrast in order or a recursive derivation: a word like

---

[6] Examples from LEWIS, p. 147; for the contextual restrictions on *-t* and basic *-dIr* (here *-dür*) see LEWIS, pp. 144f.

[7] See Pilar Vázquez Cuesta and Maria Albertina Mendes da Luz, *Gramática da língua portuguesa* (Lisbon, Edições 70, 1971), p. 133.

[8] Observation reported by Professor D. Crystal.

*sensationalisation* would still function as an uninterruptable whole within the sentence. Nor is either of these required of a minimal free form: in *sensationalisation*, *sens(e)* alone can stand by itself. But in fact these features DO tend to coincide, particularly in languages such as Latin and particularly, in English and in many others, if we restrict ourselves to words that are lexically simple. There is again no logical reason why a grammatical unit with these characteristics should also be central to phonology. Smaller units of grammar are widely independent of phonological boundaries: in a Latin word like *percontabitur* 'will ask', the divisions between roots and formatives (*per-cont-a-bi-t-ur* or *per-cont-a-b-i-t-ur*) do not coincide with syllable divisions. Larger units, like the clause, also tend not to be phonologically marked.

It is because such features tend to go together that the word has its special status. We cannot give an operational definition, which will tell us that *x* is a word if and only if it meets this test or that test. If we hanker after such definitions, we will end up by rejecting this and every other real linguistic unit. Nor can morphology and syntax be defined independently. It is precisely because so many differences centre on the word that they are separated.

## PROBLEMS AND DISCREPANCIES

Our illustrations have been largely from Latin, which is a clear example of the flectional type. What further qualifications might we have had to make if we had looked elsewhere?

In Turkish, for example, the word is a clear phonological unit. In particular, it is the unit within which rules of vowel harmony operate – within which syllables vary between Front or Back, Close Rounded or Close Unrounded, in harmony with the invariant final syllable of a Noun or other element (chapter 6). The forms we have cited are also minimal free forms. But their cohesiveness is arguably less. One striking difference between Turkish and Latin is that, in the syntax of the Noun Phrase, a Case ending only appears once. Whereas in a Latin Phrase like *meum aevum* 'my age' both *meum* 'my' and *aevum* 'age' are marked as an Accusative, the Turkish Accusative morpheme

(-*i*/*ü*/*ı*/*u*) will be added only to a Head Noun. In the same spirit, in a phrase like the following:

> Ankara ve İzmire [gideceğim]
> '[I am going] to Ankara and Smyrna'

the Dative morpheme appears only in the second member of the co-ordination (*İzmir-e*), the first (*Ankara*) being unmarked. Although -*e* is certainly not a free form, and is harmonically part of the word *İzmire*, it effectively marks both Nouns.

In its morphology, Turkish is clearly agglutinating: morpho-syntactic categories are realised as forms, generally with easily recognised boundaries between them. The word is an important unit by other criteria, and on that basis a division between morphology and syntax holds. However, constructions like this confirm that the Item and Arrangement model, in which the morpheme is an independent atomic unit, is most appropriate.

Quite different difficulties are posed by a more familiar language, French. How many words are there, for example, in the simple French phrase *des enfants* 'of the children'? The spelling will suggest that there are two: *des*, phonetically [dɛz], and *enfants* [ãfã]. But as far as phonology is concerned this is not so. Firstly, the piece as a whole carries only one accent, [dɛzã'fã]; just as there is an accent-carrying unit in Latin (the 'phonological word'), so in French there is a similar unit (whatever we call it) which carries the stress on its final syllable. From this viewpoint, therefore, the phrase is a single unit at the phonological level. In addition, the boundary between *des* and *enfants* appears to have no consequences for syllabification: in terms of these smaller phonological units the division is simply between [dɛ], [zã] and [fã]. There is no intermediate phonological unit to which *des* and *enfants* as such could belong.

Let us accept, at least, that *des* and *enfants* are distinct grammatical units. But are they distinct words? The phrase is not cohesive: for example, we might insert an Adjective to form *des grands enfants* [degrãzãfã] 'of the tall children'. But let us look further at the class of elements to which *des* belongs. In *les enfants* 'the children' we have the simple Definite Article (in this context, [lɛz]); so far so good. But in the corresponding Singular the Article is simply [l]: *l'enfant* [lãfã] 'the child'. Are we to recognise a word which can consist of one consonant only? I say 'can' since the Article would have more substance if a consonant followed: *le* [lə] *père* 'the father'. But the [ə] of [lə] is still a vowel that, unlike others, never carries the phrase accent. Further problems arise with other sets of *C* or *Cə* units. In the sentence *je ne le vois pas* 'I can't see him', there are three of them: *je* 'I', *ne* (combining with *pas* to form the negative), and *le* 'him'. These are much more cohesive with the Finite Verb (in this example, *vois* '[I] see') which follows, in that no further lexical unit – an Adverb, for instance – can intervene. Nor are any of them (or, for that matter, *des* or *les* or *le*) minimal free forms. One cannot say just *je* 'I', and the form one would use (*moi* 'me') is phonologically unrelated. It is clear at this point that our phalanx of criteria has begun to break apart. In our original example, *enfants* is at least a minimal free form, and therefore a word on one view. But do we want to say that *des*, *je*, and so on are words also?

Before we try to answer this question, it will be helpful to look at a much simpler problem in Latin. In the first clause of Virgil's *Aeneid*:

> arma virumque cano
> 'I sing of arms and the man'

the construction involves a Verb (*cano* 'I sing') which has as its Object two Nouns in the Accusative (*arma* 'arms' and *virum* 'man'). These are linked by a Conjunction (*-que*). But unlike *et*, which is another word for 'and' that we met earlier, *-que* is phonologically attached to the second member of the co-ordination. If *virum* appeared alone it would have an accent on the first syllable (*vírum*). But when *-que* is attached to it the accent shifts; not *vírumque*, but *virúmque*. Is the combination one word, as traditionally written, or two?

It seems plain that *-que* cannot be an inflection. Inflections are characteristic of particular parts of speech: Tense inflections of Verbs, Case inflections (in Latin) of Nouns, Pronouns, Adjectives and Participles, and so on. But *-que*, like *et*, combines freely with any word that can stand in a co-ordinative construction. Moreover, its form is invariable; inflections, by contrast, vary between declensions and conjugations and between one part of a paradigm and another. It therefore has an intermediate status.

Phonologically it depends on *virum*: we might say that the whole of *virúmque* 'man-and' is one **phonological word**. Grammatically it divides into two, *virum* 'man' + *-que* 'and'. But of its two parts, only *virum* can itself be a word in both phonology and grammar (thus in the alternative wording *arma et virum* 'arms and man'). If *-que* is a word, it is not one in the most complete sense.

Such intermediate units are called **clitics**. They are units which are word-like in their grammar, but phonologically must lean for support (the term is originally from the Ancient Greek word for 'to lean') on another word adjacent to them. Another clear example is the *'s* in an English phrase like *John's chances*. Traditionally it is said to mark the 'Genitive Case', and certainly, in its phonology, it is in general like the Plural suffix. But in fact it combines with units larger than words: for example, in *a man of twenty's chances* it is not an inflection of *twenty*, which is itself syntactically subordinate to *man*, but relates *chances* to the whole of *a man of twenty*. In its grammar *'s* is more like a word than an affix. But again it forms a phonological word (*John's*, *twenty's*) with the word preceding.

It is in this light that most scholars would resolve a part, at least, of our problem with French. In *je ne le vois pas* 'I can't see him', the first three elements (*je*, *ne* and *le*) are not clearly prefixes. As they are standardly described, *je* 'I' has the syntactic rôle of Subject, like, for example, *Marie* 'Mary' in *Marie ne le voit pas* 'Mary can't see him.' In standard descriptions, again, *le* is the Object and could, with some other forms of the Verb, come after it and not before (*Tuez-le* 'Kill him'). But phonologically and in their cohesiveness they are more prefix-like than word-like. Therefore they are all clitics. In our example, *vois* is preceded by a sequence of three clitics: these are, more precisely, **proclitics** – clitics that lean forwards on the word following. In *Tuez-le*, one of the same units appears as an **enclitic**: this is a clitic that leans backwards, like Latin *-que* or English *'s*, on the word preceding. In *l'enfant* 'the child', *l(e)* 'the' is another proclitic; *des*, in *des enfants* 'of the children', is arguably a clitic formed from two syntactic elements, and so on.

But clitics would then play a very large rôle in the grammar of French. In Latin, only two other units (*-ve* 'or' and the interrogative marker *-ne*), had the same status as *-que*. In English,

there are other candidates: *n't* (see earlier in this chapter) or the
*-th* of, for example, [*hundred and fifteen*]*th*. But they are not many.
In French, by contrast, they would be numerous and frequent,
and in examples like *je ne le vois pas* they pile up in sequence.
Some, moreover, are tied very closely to specific classes of words:
*je*, for example, is a clitic supported only by Finite Verbs, and
between it and them only another clitic can intervene. It is
reasonable to wonder whether, in a language like this, a distinction
between clitics and inflections (between, for example, *le* and *-ez* in
*Tuez-le*) is truly helpful.

The problem in all these examples (to put it crudely) is that
syntactic boundaries cut across word-boundaries. Thus, in *a man
of twenty's chances*, the syntactic boundary between *a man of
twenty* and *'s* cuts across *twenty's*. But there is another discrepancy
that is in a sense the opposite. In English, *sailed* is one word and
is the Past of SAIL. But what of, say, *have sailed*? It is clearly two
words: Adverbs, for example, can intervene (*I have often sailed*),
and *have* is found alone in ellipsis (*Yes, I have*). But it too is
normally treated as a Tense of SAIL, and anyone who teaches
English to foreigners will know that the contrast between *have
X-ed* (Present Perfect) and *X-ed* (Simple Past) must be tackled
directly. Similarly, as *sail(s)* is the Simple Present of SAIL,
*am/is/are sailing* is opposed to it as Present Progressive. The
implication is that English paradigms include on equal terms both
single words and sequences of words.

The same holds for the traditional accounts of other European
languages. In French, *je l'ai vu* 'I saw/have seen him' has what
is called the 'passé composé' or Compound Past Tense. But the
exponents of this are two forms, *ai* and *vu*, between which, again,
some Adverbs can be inserted (*je l'ai probablement vu* 'I probably
saw him'). In a form such as [*quand*] *je l'ai eu fait* '[when] I've
done it' there is yet another Tense (one of the 'temps
surcomposés' or Double-compound Tenses) with exponents in *ai
eu fait*. In Latin, schoolboys learned *amo* 'I love' as Present
Active, *amor* 'I am loved' as Present Passive, *amavi* 'I loved' as
Perfect Active, but then *amatus sum* (a form consisting of a
Masculine Nominative Singular Participle, *amatus*, and the form
for 'I am', *sum*) as the Perfect Passive. The last is clearly two
words, which obey separate syntactic rules (for example, of

agreement). Nevertheless they are taken together as a term in what are otherwise morphological oppositions.

It is often hard to say how many forms should be treated in this way. In the traditional account of Latin, only some of the forms with SUM are included: for example, the 'Future Infinitive Active' *amaturus esse* 'to be about to love' but not the corresponding Perfective *amaturus fuisse* 'to have been about to love'. Arguably both should be part of the paradigm, or neither. But this does not invalidate the principle, namely that a two-word form (such as *amatus sum* and its variants) may bear a semantic relationship to a single word (*amavi*) which is the same as that which other simple words (such as *amo* and *amor*) bear among themselves. In the examples from French and English we do not find parallels as close as that. But few specialists in either language would accept that the oppositions entered into by *ai vu, have sailed*, and so on are not of the same kind, from the viewpoint of meaning, as those contracted by single forms of the same lexeme. Treating them as different would make no sense of the system, either synchronically or diachronically.

What shall such forms be called? They are not inflected forms: although they are semantically within the paradigm, the formal discrepancy remains. To call them 'compound', as French 'composé', might do. But the term has already been used, as in chapter 5, for formations that are lexical rather than grammatical, and result in one word for the purposes of syntax. Moreover, one may often speak of one-word compounds in inflectional morphology: for example, the Agau Desiderative *destagi* 'I wish you studied' incorporates a particle *-gi* (here merely a means of forming the Desiderative) which also appears in syntactic constructions with the meaning 'all'.[9] An alternative, which has its basis in the classical tradition, is to talk of a **periphrasis**. Latin *amatus sum* 'I have been loved' is thus a **periphrastic form** of the Passive (a form involving periphrasis rather than a single word), and French *ai vu* 'I saw/have seen' represents a periphrastic Tense of VOIR 'to see', just as *vois* 'see' represents a

---

[9] See R. Hetzron, *The Verbal System of Southern Agaw* (Berkeley/Los Angeles, University of California Press, 1969), p. 21. Agau is a Cushitic language of Northern Ethiopia; in citing one lesser-known example I do not mean to imply that there is anything unusual in the pattern.

simple Tense. But, terminology apart, the essential point is that in such cases the paradigm of a lexeme, which is basically a morphological concept, is extended beyond the word. No other morphological concept is involved. In Latin, the inflections of *amatus* 'loved' will be described by one set of rules and those of *sum* (in itself 'I am') by another. But in a language like French, where the division of morphology and syntax is already a problem, such extensions might well be felt to weaken its validity still further.

## RELATED READING

See NORMAN, ch. 4, for a very clear sketch of the characteristics of Classical Chinese. On English *n't* see reference below to Zwicky & Pullum.

The problem of the word has been discussed many times. For what is still a useful structuralist critique see A. Martinet, 'Le Mot', *Collection Diogène* 2 (Paris, Gallimard, 1966), pp. 39–53; also MARTINET, §§4.15–17, and, for a restatement, A. Martinet, 'Que faire du "mot"?', in P. Swiggers & W. van Hoecke (eds.), *Mot et parties du discours* (Leuven, Peeters, 1986), pp. 75–84. On the historical background to discussion of the word in French see GUILBERT, pp. 105ff. For Bloomfield's definition see BLOOMFIELD, pp. 178ff.; for discussion within the later Bloomfieldian school, HOCKETT, *Course*, ch. 19. For the points made here compare in large part LYONS, *Introduction*, §5.4; also my *Inflectional Morphology*, §6.4.3 (with references to other earlier studies). BAUER's account (*Morphology* ch. 4), is similarly derivative, but has some different examples. For a fresh view of the wider issue see the rather untidy monograph by A. Di Sciullo & E. Williams, *On the Definition of Word* (Cambridge, Mass., MIT Press, 1987): although the authors seek to disguise themselves as whizz-kids, a lot of what they say is in substance sound and not unconventional.

The terms 'enclitic' and 'proclitic' originate in the description of Ancient Greek: see, for example, GOODWIN, pp. 31ff. 'Clitic' itself is relatively recent: see *OEDS*, s.v., for reference to E. A. Nida (1946), specifically on *'s* in English. For a discussion of *'s* and Latin *-que* in the context of constituency analysis compare ROBINS, *Linguistics*, pp. 226f. The status of Verbal clitics in French is another standard topic: for an earlier discussion, which I still find thought-provoking, see C. Bally, *Linguistique générale et linguistique française* (2nd edn, Berne, Francke, 1944), pp. 287–302 (especially his conclusion, §§493–4); for a useful introduction, M. B. Harris, *The Evolution of French Syntax* (London, Longman, 1978), §5.3 (pp. 118f. for their treatment as prefixes). It is perhaps worth stressing that the discrepancies between phonology and syntax can be greater than in these examples: for discussion see J. L. Klavans, 'The independence of syntax and phonology in cliticization', *Lg* 61 (1985) pp. 95–120.

On the criteria for distinguishing clitics from full words see A. M. Zwicky's very lucid paper, 'Clitics and particles', *Lg* 61 (1985), pp. 283–305; also A. M.

Zwicky & G. K. Pullum, 'Cliticization vs. inflection: English *n't*', *Lg* 59 (1983), pp. 502–13. Note Zwicky's comments ('Clitics and particles', p. 285) on the difference between a definition and a set of criteria or 'symptoms', and see again my reference to Bazell's 'Correspondence fallacy' (Reading for chapter 3).

Periphrastic forms have a syntactic structure; and, since levels are often seen as mutually exclusive, they tend to be excluded from morphology. In particular, there is little discussion of when they should be recognised. But they are well entrenched in the grammatical traditions of European languages: thus, for English, compare QUIRK *et al.*, ch. 4, on Progressive and Perfective Aspect; PALMER, chs. 3 and 4, on the interactions of Tense, Phase and Aspect.

# Iconicity

One of the oldest findings about language is that the forms of lexical elements generally do not bear a natural relation to their meanings. As Hermogenes put it in a dialogue by Plato, the names of things are justified by nothing more than rule and custom.[1] In particular, words with similar meanings have arbitrarily different forms. Not only is English *horse* different from French *cheval* or German *Pferd*; it also bears no resemblance to semantically related forms like *mare*, or *foal*, or *cow*, and so on. The reason for this is obvious enough. If similar meanings were systematically associated with similar forms, the risks of misunderstanding through mishearing – of supposing that one is being offered a stallion when in fact it is a bull, or saying that a restaurant is good but being heard as saying that it is bad – would be very great. To see this, one need only look at one of the 'natural languages' that were invented, for example, in seventeenth-century England. In one of these, the form for 'onion' is *nebghnagbana*, for 'garlic' *nebghnagmuba*; for 'cucumber' *nibmuba*, for 'gourd' *nibmoba*. The system lacks what is technically called redundancy, and is

---

[1] *Cratylus*, 384d. The character Hermogenes is not known otherwise.

very vulnerable to error. Imagine a shopping list in which just a few letters could not be made out!

But languages are less arbitrary in their grammar. Take, for example, the sentence *I lifted the dahlias yesterday*. In its formal structure, *lifted* and *the dahlias* are adjacent: one does not say *I lifted yesterday the dahlias*. By the same rule, *yesterday* and *lifted* are not adjacent: their formal relationship is more distant. But let us now look at the semantics of the construction. The Verb LIFT or 'to lift' is one that normally, at least, requires an Object: one would not simply say *I lifted yesterday*. But it does not require, nor do Verbs generally require, a Time Adverbial: one can easily say *I lifted the dahlias*, with no *yesterday*. Not every Noun will readily make sense as the Object of LIFT: what would one mean by, for example, *I lifted the breeze*? Nor is its sense entirely independent of its Object: *I lifted the dahlias* would normally mean 'I dug them up', which is not the sense of LIFT in, for example, *I lifted the bricks* or *I lifted my head*. By contrast, LIFT can be accompanied by any Time Adverbial (*I lifted the dahlias during the night, at Christmas, too late*, or whatever) and, whichever Adverbial it is, the sense of the Verb is not affected. In all this, *lifted* bears a close semantic relationship to *the dahlias*, which, as we have seen, is also formally adjacent to it. It does not bear such a close semantic relationship to *yesterday*; and, as we have seen, *yesterday* is also formally more distant. The correspondence between form and meaning is natural and not arbitrary. What is closer in meaning is closer in form; what is less close in meaning is less close in form.

This is a field in which it is very easy to imagine or manufacture correspondences. In the eighteenth century, the order of words in French seemed, to many Frenchmen, to be superbly logical. What was prior in thought (they believed) came first in the sentence, what followed in thought came later. But what was their evidence for priority in thought? Was the supposed ordering of thought more than a projection, by the grammarian, of the ordering of words? With that episode in mind, we have to take care that what we say about meanings can be justified independently of the forms to which they are related. But when we do take care, we will often be able to establish that forms and meanings stand in an **iconic** or **diagrammatic** relation. An icon (in the ordinary sense) is a picture, in which there is a schematic correspondence between the painted features and the real features of a man or woman. In a diagram of a circuit there is a similar correspondence between the representations of a switch or a condenser and the positions of a real switch or a real condenser in the circuit itself. Similarly for grammar: in our example from English, the formal distribution of Verb, Object and Adverbial corresponds as to distance with the semantic distances between the elements. It is not difficult to guess, at least, at the reason for such correspondences. Where arbitrary relations are an advantage in the lexicon, in that they increase redundancy, natural relations between form and meaning – relations like that between an icon and a man's head, or a circuit diagram and a real circuit – may be an advantage in grammar. For it is possible that rules may then be easier to learn, or speech easier to process.

In this chapter we will look for iconic relations in morphology. They are of two main kinds. The first again involves ordering: just as in syntax there is sometimes (though not always) an iconic aspect to the formal distribution of such elements as Verb, Object and Adverbial, so, in morphology, there is sometimes (though not always) an iconic aspect to the ordering of roots and affixes. In European structuralism, relations among successive elements are called **syntagmatic relations.** In SAUSSURE's formulation (p. 171), they hold between units that are present ('in praesentia') in the same stretch of speech. The first kind of iconicity may therefore be called **syntagmatic iconicity**, or iconicity on the syntagmatic dimension.

The second will involve oppositions between words. A Singular, for instance, is opposed to a Plural both in meaning and in form, and here too there may be an iconic or diagrammatic correspondence. Oppositions between units are commonly called **paradigmatic relations**. Thus, in traditional terms, there is a paradigm in which a Singular Noun-form is related to a Plural Noun-form. The second kind of iconicity can therefore be called **paradigmatic iconicity**. In morphology it is, in particular, iconicity within paradigms.

Let us take the syntagmatic dimension first.

## CENTRAL AND PERIPHERAL CATEGORIES

Suppose that a word has two or more inflections. A Verb, for example, may be inflected both for Tense and for Person and Number. How then might the categories be marked? In principle, all three might share a cumulative exponent, coming either before the root:

> Tense/Person/Number + Root

or after:

> Root + Tense/Person/Number

Alternatively, Number might have its own markers, with Tense and Person marked cumulatively. The exponents might then come in this order:

> Root + Number + Tense/Person

or in this:

> Tense/Person + Root + Number

and so on. Or, again, there might be separate markers for each category, for instance in this order:

> Root + Number + Tense + Person

Nothing in the 'Item and Process' or in any other purely formal model would rule any of these patterns out.

But let us consider the pattern that we do find in, for example, Italian. In, say, *mangiavano* '[they] were eating', the final -*no* is a cumulative marker of 3rd Plural, and it is always in this position, in the termination, that Person and Number have their exponents. The preceding stem, *mangiava*-, marks the Tense; the form is Imperfect Indicative, and these properties (or this property if Tense and Mood are seen as a single dimension) are regularly marked by -*v(a)*-. In summary, then, the pattern is like this:

> Root + Tense + Person/Number

By rules of the kind outlined in chapter 9, the stem *mangiava*- would be derived by the suffixation of -*va*-. From that, the whole form would be derived by the further suffixation of -*no*.

Why are the affixes distributed in this way? The immediate answer is, of course, historical. The pattern we find in Italian partly continues a more complicated pattern that is attested in Latin, and, by comparison with other Indo-European languages, we can project it further back into prehistory. In one sense, therefore, it is simply a persisting characteristic of this family. Not surprisingly, we can find other patterns in languages that are not Indo-European. For example, in chapter 7 we cited a few forms from an Athapaskan language in which Aspect and the Subject Person and Number are marked in this order:

Aspect + Person/Number + Root

But the pattern in Italian is also partly iconic. Let us take first the cumulative marking of Person and Number. In syntax, these are categories that go together. They characterise both Verbs and Pronouns: as *mangiavo* 'I was eating' is 1st Singular, so is the clitic Pronoun *me* 'me, myself'. Both enter into the rule by which, if a Verb has a Pronoun or Noun Phrase as its Subject, there is agreement between them. For example, in *Le donne mangiavano le uva* 'The women were eating the grapes', *le donne* 'the women' determines that the Verb is both 3rd Person and Plural. At the same time, neither is so closely related to Tense: this is a category of the Verb only, and Tenses are independent of the Subject. So, the distribution of exponents is iconic. The categories that belong together semantically are marked simultaneously; the one which is semantically separate is marked separately.

Let us now look at the ordering of the suffixes. The marker of Tense is formally more central: it is part of the stem and, as such, is close to the root. The marker of Person and Number is a termination, and is therefore formally further from the root. But this distribution also makes semantic sense. In *mangiavano*, the final -*no* identifies the participants responsible for the eating, and, although the word could stand without any further Subject (*Mangiavano* 'They were eating'), the participants could again be identified by a separate phrase (*Le donne mangiavano*). The properties marked by the termination are thus syntactically peripheral to the Verb, whose function as a lexical item is to identify the action itself. By contrast, Tense is again marked only on the Verb, and, as the category by which the action is located in time, is semantically central to it. Thus the properties of the Verb which are syntactically peripheral are also marked peripherally, by a termination. The property which is semantically central to it is marked centrally.

What conclusion can we draw from illustrations of this kind? The strongest conclusion might be to suppose that languages are subject to a law of iconicity. This would state that, if there are no disturbing factors, what is semantically more central will also be formally more central. From this, we might draw the corollary that, if categories are equally central, they will be formally cumulative. But such laws would quickly prove false. We would find that languages obeyed them in part and also, in part, disobeyed them.

At the other extreme, this might be no more than an interesting point about Italian. If there is a similar pattern in some unrelated language $X$, that will again be an interesting point about $X$. A third possibility, however, is that both Italian and $X$ exemplify a general tendency. A tendency is not a law: we would not claim that such and such 'will' be the case. But, in any individual language, we would expect to find some iconic patterning. We would also expect to find that some particular patterns are widespread. Although we know there are exceptions, we might expect that, in many other languages or families of languages, a category which is semantically like Tense in Italian will be marked more centrally (whether by suffixes or prefixes may not matter) than categories like Person and Number. We might expect that the latter will, in general, tend to be marked cumulatively.

Whatever our general hopes or expectations, it is easy to find other examples of iconicity. In Turkish, as we saw in chapter 6, the Plural morpheme (*-ler* or *-lar*) is separate from the Case morphemes, and their order, when a Noun has both, is:

Root + PLURAL + Case

Formally, then, the marking of Plural is more central – that is, closer to the root – and that of Case peripheral. But now consider the semantics of these categories. A Noun Phrase, in the simplest case, identifies a referent; this may be one man or more than one man, one village or more than one village, and so on. The distinction between 'one' and 'more than one' is part of its identification, and in that way the Plural morpheme, by whose presence or absence the distinction is made, is semantically linked to the lexical morpheme. But the function of Cases is not, in general, to establish referents. Instead they indicate relations between words or phrases – the syntactic rôles of Nouns within the sentence, the dependence of one Noun on another, and so on. In that way they belong to a wider construction. We can therefore see a semantic structure which is parallel to the formal structure. Where the Plural morpheme is part of a potential referring expression:

Root (PLURAL)

and therefore has a rôle essentially internal to the Noun Phrase, the Case supplies a syntactic modulation of the whole:

[Root (PLURAL)] (Case)

In meaning, as in form, Case is peripheral.

Lexical formatives provide another striking illustration. Take, for instance, the Italian Verb-form *verdeggiavano* '[they] were turning green'. Like *mangiavano* '[they] were eating', this has a termination *-no*, which is added to an inflectional stem *verdeggiava-*:

[verdeggiava] + no

But within the inflectional stem there is a lexical stem *verdeggi-*:

[[verdeggi] + ava]

formed by the addition of *-eggi-* to the root of VERDE 'green'. Compare *rosseggiavano* '[they] were becoming red', with the root of ROSSO 'red'; or, less perspicuously, *galleggiavano* '[they] were afloat', with a Noun root also found in the phrase *a galla* 'afloat'. Formally *-eggi-*, the lexical suffix, is closer to the root and forms an inner stage of derivation. The inflectional suffixes, both of the stem (*-a-*, *-va-*) and in the termination (*-no*) are successively peripheral.

Such patterns are so widespread that, although there are exceptions, the formal position of 'derivational' formatives has often been taken as a criterion for distinguishing them. But we can again see this as an instance of iconicity. In *verdeggiavano*, the inner stem *verdeggi-* is that of a lexeme (VERDEGGIARE) whose meaning is potentially synthetic. Although that of VERDE enters clearly into it, and the formation itself has a meaning which is paralleled at least in ROSSEGGIARE, the result is a semantic unit on its own. It is therefore natural that the formal elements *verd(e)-* and *-eggi-* should be adjacent. The meaning of the rest is analytic: *verdeggi+a+va+no* is semantically no more than a function of the complex lexeme VERDEGGIARE, plus Imperfect Indicative, plus 3rd Plural. It is therefore natural that the markers of the morphosyntactic categories should form successively outer layers.

The principle of syntagmatic iconicity has now been illustrated sufficiently. But it also has a bearing on the way in which the marking of categories overlaps. Suppose that a set of stems is formed by the main exponents of a category $A$. We may call them $A$ stems: for example, in *verdeggiavano*, the inflectional stem *verdeggiava-*, which is derived by suffixing the marker of Imperfect Indicative, is a Tense (or Tense and Mood) stem. Now it is possible that each $A$ might have a single exponent – that, morphophonemics apart, there might be no allomorphy. But suppose we do find alternation. In that case, we might expect that it should reflect only the features that are realised in the forms from which the $A$ stems are derived. So, let $A$ stems be the innermost inflectional stems. In that case, we might expect that any alternation should be lexically conditioned. For example, if $A$ is Tense, the markers of Tenses might be expected to vary between different inflectional classes. Let $A$ stems be derived instead from simpler inflectional stems: say, from stems whose formatives are the main exponents of a category $B$. In that case, we might again expect some alternations to be lexically conditioned; in addition, we would not be surprised if the marking of some values of $A$ – some Tenses, for instance – were to be conditioned by different values of $B$. But we would not expect an alternation to be conditioned by properties which, at this stage in the derivation, have yet to be realised. Let the next stage be the addition of a termination which will mark $C$. Then we would not expect that different values of $C$ would also condition the marking of $A$.

So far we have said nothing about iconicity. But suppose, in addition, that what is formally more central is also more central in meaning. So, if *A* stems are derived from *B* stems, *B* is semantically more central than *A*, and if *C* is marked by terminations, *C* is semantically peripheral. In that case, what we are saying is that, in our expectations at least, an alternation should be conditioned typically by features that are in both respects more central. For example, in a language like Italian, we would not be surprised if an alternation in the marking of Person and Number, which are peripheral categories, were to be conditioned by the class of the lexeme or by Tense. But we would not expect that the marking of Tenses should vary according to the Person and Number. Still less would we expect a lexical formative, like *-eggi-* in *verdeggiavano*, to vary in the light of any inflectional category. For they are all both semantically and formally peripheral to it.

These have been phrased as expectations only; it is therefore important that we should look at one fairly complex system to see how far they are borne out. In the Verb in Latin, the category which is at least formally most central is that of Aspect. For example, in *monueram* 'I had advised', Perfect Aspect (with a meaning in this form like that of the English Auxiliary HAVE) has as its main exponent a suffix *-u-*, which is added directly to the root *mon-*. This is the normal formation for the inflectional class that is traditionally called the 2nd Conjugation. But the Perfect stem varies strikingly from one lexeme to another. In Verbs like AMO 'love', the root is followed by a vowel plus [w]:

[am]- → [am-a:- w]-

(written *amav-*). That is the normal pattern in the regular (1st) Conjugation. In many irregular Verbs, the stem is derived by suffixing *-s*:

man- → man-s-

(MANEO 'remain'); in others by partial reduplication:

mord- → mo-mord-

(MORDEO 'bite'); in others by a lengthening of the root vowel:

[wen]- → [we:n]-

(VENIO 'come'), and so on. Thus, for the most central of the inflectional categories, we find lexical conditioning in plenty. But,

in line with our expectations, we do not find morphological conditioning. In each paradigm, the Perfect stem is constant; so too the contrasting (and more regular) Non-Perfect.

The next most central categories are those of Tense and Mood. Here too we find lexical conditioning: note therefore that, as in the case of morphosyntactic categories in chapter 9, we cannot limit the factors affecting alternations to features which are realised adjacently. But the classes involved are now very broad. For example, in *ama:bis* 'you will love' the Future Indicative is marked by *-bi-*; that is the pattern found throughout the traditional 1st and 2nd Conjugations. In *venie:s* 'you will come' it is marked by *-e:-*, and that is found throughout the remainder. At the same time, the Tense and Mood markers vary, as we might expect, with Aspect. In *ama:bis* 'you will love', *-bi-* is, in addition, a subsidiary exponent of Non-Perfect. The corresponding Perfect is *ama:veris* 'you will have loved', with (arguably) a sequence of formatives *am-a:-[w]-er-i-s*. Similarly for the Past Indicative. In the Non-Perfect *ama:ba:s* 'you were loving', it is marked by *-ba:-*; this suffix is found in every Verb except the most irregular. But it is found only in Non-Perfects: in the corresponding Perfect, *ama:vera:s* 'you had loved', there is again a form without *b* (arguably *am-a:-[w]-er-a:-s*). Once more, this is the kind of conditioning that does not surprise us, Aspect being more central.

Is there also conditioning by categories that are more peripheral? The answer is, at one point, Yes: whereas in a Future Indicative like *venie:s* 'you will come' the Tense and Mood are generally marked by *-e:-*, in the 1st Singular, and only in the 1st Singular, they are marked instead by *-a:-*. Thus *veniam* (from *-a:-m* by a morphophonemic rule of vowel shortening) 'I will come'. This exception reminds us that we are dealing with tendencies, not laws. But it is very much an exception. It affects only the smaller (3rd and 4th) Conjugations: in a regular Verb like AMO 'love' the suffix, as we have seen, is different. It is, moreover, the only case in which our expectations are not satisfied. Morphophonemics apart, the Tense and Mood stems do not vary otherwise except with respect to lexical classes and the more central category of Aspect.

Person, Number and Voice are then marked – in part cumulatively, in part separately – in the termination. For example, in *ama:ba:tur* '[he or she] was being loved' the termination *-tur* has a *-t-*, marking 3rd Singular, followed by *-ur*, which in 3rd Persons Non-Perfect is a separate exponent of Passive. Here there is little lexical conditioning; that is again what might be expected, for categories that are semantically peripheral and formally so far removed from the root. But there is rather more conditioning by Aspect, Tense and Mood. In most of the paradigm, the 1st Singular is marked by *-m* in the Active and *-r* (arguably from basic *-m-r*) in the Passive: thus *ama:bam* 'I was loving', *ama:bar* 'I was being loved'. But in the Present Indicative, in particular, it is marked in the Active by *-o:* and in the Passive by *-or* (more convincingly from basic *-o:-r*). In the terms in which we spoke in chapter 9, *-o:* in a form like *amo:* 'I love' is the main exponent of 1st Singular, but also, given that this rule would be the exception, a subsidiary exponent of Tense and Mood. First Singular has yet another marker in *ama:vi:* 'I have loved ': here the termination, *-i:*, is limited to forms that are both Present Indicative and Perfect.

In summary, then, the pattern is (with one exception) as we expected. The subsidiary marking of categories extends outwards from the formally central to the formally peripheral: Aspect conditions Tense and Mood, all three partly condition Person and Number. With the single exception, it does not extend inwards from the peripheral to the central. For any reader who has learned Latin by the traditional method, it will be clear that this largely explains the way that paradigms are set out. No one would dream of starting from the peripheral categories – of listing first, say, all 1st Singulars, then all 2nd Singulars, and so on. Instead one begins with those that are more central, listing first all forms of the Present Indicative Non-Perfect; then other Indicatives; then the Subjunctives; then similarly for the Perfects.

I have again put this without explicit reference to meaning. But the pattern we have described is also, if we leave aside the formally peripheral marking of the Passive Voice, iconic. So, what is semantically more central tends to condition the marking of what is semantically less central, not vice versa.

## MARKED AND UNMARKED

Let us now turn to the paradigmatic dimension. Here too we find iconic correspondences, and here in particular, although it would be wrong to speak of laws, there are well attested tendencies.

Let us begin with the marking of Number in Nouns. In English or in Turkish, Plural is marked regularly by an inflection: English *book + s*, Turkish *köy + ler* 'villages'. The Singulars, by contrast, are distinguished merely by the absence of an inflection: English *book*, Turkish *köy*. In languages like Latin or Russian, Number is marked cumulatively with Case. But take, for example, the paradigm of Latin PUELLA 'girl':

|            | Singular | Plural     |
|------------|----------|------------|
| Nominative | puella   | puellae    |
| Accusative | puellam  | puella:s   |
| Genitive   | puellae  | puella:rum |
| Dative     | puellae  | puelli:s   |
| Ablative   | puella:  | puelli:s   |

Throughout this, the ending of the Singular is shorter or less weighty than that of the corresponding Plural. In the Nominative, the Singular ends in a short vowel (*-a*) where the Plural ends in a diphthong (*-ae*). In the Accusative, the Singular ending is a consonant (*-m*) with a short vowel preceding; the Plural ending is an *-s* with a long vowel (*a:*) preceding. In the Dative and Ablative, the Singular has a diphthong (*-ae*) or long vowel (*-a:*); the Plural has a long vowel plus a consonant (*-i:s*). In the Genitive, the Plural has an extra syllable (*-ae* versus *-a:rum*).

There is an even neater pattern in the Russian paradigm which was given as an example in chapter 9:

|               | Singular | Plural     |
|---------------|----------|------------|
| Nominative    | stol     | stalý      |
| Genitive      | stalá    | stalóv     |
| Dative        | stalú    | stalám     |
| Accusative    | stol     | stalý      |
| Instrumental  | stalóm   | stalám ́i   |
| Prepositional | stal´é   | staláx     |

The lexeme is the Masculine Inanimate STOL 'table', and it can be seen at once that in this declension the Plural is always longer by one phoneme than the Singular. Where the Singular has the bare root (*stol*), the Plural adds a vowel (Nominative and Accusative *stal-ý*). Where the Singular has a vowel, the Plural has a vowel plus a consonant: Genitive *stalá*, *stalóv*; Dative *stalú*, *stalám*; Prepositional *stal'é*, *staláx*. Where the Singular has a vowel plus a consonant (Instrumental *stal-óm*), the Plural has a vowel plus a consonant plus another vowel (*stal-ám'i*).

These are merely observations about formal marking, which could be repeated in many other languages. But let us now look at the semantic opposition between Numbers. In English, Latin, and so on the meaning of a Plural Noun is strictly 'more than one': *the books*, for example, is a phrase that necessarily refers to more than one book. But the meaning of a Singular is not necessarily 'just one'. Some Singulars do have this meaning: in *I dropped the book*, the Object phrase will indeed refer to just one book. But take, for instance, generics: in *the migration of the arctic tern*, the phrase *the arctic tern* will usually be taken to identify not one bird individually, but the whole species. In such a use, the Singular is equivalent in reference to a Plural (*the migration of arctic terns*). The Singular is also the form taken by uncountables: thus *The bread* (it might be one loaf or it might be more than one) *is not ready*. In many languages it is also used when reference to more than one is already indicated by a Numeral. One such language is Turkish: for 'three villages' the form is *iki köy* (literally 'three village'), not usually at least (see LEWIS, p. 26) *iki köyler*. Another, close to home, is Welsh. Compare English *two books*, where *books* has the Plural ending, with Welsh *dau lyfr* (literally, again 'two book'). In general, a phrase which has plural reference can, in one circumstance or another, have a Singular Noun. But, once more, phrases which have singular reference cannot, in these languages, have a Plural Noun.

What this shows is that the semantic opposition between Singular and Plural is not symmetrical. The Plural has a positive meaning, specifically 'more than one'. So, for example in Welsh, *y llyfrau* (*y* 'the' plus *llyfr* 'book' plus Plural ending *-au*) must specifically mean 'more than one book'. But the Singular has a negative meaning: it is simply not Plural, so 'not specifically more than one'. In *dau lyfr* (*dau* 'two' plus a modified form of *llyfr* 'book'), the Noun has in itself neither the meaning 'one' nor 'more than one'; but, when it is taken together with *dau*, the whole phrase has plural reference. In the English phrase *the arctic tern*, the Singular *tern* has a meaning that is negatively opposed to that of Plural *terns*; in different contexts, the reference might be to either 'one' or 'more than one'. *The book* or *y llyfr* will normally be taken to have singular reference in opposition to *the books* or *y llyfrau*. But compare again the generic use in, say, an exhibition title: 'The Art of the Book'.

We can now see that the formal marking is iconic. In meaning, Plural is the specific or (as it is called) the **semantically marked** term in the opposition. Correspondingly, it is the term which, in English or Turkish, is formally marked or, in Latin or Russian, has longer or weightier exponents. In meaning, Singular is the non-specific or (as it is called) the **semantically unmarked** term. Correspondingly, at the level of form, it is the term which, in English and Turkish, has no formal marker or, in Latin and Russian, has shorter or less weighty exponents. What is positive and negative at the level of meaning is thus realised positively and negatively at the level of form. Alternatively, where there is cumulation, what is semantically positive is realised more positively.

Oppositions between marked and unmarked terms have been explored a great deal since the 1930s, and, although it must be emphasised that not every pattern in every language is as neat as this, and indeed we can find instances that go directly against what we are saying, paradigmatic iconicity, as we have called it, is now well established. For another illustration let us return to the periphrastic forms in Latin which were introduced in the last chapter. Formally, when finite Verbs are Active they are simple: *amo:* 'I love', *ama:vi:* 'I loved, have loved'. So too when they are Passive but not Perfect: *amor* 'I am loved'. But when they are both Passive and Perfect the form is periphrastic: *ama:tus sum* (Past Participle plus a form of 'to be') 'I have been loved'. The pattern for these forms is like this:

|  | *Active* | *Passive* |
|---|---|---|
| *Non-Perfect* | amo: | amor |
| *Perfect* | ama:vi: | ama:tus sum |

Formally – and this is generally the case – the Perfect *ama:vi:*

is longer than the Non-Perfect *amo:*). The Passive Non-Perfect is also generally longer than the Active, and *amor*, as we have seen earlier in this chapter, is arguably basic *amo:* plus a Passive suffix. The periphrastic Passive Perfect has the weightiest marking of all.

So much for the forms; what then of the meanings? In the case of Voice, it is easy to show that the Passive is semantically marked and the Active unmarked. Only some Verbs have a contrast between Active and Passive – those (like AMO 'love') that are syntactically Transitive. Others have none: for example, the verb 'to be' or the Intransitive MANEO 'remain'. But their endings are those of the Actives. Formally, *maneo*: 'I remain' is like *amo:* 'I love', not *amor* 'I am loved'; *mane:s* 'you remain' like *ama:s* 'you love' not *ama:ris* 'you are loved', and so on. The Passive is thus semantically specific. If the construction of the clause requires it, then and only then are Passive endings used. By contrast, the Active can be described negatively, as 'Non-Passive'. It is the unmarked form used when the Verb is not specifically Passive. That may be either because the construction does not require the Passive form or, in the case of SUM or MANEO, because it cannot.

The category of Aspect is semantically bound up with that of Tense, and they have to be discussed together. But consider, in particular, the marking of timeless statements ('Blood is thicker than water', 'Two and two make four', and so on). In Latin, as in English, the Verb will be in the Present Tense. More precisely, it will be in the Tense that is 'Non-Past' and 'Non-Future': whereas the Past specifically locates an action or whatever in the past, and the Future specifically locates it in the future, the Present is an unmarked term which covers both location in the present and no specific time location at all. Its general meaning is therefore negative ('not specifically located in time at a point earlier than or later than the moment of speaking'). In timeless statements the Verb will also be Non-Perfect. In Latin, a Perfect like *ama:vi:* 'I loved, have loved' had a positive meaning. It was, more exactly, a Perfect Present, and located the experience of loving in a period whose commencement, at least, is displaced backwards in time (Perfect) from a period not removed (Non-Past, Non-Future) from the moment of speaking. The form we have already called Non-Perfect is again the negation of the

Perfect ('not specifically displaced backwards'). This can cover
what is happening at the moment of speaking (*amo*: 'I am [now]
in love with') and what holds then and always: 'Two and two
make (Present Non-Perfect *faciunt*) four'.

In a notation which is widely used, positive terms are indicated
with a plus and negative with a minus. So for 'Singular', in our
earlier illustration, read −Plural and for 'Plural' read +Plural;
for 'Present' in Latin read −Past, −Future, and so on. Our table
of simple and periphrastic forms can therefore be rewritten like
this:

|  | −*Passive* | +*Passive* |
|---|---|---|
| −*Perfect* | amo: | amor |
| +*Perfect* | ama:vi: | ama:tus sum |

The more the form is semantically marked – the more plusses
there are – the more it is formally marked. The form which has
semantically the most plusses is periphrastic.

In all these examples, the formal difference is quite striking:
suffix versus no suffix, weightier versus lighter ending, periphrastic versus simple. But it can be more subtle. The table which
follows:[2]

|  | *Present* | *Past* |
|---|---|---|
| 1*st Sg.* | -o | -a |
| 2*nd Sg.* | -is | -es |
| 3*rd Sg.* | -i | -e |

shows a set of six Verb endings in Modern Greek. On the face of
it, the weightiest are those of the 2nd Singulars: *yráf-is* 'you
write, are writing' (γράφεις), *é-yraf-es* 'you were writing'
(έγραφες). Those of the 1st and 3rd Singulars are less weighty:
*yráf-o* 'I write, am writing' (γράφω), *é-yraf-a* 'I was writing',
(έγραφα), *yráf-i* '[he or she] writes, is writing' (γράφει) and
*é-yraf-e* '[he or she] was writing' (έγραφε). Past Tense has
extended exponents, a prefix *e-* which carries the accent plus
endings different from the Present. But, on the face of it, the Past
and Present endings are of equal weight.

---

[2] The example was suggested to me by work by Irene P. Warburton. Compare her
article, 'Modern Greek Verb Conjugation', *Lingua*, 32 (1973), pp. 193–226.

So much 'on the face of it'. But let us begin by looking more closely at the category of Person. The forms which are traditionally '1st Person' refer to the speaker, alone (Singular) or with others (Plural). A 2nd Person refers to whoever the speaker is addressing, sometimes one and sometimes more, again with or without others. For both these values the meanings are positive. But that of the 3rd Person can best be defined negatively. A form like *yráfi* '[he or she] is writing' refers to an individual who is 'not the speaker' and 'not the person addressed'. In uses like this, the 3rd Singular is already opposed negatively to the 1st Singular and 2nd Singular. But it is also used as an Impersonal. *Vréxi* (βρέχει) 'it is raining' is morphologically like *yráfi*; but here no individual – no one, as it were, who 'does' the raining – is referred to. The Verb 'ought' is consistently Impersonal: *prépi ná* (literally 'it-oughts that'), say, I shut up (πρέπει νά...). *Prépi* 'it oughts' is again formally 3rd Singular. If the meaning of 1st Person is 'specific reference to the speaker' and that of the 2nd is 'specific reference to a person or persons addressed', the 3rd Person simply means 'no such specific reference'.

Let us now consider an aspect of Modern Greek that is at first sight unrelated. Take, for example, the sequence of words *to ákusa* 'I heard it' (τὸ ἄκουσα).[3] By a rule of sandhi that operates across word boundaries, this is phonetically not [to'akusa] but ['takusa]: the vowel of *to* 'it' is 'elided' (to use the traditional term) before the initial *a* of *ákusa* 'I heard'. Now take another sequence, *ta évlepa* 'I saw them' (τὰ ἔβλεπα). Here the form is phonetically ['tavlepa]: whereas, in *to ákusa*, an *o* was elided before an *a*, in this example the initial *e* of *évlepa* 'I saw' is 'prodelided' – to use again the traditional term – after the *a* of *ta* 'them'. The rule is in fact conditioned by the qualities of the vowels. If two successive vowels are the same, they will simply collapse into a single vowel of the same quality: hence, for example, *ta* (τὰ) 'the' [Neuter Plural] + *arxéa* (αρχαία) is phonetically [tar'xea]. But if they are different, the choice between elision and prodelision is determined by their position on a scale of phonological strength or dominance. According to this scale,

---

[3] Examples are taken from MIRAMBEL, pp. 43f. See also F. W. Householder, K. Kazazis & A. Koutsoudas, *A Reference Grammar of Literary Dhimotiki* (Supplement to *IJAL*, Bloomington, 1964), pp. 12ff.

the single open vowel *a* is 'stronger' than any of the others: hence the *a* of *ákusa* 'wins' over the *o* of preceding *to*, but conversely the *a* of *ta* also 'wins' over the *e* of following *évlepa*. By the general rule it is dominance and not position that is decisive.

Of the other combinations of vowels that are possible, a back vowel (*o* or *u*) is stronger or more dominant than a front (*e* or *i*). Hence, for example, *to* and *éleya* 'I was saying' (ἔλεγα) combine or fuse to *tóleya*, and likewise *tu* (τοὺ) + *éleya* ('I was saying to him') → *túleya*. We may also generalise by saying that mid vowels are stronger than close, although the order of *i* and *e* is not so certain (see examples in Householder *et al.*, *Dhimotiki*, p. 12). To sum up, therefore, the scale of dominance might be shown by a diagram of the following form:

(dotted line for the less certain case), in which vowel *x* is weaker than vowel *y* if there are one or more arrows (one, e.g., for *o* and *e*; two e.g., for *a* and *u*) leading from *y* to *x*. In phonetic terms, the more sonorous open and back vowels 'win' over the less sonorous mid/close and front.

What bearing does this have on the Verb terminations? Recall, firstly, that 3rd Singulars are semantically unmarked. But they are also marked formally by the vowels which come lowest on this scale of sonority: 3rd Singular Present -*i*, 3rd Singular Past -*e*. In the 2nd Singular, which is semantically marked, we have the same vowels plus a consonant: Present -*is*, Past -*es*. In the 1st Singular, which is also marked semantically, we find the vowels which are highest on the scale of sonority: Present -*o*, Past -*a*. Despite initial appearances, the formal marking does reflect the semantic relations. The two marked Persons have respectively a -*VC* ending or a vowel which is more sonorous; the unmarked Person a -*V* ending with a vowel that is less sonorous.

But there is more. In Greek, as in Latin or in English, the Past Tense is semantically marked in opposition to the Present. In the forms which we cited, it is also marked formally by an accent-bearing prefix: *yráf-o* 'I write, am writing' versus *é-yraf-a* 'I wrote'. But we can now point to a further parallel in the endings. In the 1st Singular, Past -*a* is opposed to Present -*o*; of the two vowels which are phonologically most dominant, the semantically marked form has the one which is most dominant of all. Between Past -*e*(*s*) and Present -*i*(*s*) the phonological weighting is less certain (broken line in the diagram). But if it can be demonstrated, it again fits: Past *e* stronger, Present or Non-Past *i* weaker.

For a final illustration, and one that, though more obvious on the surface, is especially elegant, let us look at the marking of Person in Italian. The 3rd Singular is semantically unmarked: there is, for instance, a straightforward parallel between Modern Greek *vréxi* 'it is raining' and its Italian translation *piove*. We can add that the Singular is again the unmarked Number. As in Nouns, the Plural implies specific reference to more than one individual. (Note that the 2nd Plural is not used, as in French, as a formal or polite form.) In the unmarked Singular, the reference may again be strictly to one individual, or to many, or (in some Impersonals) to none.

What then of the formal markers? In the paradigm of CANTARE 'sing', the forms of the Present Indicative are:

|  | *Singular* | *Plural* |
|---|---|---|
| 1*st* | cánto | cantiámo |
| 2*nd* | cánti | cantáte |
| 3*rd* | cánta | cántano |

(acute accent added to indicate the position of the word-stress). Two points of interest can be noted already. Firstly, the Plural endings are longer by one syllable. This is in line with the pattern noted earlier in Latin Nouns, where Number was marked cumulatively with Case. Secondly, in both the 1st and 2nd Plural the stress shifts to the penultimate syllable. These are both semantically marked. In the 3rd Plural, which is semantically unmarked, it does not shift.

The rest requires some further analysis. Briefly, a Verb like CANTARE belongs to an inflectional class or Conjugation whose forms are based on a stem in -*a*. This appears directly in, for example, *cant-á-te* (2nd Pl.); also in the Infinitive (*cant-á-re* 'to sing'), in the Imperfect Indicative (*cant-á-vo* 'I was singing'), in most forms of the Past Definite (*cant-á-i* 'I sang') and so on. We met it earlier in this chapter in, for example, *mangi-a-va-no* '[they] were eating'. But in two other conjugations the inflections are based on stems in *-e* or *-i*. Compare, for example, *ved-é-te* 'you see, can see' and *ven-í-te* 'you come, are coming'; *ved-é-re* 'to see' and *ven-í-re* 'to come'; *ved-é-vo* 'I was seeing' and *ven-í-vo* 'I was coming'. CANTARE thus belongs to the '*a* class', which is also the one that is open and thus maximally regular. VEDERE 'see' and VENIRE 'come' belong respectively to the '*e* class' and the '*i* class'.

Let us now return to the forms in our table. The 3rd Singular, *cánta*, plainly consists of the stem in *-a* with no termination: *cánta*+zero. By contrast, the 3rd Plural has a termination *-no*: *cánta*+*no*. Again the semantically marked property (+Plural) has an explicit formal marker, while the maximally unmarked 3rd Singular has none. Similarly for the *e* class: 3rd Singular *véde* (*vede*+zero); 3rd Plural *véd-o-no* (or *véd(e)-o-no*). In the 1st Singular, *cánto*, the vowel is different; also in the 2nd Singular, *cánti*. We might posit an operation by which the stem vowel is changed (*-a* → *-o*, *-a* → *-i*); alternatively, the forms are morphophonemically ← *cánta*+*o* (fusion of successive vowels in unstressed position) and *cánta*+*i*. But in either case the *-o* and *-i* are positive exponents of 1st Singular and 2nd Singular. Compare, for VEDERE, *véd-o* (or *véde*+*o*) and *véd-i*; even, for the irregular Verb 'to be', *sóno* 'I am', *séi* 'you are'. Here too, the semantically marked forms (+1st or +2nd) are distinguished by the presence of a formative; the unmarked form (−1st, −2nd) once more has none.

We can extract the endings and display them in a table:

|                | −*Plural* | +*Plural* |
|----------------|-----------|-----------|
| +1*st*         | -o        | ´-mo      |
| +2*nd*         | -i        | ´-te      |
| −1*st*, −2*nd* |           | -no       |

The forms which are semantically marked are the 1st Plural (+1st, +Plural) and the 2nd Plural (+2nd, +Plural). These, as we have seen, are also formally most marked, by a *-CV* termination (*-mo*, *-te*) plus a shift of word-stress, shown in the table by an acute before the termination, to the syllable preceding. The 3rd Plural, though marked as to Number, is unmarked in respect of Person ($-$1st, $-$2nd, $+$Plural). It has a *-CV* termination *(-no)*, but without a stress shift. The 3rd Singular is maximally unmarked ($-$1st, $-$2nd, $-$Plural) and we have seen that it has no termination. The 1st and 2nd Singular are marked as to Person ($+$1st or $+$2nd) but unmarked as to Number ($-$Plural). They have terminations *(-o, -i)*, but their form is *-V* not *-CV*.

The pattern has been illustrated for the Present Indicative. But the Imperfect Indicative has identical endings, and, although there are complications and some partly contradictory tendencies in other Tenses, much of the iconicity runs right through the paradigm. In the Future, for example, the 3rd Plural is again marked formally in opposition to 3rd Singular: Singular *canterá* (spelled *canterà*) '[he or she] will sing'; Plural *canteránno* '[they] will sing'. But in the 1st and 2nd Plurals (*canteré-mo* 'we will sing', *canteré-te* 'you will sing') there is no shift of stress, since the Future stem (*canteré-* in these forms) is already stressed on its last syllable. In the Conditional, the 1st Singular has a shorter form than the 3rd Singular: *canteréi* versus *canterébbe*. That goes against our pattern. But the 3rd Plural (*canterébbero*) again adds a formative (*-ro*) to the Singular. There is indeed no Plural form, at any point in the paradigm, which is phonologically less marked than the corresponding Singular, and in all but three pairs (the 2nd Persons in the Conditional, Past Definite and Imperfect Subjunctive) the Plural has at least one more syllable.

What, finally, is the theoretical significance of iconicity? Two words I have eschewed throughout this chapter are 'explain' and 'explanation'. This is because they raise philosophical complications: to many scholars, it does not seem right to speak of explanation, even in what is plainly a branch of the humanities, unless there are laws that cover every instance. But we have stressed that there are no laws, only tendencies. So, if one takes that view, nothing that we have said can lead to any explanatory theory.

Suppose, however, that we take what might be seen as a more realistic view. In that case, it seems likely that the principle of iconicity will help to explain aspects of the history of languages. Consider, for example, the development of Italian. The Verb CANTARE 'sing' is the reflex of a similar Verb in Latin, whose endings, in the Present Indicative Non-Perfect, may be extracted as follows:

|  | Singular | Plural |
|---|---|---|
| 1st Person | -oː | -mus |
| 2nd Person | -s | -tis |
| 3rd Person | -t | -nt |

Some forms, like the 1st Singular, have changed little: *canto*: 'I sing' (← *cantaː-oː*). But the 3rd Singular ended in a consonant: *cantat* '[he or she] sings' (← *cantaː-t*). It was thus no shorter, apart from the morphophonemic shortening of *-aː-* to *-a-*, than the 2nd Singular *cantaːs* 'you sing'. Another difference is that the 3rd Plural (*cantant* '[they] sing') ended in a cluster of consonants, not in a separate syllable. Now a philologist will identify several changes that have led from the Latin system to the Italian. Some are purely phonological (the loss, for example of final consonants or of the distinction of vowel length). But where they are more particular, it is hard to believe that the maintenance and enhancement of what we have called paradigmatic iconicity have not sometimes entered into them.

## RELATED READING

On the terms 'iconic' and 'iconicity' see LYONS, *Semantics*, vol. 1, pp. 102ff. For the application of this notion to grammar see, for example, J. Haiman, *Natural Syntax : Iconicity and Erosion* (Cambridge, Cambridge University Press, 1985); also a short and useful essay by N. B. Vincent, 'Iconic and symbolic aspects of syntax: prospects for reconstruction', in P. Ramat (ed.), *Linguistic Reconstruction and Indo-European Syntax* (Amsterdam, Benjamins, 1980), pp. 47–68. For 'arbitrariness' it is customary to refer to SAUSSURE, but he did not himself pretend that the concept was new. Those who think that it was should read, for instance, Rabelais, part 3, ch. 19; for the history of the idea see E. Coseriu, 'L'Arbitraire du signe: zur Spätgeschichte eines aristotelischen Begriffes', *Archiv für das Studium der neueren Sprachen* 204 (1967), pp. 81–112. The example of an invented 'natural vocabulary' is from M. M. Slaughter, *Universal Languages and Scientific Taxonomy in the Seventeenth Century* (Cambridge, Cambridge University Press, 1982), p. 150, one of a number of fascinating studies of the 'universal language movement'.

I am using the term 'paradigmatic' in a wide sense: for a narrower usage, in which paradigmatic relations hold only among items that can be substituted one for another, see LYONS, *Semantics*, vol. 1, pp. 240ff. Note that Lyons's concept is not, as he implies, in SAUSSURE.

Markedness, especially, has been extensively studied within 'natural morphology'. See MAYERTHALER; WURZEL, ch. 1 especially; DRESSLER, *Leitmotifs* (in part); also, for a programmatic account, W. U. Dressler, 'On the predictiveness of natural morphology', *JL* 21 (1985), pp. 321–37. For a textbook survey, which goes somewhat wider, see BAUER, *Morphology*, ch. 12. But note an important difference. In most work on natural morphology, it is assumed that there are substantive laws that operate directly in the development of languages. For example, it is a universal law that Plural is marked and Singular unmarked, and, all else being equal, this will be reflected in each system. Thus MAYERTHALER; also WURZEL, §6.1, who argues, however, that other factors which are internal to the system have priority. As WURZEL points out in ch. 1, this view is parallel to that taken earlier by the short-lived school of 'natural phonologists'. In the view that I have expounded there are no laws; though, naturally, a particular pattern, or the tendency for languages to show one pattern rather than another, may be explicable at a higher level.

For wider discussion of laws see my inaugural lecture, *Do Languages Obey General Laws?* (Cambridge, Cambridge University Press, 1981). In his article in *JL* Dressler contrasts this with the view of natural morphologists; but the disagreement may be subtler than he implies.

Syntagmatic iconicity has been studied less than paradigmatic: but see, in particular, BYBEE, §2.6, on the ordering of markers in Verb-forms in a sample of languages, and §9.2, on Aspect, Tense and Mood. For marked/unmarked oppositions the leading studies are two pre-war papers by Jakobson: R. Jakobson, 'Zur Struktur des russischen Verbums' (1932), 'Beitrag zur allgemeinen Kasuslehre' (1936); both are reprinted in *RiL II* (pp. 22–30, 51–89), and in R. Jakobson, *Selected Writings*, vol. II. (The Hague, Mouton, 1971), pp. 3–15, 23–71. On markedness in general see LYONS, *Semantics*, vol. 1, §9.7. As he remarks (p. 305), the concept 'covers a number of disparate and independent phenomena': in particular, the use of these terms in Chomskyan linguistics (dating from CHOMSKY & HALLE) does not concern us here. Of the categories discussed, Person is the subject of a classic paper by Benveniste: see E. Benveniste, 'Structure des relations de personne dans le verbe', in BENVENISTE, pp. 225–36. See also LYONS, *Introduction*, pp. 276f., for a brief discussion of Person (and ch. 7 generally for other categories).

It has always astonished me that writers on English (like PALMER on the Verb) have been able to make so little use of the notion of semantic markedness.

# INDEX